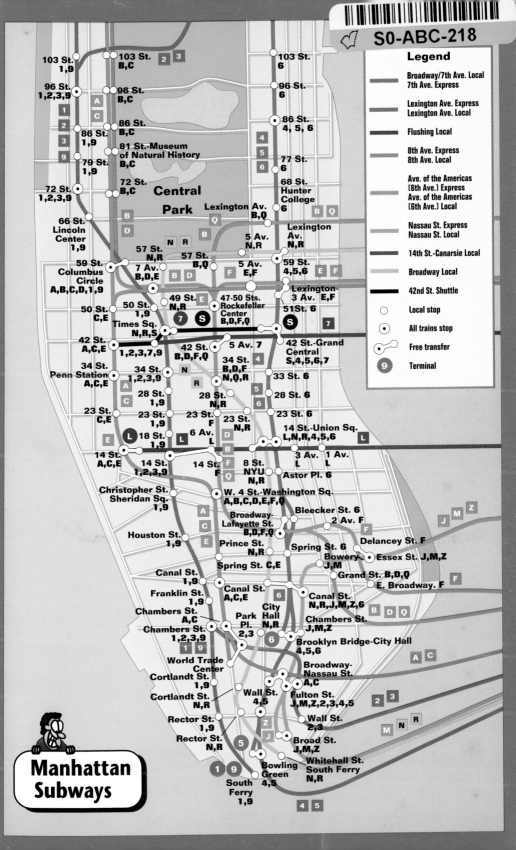

Manhattan Subways

Midtown Manhattan

0 .2 mi
0 .32 km

Hudson River

East River

Roosevelt Island Tram
Queensboro Bridge
Queens-Midtown Tunnel

Subway stop Ⓜ

York Av
Sutton Pl South   Sutton Pl
Beekman Place
Mitchell Place
First Av
United Nations

Second Av
Third Av
Lexington Av
Depew Pl
Park Av
Vanderbilt Av
Grand Central Terminal
Chrysler Building
E 43rd St
E 42nd St

MURRAY HILL

Tunnel Exit
Tunnel Entrance

E 66th St
E 65th St
E 64th St
E 63rd St
E 62nd St
E 61st St
E 60th St
E 59th St
E 58th St
E 57th St
E 56th St
E 55th St
E 54th St
E 53rd St
E 52nd St
E 51st St
E 50th St
E 49th St
E 48th St
E 47th St
E 46th St
E 45th St
E 44th St
E 41st St
E 40th St
E 39th St
E 38th St
E 37th St
E 36th St
E 35th St
E 34th St
E 33rd St
E 32nd St

MIDTOWN EAST

St. Patrick's
Museum of Modern Art
Rockefeller Center
Fifth Av
Madison Av
Sixth Av
Bryant Park
New York Public Library
Empire State Bldg.

Central Park
East Drive
Center Drive
West Drive
The Pond
Central Park S

Carnegie Hall
Seventh Av
Broadway
W 46th St
Restaurant Row
Columbus Circle
Central Park W

THEATER DISTRICT

TIMES SQUARE

Port Authority
Eighth Av
Penn Station
Broadway

W 66th St
W 65th St
W 64th St
W 63rd St
W 62nd St
W 61st St
W 60th St
W 59th St
W 58th St
W 57th St
W 56th St
W 55th St
W 54th St
W 53rd St
W 52nd St
W 51st St
W 50th St
W 49th St
W 48th St
W 47th St
W 45th St
W 44th St
W 43rd St
W 41st St
W 40th St
W 39th St
W 38th St
W 37th St
W 36th St
W 35th St
W 34th St
W 33rd St
W 32nd St

Columbus Av
Amsterdam Av
Ninth Av
Tenth Av
West End Av
Eleventh Av
Twelfth Av

Lincoln Center
DeWitt Clinton Park

MIDTOWN WEST

Javits Convention Center

INTREPID MUSEUM
CIRCLE LINE CRUISES

Lincoln Tunnel

FDR Drive

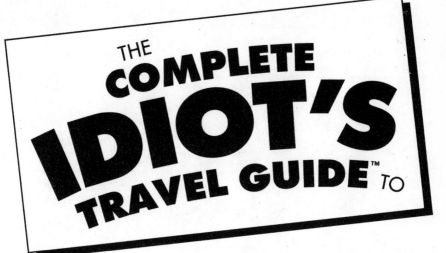

New York City

by Bruce Murphy
and Alessandra de Rosa

Macmillan Travel   Alpha Books
Divisions of Macmillan Reference USA
A Simon & Schuster Macmillan Company
1633 Broadway, New York NY 10019-6785

MACMILLAN is a registered trademark of Macmillan, Inc.
FROMMER'S is a registered trademark of Arthur Frommer. Used under license.
THE COMPLETE IDIOT'S GUIDE name and design are trademarks of Macmillan, Inc.

ISBN 0-02-862297-9
ISSN 1096-7613

Editor: Matt Hannafin
Production Editor: Robyn Burnett
Design by designLab
Page Layout: Daniela Raderstorf & Regina Rexrode
Proofreader: Megan Wade
Digital Cartography by Peter Bogaty & Ortelius Design
Illustrations by Kevin Spear

Special Sales
Bulk purchases (10+ copies) of Frommer's and selected Macmillan travel guides are available to corporations, organizations, mail-order catalogs, institutions, and charities at special discounts, and can be customized to suit individual needs. For more information write to: Special Sales, Macmillan General Reference, 1633 Broadway, New York, NY 10019.

Manufactured in the United States of America

Contents

Part 1 **What You Need to Do Before You Go**   **1**

  1 **How to Get Started**   **2**

Information, Please 2

    Crawling the Web 3

When Should I Go? 3

    It's Not the Heat, It's the Humidity—NYC Summers 3

    It's Not the Cold, It's the Wind Chill—NYC Winters 4

Hitting the Big Events & Exhibitions 4

We Are Family—Traveling with Your Kids 8

    Preparation 8

    Arriving & Finding Transportation 8

    Finding a Babysitter 9

    Keeping the Kids Entertained 9

Travel Advice for the Senior Set 9

Advice for Travelers with Disabilities 10

    Building Accessibility 12

Advice for Gay & Lesbian Travelers 12

Big Apple Safety Tips 13

  2 **Money Matters**   **14**

Should I Carry Traveler's Checks or the Green Stuff? 14

    ATMs to the Left of Me, ATMs to the Right of Me 15

    Check It Out 15

Plastic Money 16

Stop, Thief! (What to Do If Your Money Gets Stolen) 16

So What's This Trip Gonna Cost? .17

    Lodging 17

    Transportation 17

    Restaurants 17

    Attractions 18

    Shopping 18

    Entertainment 18

    Tipping 19

    What Are All Those Dollar Signs? 19

What If I'm Worried I Can't Afford It? 20

    Convenience Costs 21

Budget Worksheet: You Can Afford This Trip 23

  3 **How Will I Get There?**   **24**

Travel Agent—Friend or Foe? 24

Should I Join an Escorted Tour or Travel on My Own? 25

    Hey, Mister Bus Driver! 26

    Plush Bus or Busted Buggy? 26

The Pros & Cons of Package Tours 27

    Pick a Peck of Pickled Packages 27

Fighting the Airfare Wars 28

    Surfing the Web to Fly the Skies 29

Happy Landings 30

The Inside Scoop on the Comfort Zone 30

Getting There by Car 31

Getting There by Train 32

Getting There by Bus 32

Fair Game—Choosing an Airline .32

4 Tying Up the Loose Ends   **37**
Do I Need to Rent a Car in New York? 37
What About Travel Insurance? 38
What If I Get Sick away from Home? 38
Making Reservations & Getting Tickets Ahead of Time 39
    So What's Goin' on Here?—New York Entertainment . . .39
    You Make the Call 41
Pack It Up 41
Packing Checklist—Don't Forget Your Toothbrush 43

Part 2 Finding the Hotel That's Right for You   **45**

5 Pillow Talk—The Lowdown on the New York Hotel Scene   **46**
Location! Location! Location! 46
    Midtown 46
    Upper West Side 48
    Upper East Side 49
    Downtown 49
The Price Is Right 50
    What Off Season? 51
    Taxes & Service Charges 51
What's in It for Me?—What You Get for Your Money 52
What Kind of Place Is Right for You? 53
    Bed & Breakfasts 54
Getting the Best Room 54
Hotel Strategies for Families Traveling with Kids 55
Hotel Strategies for Travelers with Disabilities 55
What If I Didn't Plan Ahead? 55

6 New York Hotels from A to Z   **57**
Quick Picks—New York's Hotels at a Glance 58
    Hotel Index by Location 58
    Hotel Index by Price 62
Our Favorite New York Hotels 64
Help! I'm So Confused! 79
Hotel Preferences Worksheet 80

Part 3 Learning Your Way Around New York   **83**

7 Getting Your Bearings   **84**
Fly Me to the Moon...or New York...whichever... 84
    Yo, Taxi! 86
    The Magic Bus 87
Airport Bus Schedule 88
    May I Call You a Limousine, Ma'am? 88
The Bronx Is Up & the Battery's Down (and All the Other
Directions You'll Need) 89
    Downtown 89
    Greenwich Village (East and West) 90
    Chelsea 90
    Midtown 90
    The Upper West Side 92
    The Upper East Side 92
Street Smarts—Where to Get Information once You're
in the City 92

Contents

8 Getting Around the Apple   **94**
Going Underground—Using the Subway System 94
   Subway Hints 96
Traffic, Schmaffic—Using the City Buses 97
Public Transportation for People with Disabilities 98
I'm Walkin' Here!—Getting Around on Foot 99

Part 4 New York's Best Restaurants   **101**

9 The Lowdown on the New York Dining Scene   **102**
What's Hot 102
Location! Location! Location! 103
   The West Village 103
   The East Village & NoHo 104
   SoHo 104
   Tribeca 105
   Gramercy Park & the Union Square Area 105
   Midtown 105
   The Upper West Side 106
   The Upper East Side 106
Unchain My Lunch 107
Fine Dining in the Melting Pot—Ethnic Eats in NYC 108
   Little India 108
   Chinatown 108
   Little Italy 109
   Koreatown 109
The Price Is Right 109
Top Hat, White Tie, & Tails? Dressing to Dine 111
Mind if I Smoke? 111
Paying Your Taxes & Giving Your Tip 111
Do You Have a Reservation, Sir? 111

10 New York Restaurants from A to Z   **112**
Quick Picks—New York's Restaurants at a Glance 113
   Restaurant Index by Location 113
   Restaurant Index by Price 116
   Restaurant Index by Cuisine 117
Our Favorite New York Restaurants 121

11 Light Bites & Munchies   **145**
Afternoon Tea 145
Brunch 146
Snacking While Shopping 146
Coffee Break 146
Best Bagels in New York 147
A Slice of Heaven 148
Delis & Salad Bars 148
Fast & Cheap 149
A Dog with Everything 150
Street Carts 150
You Want Some Fries with That? 150
A Nice Bowl of Chicken Soup—and More 151
I Scream, You Scream 151
Pastries & Sweet Breaks 152
Brew Me a Cold One—NYC Microbreweries 153

PART 5   Ready, Set, Go! Exploring New York   155

12   Should I Just Take a Guided Tour?   156
Here's the Church & Here's the Steeple—
  Orientation Tours 157
Rollin' on the River—Cruises Around Manhattan 158
George Washington Slept Here—Architectural &
  Historical Tours 160
Special-Interest Tours 161
Free Walking Tours 161
Don't Forget 162

13   New York's Top Sights from A to Z   163
Quick Picks—New York's Top Attractions at a Glance 164
  Index by Location 164
  Index by Type of Attraction 164
The Top Sights 170
Worksheet: Your Must-See Attractions 190

14   More Fun Stuff to Do   196
New York for the Art Lover 196
Where the Wild Things Are—New York Zoos 197
New York for the History Buff 198
New York for the Bookish 199
Ice Skating, Rock Climbing, & Other Ways to Work
  off Dessert 199
New York's Corridors of Power 200
More Gorgeous Buildings to Stare at 201
Take Me out to the Ball Game 201
Museums of Many Cultures 202
Pictures That Move & Pictures That Don't 202
Who Lived Where? 203
Good Bets if You've Got the Kids in Tow 203

15   Charge It! A Shopper's Guide to New York   205
Shopping Hours 206
Paying Your Taxes 206
The Big Names 206
Prime Hunting Grounds 208
  Madison Avenue 208
  SoHo 210
  Fifth Avenue and 57th Street 212
  South Street Seaport and Pier 17 212
  8th Street 213
Where to Find That Thingie You Wanted—
  Specialty Shopping 216
  Antiques 216
  Bookstores 216
  Discount Stores 217
  Electronics 218
  Food 218
  Jewelery 219
  CDs and Tapes 219
  Musical Instruments 220

**16 Battle Plans for Seeing the Sights—
     Eight Great Itineraries   221**
Itinerary #1—Central Park & the East Side Museums 222
Itinerary #2—The Museums, the Park, & Times Square 223
Itinerary #3—The Statue of Liberty, South Street, &
     Chinatown 226
Itinerary #4—The Statue of Liberty, Wall Street, &
     the Village 228
Itinerary #5—The World Trade Center, Chinatown,
     Little Italy, & the Village 230
Itinerary #6—Fifth Avenue, MOMA, Rockefeller Center,
     & Times Square 232
Itinerary #7—The Village, the Flatiron District, &
     the Empire State Building 233
Itinerary #8—The U.N., Grand Central, the *Intrepid*,
     & Times Square 236

17 Designing Your Own Itinerary   238
Back to the Drawing Board—Your Top Attractions 238
Budgeting Your Time . . . . : . . .240
Am I Staying in the Right Place? 241
Getting All Your Ducks in a Row 242
Fill-Ins 242
Sketching Out Your Itineraries 243
Planning Your Nighttime Right 245

PART 6   On the Town—Nightlife & Entertainment   247

18 The Play's the Thing—Theatergoing in NYC   248
Getting Theater Information 248
Buying Your Tickets 249
     Getting the Right Seats 250
Enter the Ticketmonger 251
Broadway 251
Off-Broadway 251
Dressing for the Big Show 252
Missing the Curtain 254
Tipping 254
Having Dinner Before or After the Show 254
     When to Eat 254
     Where to Eat 255
     What to Eat 255
Taking Your Children to the Theater 256

19 The Performing Arts   257
Finding out What's On 257
Getting Your Tickets 258
For Every Thing There Is a Season 258
For Every Venue There Is a Subway .259
Where Classical Music Is King 260
A Night at the Opera 261
Music That Defies the Melting Pot 261
Dance (and We Don't Mean the Funky Chicken) 262

From Blue Men to Can-Can—All Those Other
    Performing Arts 262
Wait a Minute—What About Movies? 263

20 Hitting the Clubs & Bars   264
Hey, Hepcats—Where to Go for Jazz 264
Shake Your Booty—Where to Go to Dance 265
Getting the Blues 265
Life Is a Cabaret—and So Are These Places 266
Country, Folk, & Bluegrass in New York? You Bet 266
Where to Go if You Could Use a Laugh 266
The World Music Scene 267
Lawdy Miss Claudy—The Rock & Roll Scene 267
Where the Avant Garde Is Probably Old Hat 267
Where Have All the Pubs Gone? 267
Martinis & Manhattan 268
Other Watering Holes 268
Gay Clubs & Bars 268
Staying out Late—The Velvet-Rope Scene 269

Appendices

A New York A to Z—Facts at Your Fingertips   270

**B Toll-Free Numbers & Web Sites for Airlines
    & Hotels   273**

Index   275

Maps

Downtown Orientation xiv
Midtown Orientation xvi
Uptown Orientation xviii
Downtown Hotels 59
Midtown Hotels 60
Uptown Hotels 63
New York Metropolitan
  Area 85
Manhattan Neighborhoods 91
Downtown Dining 114
Midtown Dining 118
Uptown Dining 122
Downtown Attractions 165
Midtown Attractions 166
Uptown Attractions 168
Brooklyn Heights & the
  Promenade 172
Central Park Attractions 175
Greenwich Village & SoHo 179
Chinatown & Little Italy 181
Wall St. & the Financial
  District 188
Madison Avenue Shopping 209
Downtown Shopping 211
Midtown Shopping 214

Itinerary #1—Central Park &
  the East Side Museums 222
Itinerary #2—The Museums,
  the Park, & Times Square . . .224
Itinerary #3—The Statue of
  Liberty, South Street, &
  Chinatown 227
Itinerary #4—The Statue of
  Liberty, Wall Street, &
  the Village 229
Itinerary #5—The World Trade
  Center, Chinatown, Little
  Italy, & the Village 231
Itinerary #6—Fifth Avenue,
  MOMA, Rockefeller Center,
  & Times Square 232
Itinerary #7—The Village, the
  Flatiron District, & the
  Empire State Building 235
Itinerary #8—The U.N., Grand
  Central, the Intrepid, &
  Times Square 237
The Theater District 253
Lincoln Center 260

About the Authors
Bruce Murphy was born in New York City, where he now works as a free-lance writer.

Alessandra de Rosa is a world traveler and professional tourist who has also worked for the United Nations.

An Invitation to the Reader
In researching this book, we discovered many wonderful places—hotels, restaurants, shops, and more. We're sure you'll find others. Please tell us about them so that we can share the information with your fellow travelers in upcoming editions. If you were disappointed with a recommendation, we'd love to know that, too. Please write to:

Bruce Murphy & Alessandra de Rosa
The Complete Idiot's Travel Guide to New York City
Macmillan Travel
1633 Broadway
New York, NY 10019

An Additional Note
Please be advised that travel information is subject to change at any time—and this is especially true of prices. We therefore suggest that you write or call ahead for confirmation when making your travel plans. The authors, editors, and publisher cannot be held responsible for the experiences of readers while traveling. Your safety is important to us, however, so we encourage you to stay alert and be aware of your surroundings. Keep a close eye on cameras, purses, and wallets—all of which are favorite targets of thieves and pickpockets.

The following abbreviations are used for credit cards:

AE	American Express	EURO	Eurocard
CB	Carte Blanche	JCB	Japan Credit Bank
DC	Diners Club	MC	MasterCard
DISC	Discover	V	Visa
ER	enRoute		

Introduction

New York is a city that could make anyone feel like an idiot. It's big, loud, fast, and can be more than a little intimidating. If New Orleans is "The Big Easy," New York is "The Even Bigger Difficulty."

Despite this bad reputation, we've got some good news: You couldn't have picked a better time to visit (except maybe the 1920s, but that's not an option). New York is currently undergoing a renaissance. Crime is down, business is up, the incessant building and renovation continues, and people are in an uncharacteristically good mood (most of the time, anyway—just don't get in their way on the sidewalk). The hotel industry is developing newer and better facilities for families, new restaurants are popping up every week, and even notorious 42nd Street is scrubbed clean and wearing its best suit.

As a tourist, you won't have to do the horrible things that people who live here do—like find an apartment or a job—but, just like us, you'll have to learn what's where, and how to get there. Fortunately, you have this easy-to-use guide, which is set up to make your first bite of the Big Apple as palatable as possible. Unlike those monstrous travel tomes in which you need 11 or 12 fingers to keep track of all the information on a single topic, we start from the beginning and put all the information you need for a specific task, such as finding a hotel, in one place.

Part 1 answers all those nagging questions you've been asking yourself, such as when to go, how to get there, whether or not to join a tour, and how much it's all going to cost. It also gives you addresses, phone numbers, and Web sites where you can get more information.

Part 2 is all about hotels. We discuss New York neighborhoods from the perspective of lodging, and we pose questions to help you determine your needs and the kind of accommodation you want. A special feature of this book is the use of indexes, so after you've gone through all those descriptions you don't have to pull out your scratch pad and list all the ones in Midtown, all the cheap ones, and so on. The work has already been done for you.

Part 3 is about geography—where things are, and how to get around in the city. The neighborhoods are described in terms of their attractions.

Part 4 is all about food, from the humble hot dog stands to the elegant dining rooms. Once again, indexes are provided to help you narrow down your choices.

Part 5 describes the sights, from museums to the main pilgrimage sites for shoppers. In order to help you fit in all that you want to see without getting worn out, we provide some sample itineraries throughout the city, and then lead you through the process of planning an itinerary of your own.

Part 6 belongs to the night. It covers the major artistic attractions, from Broadway shows to jazz clubs, and gives you an idea of what each costs, as well as ways to get discount tickets (and for big hits, how to get tickets, period). There is also a chapter on places to have a drink, night clubs, and other more or less civilized relaxations.

Extras

This book has several special features that you won't find in other guidebooks—features that will help you make better use of the information, and find it faster.

As mentioned above, **indexes** cross reference the information in ways that let you see at a glance your options in a particular subcategory: Italian restaurants, downtown hotels, hotels for people with disabilities.

We've also sectioned off little tidbits of useful information in **sidebars,** which come in five types:

Sometimes the best way to fix something in your mind is to write it down, and with that in mind we've provided **worksheets** to help you concretize your thinking and make your decisions. (Underlining or highlighting as you read along isn't a bad idea, either.)

A **kid friendly icon** is used throughout the book to identify those activities, attractions, and establishments that are especially suited to people traveling with children.

Appendixes at the back of the book list important numbers and addresses covering every aspect of your trip, from reservations to emergencies.

New York Stories

These boxes offer you interesting historical facts or trivia about the city.

Extra! Extra!

Check these boxes for handy facts, hints, and insider advice.

Tourist Traps

These boxes steer you away from rip-offs, activities that aren't worth the trouble, shady dealings, and other pitfalls.

Dollars & Sense

Here you'll find tips on saving money and cutting corners to make your trip not only enjoyable but also affordable.

Time-Savers

Here you'll find ways to save time, avoid lines and hassles, and streamline the business of traveling.

Downtown Orientation

0   333 y

0   152 m

Downtown is where New York City began, with the first Dutch settlements back in the early 17th century. Today, it's home to both Wall Street stockbrokers and East Village skate-punks, bustling Chinatown markets and quiet SoHo galleries. Almost everywhere you look, there's some great New York experience to be had. Here's a few of them.

Classic Downtown Experiences

- Visiting the **Statue of Liberty** and **Ellis Island**
- Going to the top of the **World Trade Center**
- Walking across the **Brooklyn Bridge**
- Strolling in **Greenwich Village**
- Eating dim sum in **Chinatown**
- Taking a **cruise** on the harbor
- Going to the **art galleries in SoHo**
- Having lunch in a **sidewalk cafe**
- Seeing **Wall Street** in action
- Checking out the scene in **Washington Square Park**
- **Shopping** in the Village and SoHo boutiques
- Going to the **South Street Seaport**
- Going to a **jazz club** in Greenwich Village or a **rock club** in the East Village

Information on these and other New York adventures can be found throughout the book; check the index to find one quickly.

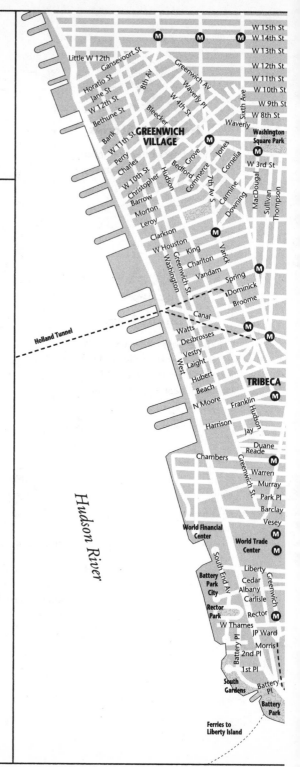

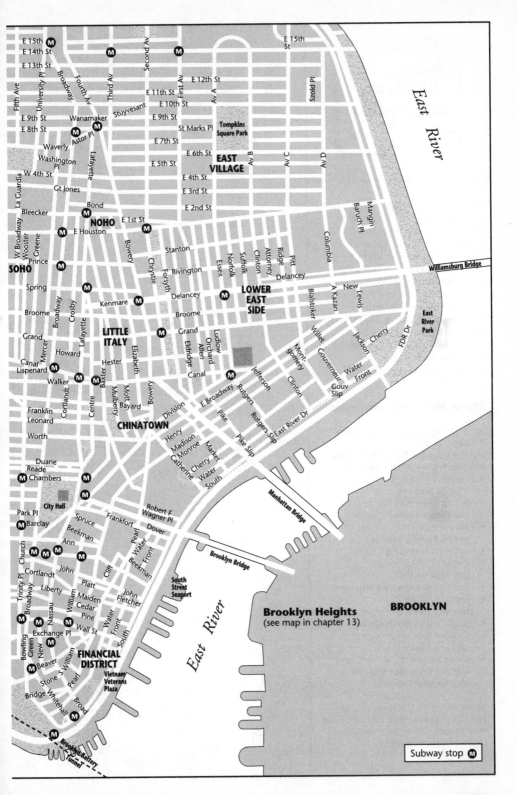

East River

E 15th
E 14th St
E 13th St
Second Av
E 12th St
E 11th St
E 10th St
E 9th St
St Marks Pl
E 8th St
Waverly
Washington Pl
W 4th St
Gt Jones
Bleecker
Bond
NOHO
E Houston
Stanton
Forsyth
Rivington
Delancey
Broome
Grand
Eldridge
Canal

Fifth Av
University Pl
Broadway
Fourth Av
Third Av
First Av
Av A
Wanamaker
Stuyvesant
Astor Pl
Lafayette
La Guardia
W Broadway
Wooster
Greene
Prince
Spring
Broome
Grand
Canal
Lispenard
Walker
Franklin
Leonard
Worth
Duane
Reade
Chambers

E 15th
St

Szold Pl

Tompkins
Square Park

EAST
VILLAGE

Av B
Av C
Av D

Mangin
Baruch Pl

Columbia

Williamsburg Bridge

Pitt
Ridge
Attorney
Clinton
Suffolk
Norfolk
Essex

SOHO

Chrystie
Bowery

Kenmare
Broadway
Crosby
Mercer

LITTLE
ITALY
Howard
Hester
Elizabeth
Mott
Bayard
Bowery
Baxter
Centre
Mulberry
Cortlandt
Lafayette

E 1st St

Delancey

LOWER
EAST
SIDE

Bialstoker
A Kazan
New
Lewis

Jackson
Cherry

East
River
Park

Willet
Gouverneur

Mont-
gomery
Clinton
Jefferson
Rutgers
Rutgers Slip
East River Dr
Pike
Pike Slip

Water
Front
Gouv
Slip

FDR Dr

Ludlow
Orchard
Allen

E Broadway

Division
Henry
Madison
Monroe
Catherine
Cherry
Water
South

CHINATOWN

Market

Manhattan Bridge

City Hall

Park Pl
Barclay
Spruce
Beekman
Frankfort
Ann
John
Church
Cortlandt
Liberty
Platt
Maiden
Cedar
Pine
Wall St
Cliff
Beekman
Pearl
Water
Front
John
Fletcher

Robert F
Wagner Pl
Dover

Brooklyn Bridge

South
Street
Seaport

Trinity Pl
Broadway
Nassau
William
Exchange Pl
Bowling
Green
New
Beaver

Stone
S William
Pearl
Bridge
Whitehall
Broad

FINANCIAL
DISTRICT

Vietnam
Veterans
Plaza

East River

Brooklyn Heights
(see map in chapter 13)

BROOKLYN

Brooklyn Battery
Tunnel

Subway stop Ⓜ

XV

Midtown
Orientation

0 ————— 330 y

0 ————— 301 m

Midtown Manhattan is the
crossroads of the world, where
big business gets busy 24 hours
a day, where Times Square
rings in the new year, and where
every actor in the world dreams
of hitting the stage. Some of the
biggest attractions in the city are
located here, including the
Empire State Building, the United
Nations, and Rockefeller Center,
and since most of the big hotels
are in this part of town, why
not just consider it home...

Classic Midtown Experiences

- Catching a **Broadway show**
- Going to the top of
  the **Empire State Building**
- Shopping on **Fifth Avenue**
- Seeing the lights in
  Times Square
- Having afternoon tea at
  the **Plaza Hotel**
- Eating lunch on the steps
  of the **Public Library**
- Getting a **hot dog** ("with
  everything") from a
  sidewalk vendor
- Going to the **United Nations**
- Seeing a movie in
  Bryant Park (summer only)
- Ice skating at **Rockefeller
  Center** (winter only)
- Going to **Macy's**
- Seeing architectural wonders
  like the **Chrysler Building**
  and **Grand Central**

Information on these and other
New York adventures can be found
throughout the book; check the
index to find one quickly.

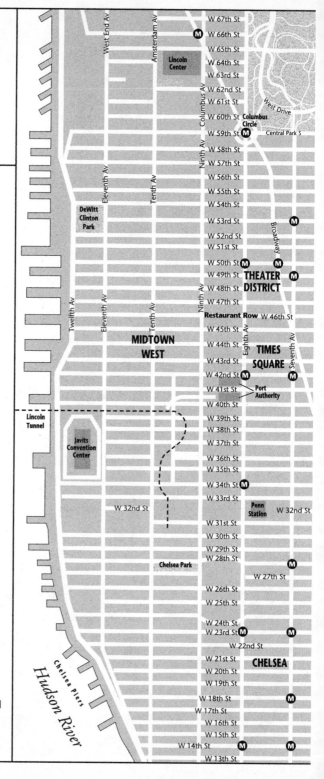

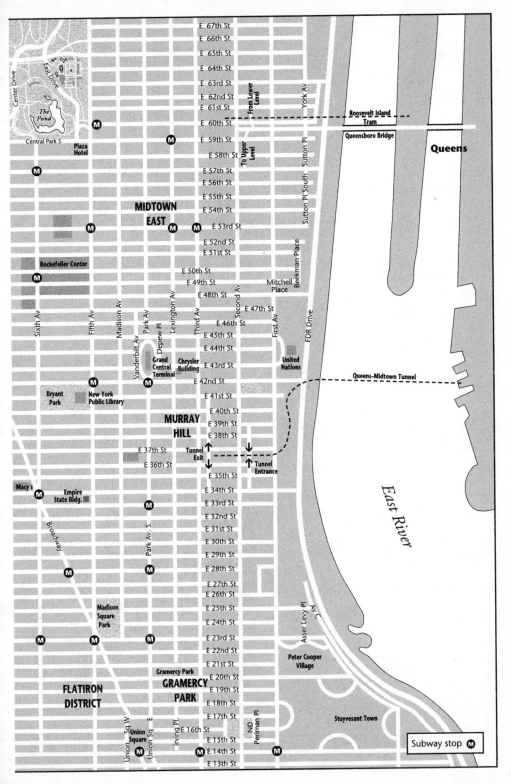

Uptown Orientation

```
0          330 y
0          301 m
```

Uptown is where we keep the museums here in New York—and where we keep a lot of the New Yorkers, too. Divided by Central Park, the Upper East Side and the Upper West Side are both big residential areas full of beautiful 19th- and early 20th-century architecture, interspersed with some of the best museums and concert halls in the world. Whether it's boutiques, bookshops, or bagels you're looking for, a trip Uptown is sure to get you in a New York state of mind.

Classic Uptown Experiences

- Going to the opera, ballet, or symphony at **Lincoln Center**
- Going for a walk in **Central Park**
- Going to the **Metropolitan Museum of Art**
- Having lunch at Central Park's **Boathouse Cafe**
- Strolling down **Museum Mile** and checking out the art
- Going food shopping at **Zabar's** and getting bagels at **H&H**
- Taking the tram to **Roosevelt Island**
- Going to the **Cafe Carlyle** for a dinner show
- Shopping on **Madison Avenue**
- Going to **Riverside Park** and watching the boats on the Hudson
- Visiting the **Cathedral of St. John the Divine**
- Going to the **Central Park Zoo**

Information on these and other New York adventures can be found throughout the book; check the index to find one quickly.

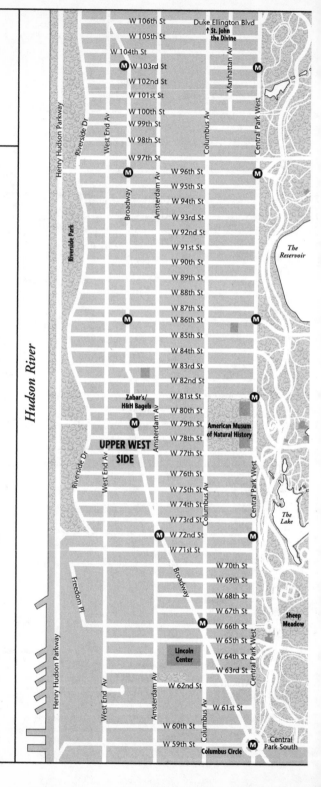

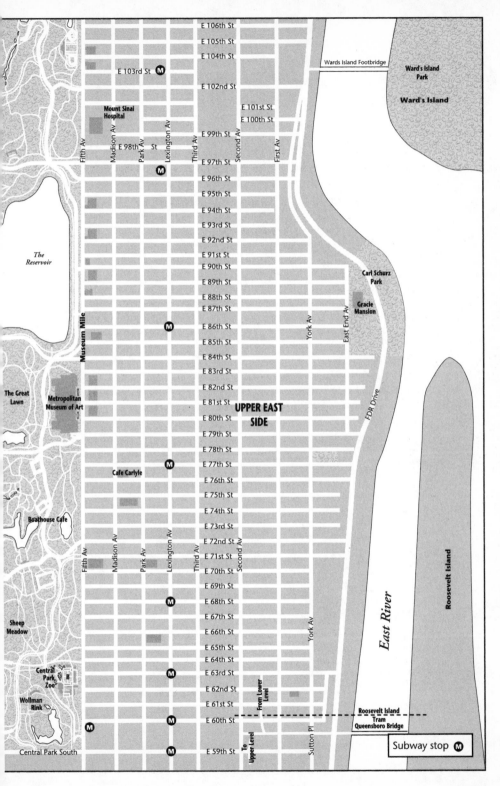

Part 1

What You Need to Do Before You Go

The Big Apple, The City That Never Sleeps, Sin City—whatever you call it, there's a mystique about New York that leads 16.4 million people to live in its metropolitan area and millions more to visit. You want art? It's here. Theater, music, and dining? All here. There's so much here, in fact, that you could keep yourself amused for years.

But it would cost you. Let's get our cards right out on the table: New York ain't cheap. That's one of the reasons you need to plan your visit well: so that you can take advantage of whatever bargains are available. Remember that New York is classified as a "megacity"—one of only 16 in the world. It's not the kind of place where you can just drop in and have it all waiting for you. As the center of international finance, New York is busy all the time, and during a busy season or convention you might have a nasty surprise if you haven't booked a room in advance. (That said, we'll still give some tips in chapter 5 on what to do if you haven't planned ahead.)

If you read this book and do your homework, you shouldn't have any problem. Part 1 will help you "know before you go" and guide you through selecting transportation. Part 2 will help you find food, clothing, and shelter (also known as dining, shopping, and lodging), as well as give you the lowdown on entertainment and tips on how to get around the city like a real New Yorker.

Chapter 1

How to Get Started

In This Chapter

➤ What you need to find out

➤ Where to go for information

➤ Thinking ahead

➤ When to go

➤ Who do you think you are? (Evaluating your special needs and interests)

Information, Please

Your visit begins long before you set foot on a plane, train, or car; it begins when you first begin to accumulate travel facts. If you have a phone, a computer, or a pen and some stamps, you can assemble a wealth of information about the city from the privacy of your own home; your mailbox will be full of tourist brochures in no time. Just remember, though, that almost every one of the brochures will have been produced by someone with a vested interest in luring you in, so they're not going to be what you call unbiased. Take everything they promise with a grain of salt, and compare your data with information in this book (or, if you want to augment our info, with the listings in one of those super mondo complete, explore-every-nook-and-cranny guidebooks, like Frommer's).

A good place to begin your search is the **New York Convention & Visitors Bureau,** 810 Seventh Ave., New York, N.Y. 10019. Their 24-hour telephone hotline (☎ **800/NYC-VISIT;** outside North America and from

NYC dial 212/397-8200), is for ordering New York City literature only. You can order a Big Apple Visitors Kit (hotels, restaurants, theaters, events, etc.) from them for $5, but allow 4–6 weeks for delivery. If you want to talk to a real live person, call the local number (☎ **212/484-1222**) Monday through Friday, 9am to 5pm They can tip you off to upcoming city events and transportation, too. For those of you who are wired into the World Wide Web, you can reach the Visitors Bureau Web site at **www.nycvisit.com**.

For New York State information, call ☎ **800/225-5697.**

Big Apple Greeters is a non-profit organization with a staff of volunteer New Yorkers who will take you around their beloved neighborhoods for 3 or 4 hours on a free tour. Call them at ☎ **212/669-2896** (or fax 212/669-3685) Monday to Friday from 9am to 5pm before you leave; they get a lot of requests, so you have to reserve at least a week in advance.

Crawling the Web
Here are three of the more useful on-line sources:

➤ The *New York Times* Web site at **www.nytimes.com** is a prime site for gathering cultural information, reading reviews, and checking out the Sunday "Arts & Leisure" section. (The only drawback is that you have to register and may have to pay for access to certain sections.)

➤ **www.newyork.sidewalk.com** is great for checking out the entertainment and dining prospects.

➤ You can find out about lots of other New York–related Web sites—a couple thousand of them—through the index **www.panix.com/clay/nyc/**.

For more Web sites, see chapters 4 and 19. Whether or not you did your homework, once you arrive in New York you'll have several more sources of information. You'll find information on real-person, visitor's bureau–type sources in chapter 7 and info on informational magazines and newspapers in chapter 4.

When Should I Go?
New York always has great things going on, summer or winter, rain or shine, so there's no real "best" time to go. Various factors will affect your choice, however, so it might be easier to think about when *not* to go.

It's Not the Heat, It's the Humidity—NYC Summers
The worst weather in New York is during that long week or 10 days that seems to arrive each summer—sometime between, say, mid-July and mid-August—when temperatures go up to around 100°F (38°C) with 100% humidity. Then the city absolutely stinks: You feel sticky all day, the streets smell horrible, everyone's cranky, and locals slink from one air-conditioned place to another or just leave town entirely. Don't get put off by this

drawback—summer has its compensations, such as wonderful free open-air concerts and other events that the city hosts to soothe boiling spirits—but bear it in mind. If you're planning to visit in the summer and are at all temperature sensitive, your odds of getting comfortable weather are better at the end of the summer.

It's Not the Cold, It's the Wind Chill—NYC Winters
Another period when you might not like to stroll around the streets of the Big Apple is during the freezing-cold period in January or February, when temperatures are in the 20s (–6°C) or below and the wind whipping down the canyons between buildings makes it feel well below zero. Stimulating for a visit to Central Park! Of course, you might get lucky and hit mild weather. Consult your *Farmer's Almanac*.

Fall and spring are the Shangri La times in New York. From April to June and September to November, temperatures are mild and pleasant and the light is beautiful. Also, sometimes around the middle of October the city experiences an Indian Summer—our reward for getting through that summer hot spell. Note that the worse the weather, the more anxious hoteliers and merchants are to lure you here, so traveling in the off season has the enticement that you won't have to fight so hard for a room or a table (in summer, restaurants sometimes feel *empty*) and you may get better deals.

NYC Average Temperature & Rainfall

	Jan	Feb	Mar	Apr	May	June	July	Aug	Sept	Oct	Nov	Dec
Daily Temp. (°F)	38	40	48	61	71	80	85	84	77	67	54	42
Days of Rain	11	10	11	11	11	10	11	10	8	8	9	10

Hitting the Big Events & Exhibitions
If you're passionately interested in one field or another—art, music, dance, opera, theater—then the whole weather discussion may be academic: You'll be gearing your trip to take advantage of the best events, and weather be damned. If it's Broadway theater you're looking to see, fall through early spring is the best time for a visit. (Tickets are easiest to come by in the first two months of the new year.) If it's museums and the gallery scene that you want, be aware that the major cultural institutions hibernate in summer rather than winter. (As we said earlier in this chapter, however, the city takes up some of the slack by offering free concerts and events in the summertime.)

But the arts aren't everything. There are dog shows, boat shows, famous parades, weird parades, and fireworks displays. Following is a list of high points, arranged chronologically. For more information, consult chapters 13 and 14.

January
➤ **New York National Boat Show,** Javits Convention Center. Call
☎ **212/922-1212** for information. A virtual recreational navy under
glass. Jan 3–11.

➤ **Winter Antiques Show at the Seventh Regiment Armory,** 643
Park Ave. at 66th St. Call ☎ **212/879-9713** for information. Calling
this show tony is an understatement. Take a couple hundred thousand
bucks out of the mattress and buy that Louis XVI footstool you always
wanted. Jan 15–25.

➤ **Chinese New Year,** Chinatown. Two weeks of fun, with the famous
dragon parade, as well as fireworks (but only the big, legally sanctioned
kind—the city is cracking down). Late Jan/early Feb.

February
➤ **Westminster Kennel Club Dog Show,** Madison Square Garden.
Call ☎ **212/255-0020** for information. The fur flies with 2,500 canine
competitors and their owners. Who will be Top Dog? Mid-Feb.

March
➤ **International Cat Show,** Madison Square Garden. Call ☎ **212/
465-6741** for information. The other *Cats*—only here there are 800
of 'em, and they don't jump in your lap.

➤ **New York Flower Show.** It was canceled in 1997 and 1998, but
they're considering reviving it for 1999. Keep your fingers crossed.
Sponsored by the Horticultural Society (☎ **212/757-0915**).

➤ **St. Patrick's Day Parade,** Fifth Avenue. Umpteen thousand specta-
tors line the route to watch 150,000 marchers dressed in varying shades
of green. The parade has been controversial in recent years due to a dis-
pute between Catholic and parade hierarchy and a gay Irish group
that's been banned from marching. Mar 17.

➤ **Ringling Brothers and Barnum & Bailey Circus,** Madison
Square Garden. Call ☎ **212/465-6741** for information. The morning
before the show opens, elephants and other animals troop from
Twelfth Avenue and 34th Street to the Garden in one of New York's
most unusual parades. March through April.

April
➤ **The Easter Parade,** Fifth Avenue. Not exactly like the Fred Astaire
movie, but still fun. April 12.

➤ **Greater New York International Auto Show,** Javits Convention
Center. Call ☎ **212/216-2000** for information. The largest such show
in the country. Apr 11–19.

May

➤ **International Fine Arts Fair,** Seventh Regimental Armory, 643 Park Ave. at 66th St. Call ☎ **212/472-0590** for information. A relatively new but prospering show with dozens of galleries participating. Early May.

➤ **Fleet Week,** *Intrepid* Sea-Air-Space Museum. Call ☎ **212/245-0072** for information. A plethora of ships and thousands of crew visit New York, offering demonstrations. May 20–27.

➤ **Ninth Avenue International Food Festival,** 37th to 57th Streets. Twenty blocks of food, as well as street entertainment and music. May 23–24.

June

➤ **Lesbian and Gay Pride Week and March,** Fifth Avenue/West Village. Call ☎ **212/807-7433** for information. Commemorating the Stonewall Riot of 1969—birth of the gay rights movement—with a week of events and a lengthy parade (52nd Street to the West Village). June 21–28.

➤ **Restaurant Week.** Participating fine restaurants offer dinner for $19.98. Check informational publications (see chapter 4) for times and the list of restaurants.

July

➤ **Fourth of July.** A downtown street festival in the daytime; a parade of tall ships as well as fireworks at night.

➤ **Rockefeller Center Flower and Garden Show,** 48th and 51st Streets. Call ☎ **212/632-3975** for information. A premier horticultural event, especially given the apparent demise of the Flower Show (see above). Mid-July.

➤ **Lincoln Center Festival,** Lincoln Center. Call ☎ **212/546-2656** for information. Dance, opera, ballet, theater, music, and more. July and August.

➤ **Mostly Mozart,** Avery Fisher Hall. Call ☎ **212/875-5030** for information. Many world-class musicians have performed in this festival. July or Aug.

August

➤ **U.S. Open Tennis Championships,** Flushing Meadows, Queens. Call ☎ **718-760-6200** for information. One of tennis's "grand slam" events. Aug through Sept.

September

➤ **Wigstock,** 11th Street Pier. Call ☎ **212/213-2438** for information. A drag queen extravaganza. The costumes put Vegas showgirls to shame. Location varies from year to year. Labor Day weekend.

➤ **New York Film Festival,** sponsored by the Film Society of Lincoln Center. Call ☎ **212/875-5610** for information. A two-week festival that's seen many important premieres over the years. Get your tickets in advance. Sept through Oct.

October

➤ **Next Wave Festival,** Brooklyn Academy of Music. Call ☎ **718/636-4100** for information. Experimental dance, theater, and music. Oct through Dec.

➤ **Greenwich Village Halloween Parade,** West Village/Chelsea. Not your average group of trick-or-treaters, this parade features outrageous costumes and people. Oct 31.

November

➤ **New York City Marathon.** Ends in Central Park. Call ☎ **212/860-4455** for information. Some 30,000 runners, including the best in the world, zip through all five boroughs while a million onlookers cheer. Nov 1.

➤ **Macy's Thanksgiving Day Parade,** Central Park West/Broadway. Call ☎ **212/494-5432** for information. You can watch it on TV at home, but it's not the same (especially if you go the night before and watch them inflate the balloons). Nov 26.

➤ **Big Apple Circus,** Lincoln Center. Call ☎ **212/268-2500** for information. A native circus, and a favorite with New Yorkers. Nov through Jan.

December

➤ **Rockefeller Center Christmas Tree Lighting,** Rockefeller Center. The lighting of the huge tree, which is trucked in from distant parts, draws huge crowds. Early Dec.

Tourist Traps

Untold hordes converge on Times Square each **New Year's Eve** for "the dropping of the ball." If you feel you have to see it, call ☎ **212/768-1560** or 212/354-0003 (the hotline) for information. Some people will tell you it's exciting; others report the crowd is huge (about half a million people), mostly drunk, and often violent. You may take away great memories or a black eye.

We Are Family—Traveling with Your Kids

The good news is that there are more "family-friendly" accommodations and sights in New York than there used to be. However, if you are traveling with kids, special planning is involved. (As we're sure you already knew.)

Your family is as individual as you are. Common sense says that whatever your kids like to do at home, they might like to do in New York (or might dislike *not* being able to do). Only you know whether it will be important to have electronic babysitters like television and computers in your hotel room, or if your rambunctious offspring would go crazy cooped up and would rather romp in Central Park. These are factors you must not forget when you choose a hotel (see chapter 6) or restaurant (see chapter 10). Throughout the book, look for the child icon identifying family-friendly options.

Preparation

As you're planning your trip, get your kids involved. There are plenty of children's books set in New York, going back to *To Think That I Saw It On Mulberry Street*. Show them some movies set in New York (not *Escape from New York*, however; how about *Miracle on 34th Street*?). You can also get them involved in going over the brochures, and hook them up to the New York City Reference Web site (www.panix.com/clay/nyc), where they can see pictures transmitted almost live from various vantage points around the city.

There are several publications you may want to grab before you visit:

➤ *Big Apple Parents' Paper,* 36 E. 12th St., New York, NY 10003. ☎ 212/533-2277; fax 212/475-6186. $28 per year. Monthly calendar on-line at **www.family.com/hompage.html**.

➤ *ParentGuide,* Parent Guide Network Corp., 419 Park Ave. S., New York, NY 10016. ☎ **212/213-8840**; fax 212/447-7734. $19.95 per year.

➤ *New York Family,* 141 Halstead Ave., Suite 3D, Mamaroneck, NY 10543. ☎ **914/381-7474**. $30 per year. On-line calendar: **www.starwave.com**.

Free copies of these publications can be found at children's stores and other locations in Manhattan.

For a guide book all about traveling to the Big Apple with children, look for *Frommer's New York City with Kids*.

Arriving & Finding Transportation

Your children may have even less patience than you do about waiting for public transportation to get into the city. If so, take a cab. If you have teenagers, then one of the bus options should be fine (see chapter 3). Once you get into the city, there's no reason you shouldn't travel by subway and bus.

Finding a Babysitter

You'll have to decide how much time you
want to spend with your kids in New York.
100%? Then you have no problem. If you
want to sneak off for a romantic dinner
and a show and you have younger children, however, you need to think about
babysitting.

New York Stories

New York is the fourth
largest city in the world in
terms of population. Only
Tokyo, Mexico City, and São
Paulo are larger.

The first place to look for babysitting is in
your hotel (better yet, ask about babysitting when you reserve). Many hotels have
babysitting services or will provide you
with lists of reliable sitters. If this doesn't
pan out, there's the **Baby Sitters Guild,** which you can reach at
☎ **212/682-0227,** or the **Frances Stewart Agency** (☎ **212/439-9222**).
They will also take your child on an outing. The sitters are licensed, insured,
and bonded.

Keeping the Kids Entertained

Given that your child probably isn't going to want to spend an hour looking
at medieval altarpieces in the Met, you'll need to plan some activities around
him/her/them. Look for the child icon throughout this book for places of
particular interest to children. Some child-friendly attractions are obvious,
like the Empire State Building, the Bronx Zoo (don't forget small and charming Central Park Zoo if you can't make it to the Bronx), the Statue of Liberty,
the Museum of Natural History, and Central Park.

If you have teenagers, you might want to consider that they'll be more interested in Downtown than Uptown, and Midtown may bore them stiff after
they've stared up at the buildings for a few hours. Downtown has a younger
crowd, lots of alternative music, coffee shops (if your kids drink coffee),
funky music stores, bookstores, and popular kids' hangouts. If you don't
want them wandering around the East Village alone, then prepare to go with
them; set aside some time to explore with them (and consult the restaurant
and attractions chapters later in the book).

Travel Advice for the Senior Set

People over the age of 60 are traveling more than ever before. And why not?
Being a senior citizen entitles you to some terrific travel bargains. If you're
not a member of **AARP (American Association of Retired Persons)**,
601 E St. NW, Washington, DC 20049 (☎ **202/434-AARP,** Web site
www.aarp.org), do yourself a favor and join. You'll get discounts on car
rentals and hotels.

Mature Outlook, P.O. Box 9390, Des Moines, IA 50306-9519 (☎ **800/
336-6330;** fax 847/286-5024), is a similar organization, offering discounts on
car rentals and hotel stays at many Holiday Inns, Howard Johnsons, and Best

Westerns. The $20 annual membership fee also gets you $100 in Sears coupons and a bimonthly magazine. Membership is open to all Sears customers 18 and over, but the organization's primary focus is on the 50-and-over market.

In addition, most of the major domestic airlines, including American, United, Continental, US Airways, and TWA, all offer discount programs for senior travelers—be sure to ask whenever you book a flight. Seniors get a 50% discount on bus and subway fares in New York, and certain theaters, museums, and other attractions give a senior discount as well—always inquire when buying your tickets, and be sure to carry identification with proof of age.

New York Stories

Of the 30 million or so visitors who come to New York every year, the largest category of visitors (other than U.S. citizens) is Canadians. The U.K. and Germany are second and third among foreign visitors.

The Mature Traveler, a monthly 12-page newsletter on senior citizen travel, is a valuable resource that's available by subscription ($30 a year) from GEM Publishing Group, Box 50400, Reno, NV 89513-0400. GEM also publishes *The Book of Deals,* a collection of more than 1,000 senior discounts on airlines, lodging, tours, and attractions around the country; it's available for $9.95 by calling ☎ **800/460-6676.** Another helpful publication is *101 Tips for the Mature Traveler,* available from Grand Circle Travel, 347 Congress St., Suite 3A, Boston, MA 02210 (☎ **800/221-2610** or 617/350-7500; fax 617/350-6206).

Grand Circle is also one of the literally hundreds of travel agencies specializing in vacations for seniors. But beware: Many of them are of the tour bus variety, with free trips thrown in for those who organize groups of 20 or more. Seniors seeking more independent travel should probably consult a regular travel agent. **SAGA International Holidays,** 222 Berkeley St., Boston, MA 02116 (☎ **800/343-0273**), offers inclusive tours and cruises for those 50 and older.

Advice for Travelers with Disabilities

There are more options and resources out there than ever before, so a disability shouldn't stop anybody from traveling. *A World of Options,* a 658-page book of resources for disabled travelers, covers everything from biking trips to scuba outfitters. It costs $30 plus $5 shipping and is available from **Mobility International USA,** P.O. Box 10767, Eugene, OR, 97440 (☎ **541/343-1284,** voice and TDD; Web site www.miusa.org). For more personal assistance, call the **Travel Information Service** at ☎ **215/ 456-9603** or 215/456-9602 (for TTY).

Many of the major car rental companies now offer hand-controlled cars for disabled drivers. Avis can provide such a vehicle at any of its locations in the U.S. if given 48-hour advance notice; Hertz requires 24–72 hours of advance reservation at most of its locations. **Wheelchair Getaways (☎ 800/ 873-4973;** Web site www.blvd.com/wg.htm) rents in more than 100 cities across the U.S. specialized vans with wheelchair lifts and other features for the disabled.

Travelers with disabilities may also want to consider joining a tour that caters specifically to them. One of the best operators is **Flying Wheels Travel,** 143 West Bridge (P.O. Box 382, Owatonna, MN 55060, ☎ 800/533-0363). The company offers various escorted tours and cruises, as well as private tours in minivans with lifts. Another good company is **FEDCAP Rehabilitation Services,** 211 W. 14th St., New York, NY 10011. Call ☎ 212/727-4200 or fax 212/727-4374 for information about membership and summer tours.

New York Stories

Ever wonder why New York is called **"The Big Apple"**? The general idea is that, like an apple, the city is "ripe with possibilities." Most people credit the term to journalist John J. FitzGerald of the long-defunct *Morning Telegraph,* who heard it used by stable hands at a New Orleans racetrack in the 1920s and thereafter used it to refer to New York's own tracks. Jazz musicians used it to refer to New York in general (and Harlem in particular) throughout the 1930s, but the term slowly fell out of use thereafter and was more or less forgotten by the 1970s, when it was used in an ad campaign run by the New York Convention and Visitors Bureau.

Vision-impaired travelers should contact the **American Foundation for the Blind,** 11 Penn Plaza, Suite 300, New York, NY 10001 (☎ 800/ 232-5463), for information on traveling with seeing-eye dogs.

In general, New York is progressive in its efforts to provide accessibility for the disabled. Equal access is now mandated by law, but implementation has been gradual and is not complete. All buses in New York have wheelchair lifts and "kneel" closer to the curb to enable those who are less mobile to step up into the bus. The subway is a different story: Some stations are wheelchair accessible, others not. You can get a free brochure, ***Accessible Transfer Points,*** from MTA Customer Assistance, 370 J St., Room 702, Brooklyn, NY 11201 (☎ 718/330-3322; TTY 718/596-8273). Braille subway maps are available from **The Lighthouse, Inc.,** 111 E. 59th St., New York, NY 10022 (☎ 800/334-5497 or 212/821-9200), which also produces concerts and exhibitions by the vision impaired.

For getting into the city from the airports, consider the **Gray Line Shuttle** (☎ **800/451-0455** or 212/315-3006), which has minibuses with lifts. The vans go only to Midtown hotels, and a reservation is necessary. Taxis should take disabled persons, wheelchairs, and guide dogs—they are required to by law.

Special guided tours for the disabled are provided by **Big Apple Greeters** (☎ **212/669-2896;** TTY 212/669-8273). As with their other tours (see above), advance reservations are necessary.

Building Accessibility

To find out which hotels, restaurants, and cultural institutions are accessible to the disabled, contact these organizations:

➤ **Hospital Audiences, Inc.,** 220 W. 42nd St., 13th Floor, New York, NY 10036 (Hotline ☎ **888/424-4685;** local 212/575-7676; TDD 212/575-7673). You can also order the accessibility guidebook on city cultural institutions, *Access for All*, for $5.

➤ **Society for the Advancement of Travel for the Handicapped,** 347 Fifth Avenue, Suite 610, New York, NY 10016 (**212/447-7284,** fax 212/725-8253). The society will send you information on accessible hotels, restaurants, and institutions.

Other helpful organizations, in addition to The Lighthouse (see above), are

➤ **New York Society for the Deaf,** 817 Broadway, 7th Floor, New York, NY 10003 (☎/TDD **212/777-3900**).

➤ **American Foundation for the Blind,** 11 Penn Plaza, Suite 300, New York, NY 10001 (☎ **800/232-5463** or 212/502-7600).

Advice for Gay & Lesbian Travelers

New York has had an important gay population at least since the days when Walt Whitman lived here, and has had a vocal gay population at least since June 27, 1969, when patrons of the Stonewall Bar on Christopher Street decided they weren't going to take another anti-gay rousting by the police. The violent protest that ensued gave birth to the gay rights movement. Today, New York ranks with San Francisco as one of the most hospitable and tolerant cities as far as gay people are concerned, and the communities of Greenwich Village and Chelsea have large gay populations. (It's not utopia, however; bias incidents, unfortunately, still do occur.)

New York Stories

New York City is believed to have the largest gay population of any city in the United States.

The following are a few of the major gay organizations in the city:

➤ The **Lesbian and Gay Community Services Center,** 208 W. 13th St., between Seventh and Eighth Avenues (☎ **212/620-7310**), can supply you with a calendar of cultural and other events. They sponsor dozens of programs and host 400+ other gay, lesbian, and bisexual organizations.

➤ **Gay Men's Health Crisis (GMHC),** 119 W. 24th St., has an AIDS hotline (☎ **212/807-6655**) and serves anyone with HIV, not just gays.

➤ **The Organization of Lesbian and Gay Architects and Designers** (☎ **212/475-7652**); by calling the organization you can obtain a free map of lesbian and gay historical landmarks.

Gay nightlife is centered in the West Village and Chelsea. *Homo Xtra* is a free publication that's distributed in restaurants, clubs, and bars and carries information about what's going on in town. A couple of other gay publications that have popped up are *LGNY* (*Lesbian & Gay New York*), which appears on alternate Tuesdays, and *The New York Blade News*, a weekly newspaper that comes out on Fridays and is only a few months old.

Big Apple Safety Tips

New York is not as threatening as you might think from the movies that are made about it. The good thing is that you usually can sense whether or not you are in the wrong place (unlike some other innocent-seeming towns we could mention). If it feels unsafe, it probably is; go elsewhere.

Some other ideas:

➤ In the subway, off-hours waiting areas are marked with signs. Use them. Also, sit in the middle rather than at the ends of the cars, and don't ever get on an empty car; there's safety in numbers.

➤ Be discreet when looking at maps, checking to see how much money you have, and so on. Don't advertise yourself as an out-of-towner.

➤ Don't wear valuable jewelry.

➤ Keep the door of your hotel room locked; don't assume hotel security will spot every shady character who walks in.

➤ Avoid deserted or dark streets.

➤ Take yellow cabs with city medallions only (not "gypsy" cabs).

➤ If accosted on the street by someone with a long story to tell, say "sorry" and keep going.

➤ Don't leave purses or jackets with wallets in them hanging on your chair in a restaurant.

➤ Use the main exits of theaters.

➤ Don't play three-card monte or other con games. You'll lose.

➤ Jack Benny's joke answer to "Your money or your life" ("Wait, I'm thinking it over") was a lot funnier 30 years ago. If you actually are mugged by someone who means business, don't be so foolish as to resist.

Chapter 2

Money Matters

In This Chapter

➤ Money: How much and what kind?

➤ Budgeting your trip

➤ Pinching pennies

Money matters, all right, especially in New York. One thing is certain: This city is well set up for separating you from your bread. There are plenty of places to get it—cash machines galore—and even more places to spend it. New York is an expensive city to visit, and you need to have your wits about you to keep your budget on track.

Should I Carry Traveler's Checks or the Green Stuff?

Traveler's checks are something of an anachronism from the days when people used to write personal checks all the time instead of going to the automated teller machine (ATM). In those days, travelers could not be sure of finding a place that would cash a check for them while they were on vacation. Also, because they could be replaced if lost or stolen, traveler's checks were a sound alternative to filling your wallet with cash at the beginning of a trip. These days, traveler's checks are less necessary because most cities have 24-hour network-linked ATMs that allow you to withdraw money from your account at home.

ATMs to the Left of Me, ATMs to the Right of Me...

The good thing about cash is that everybody takes it. That's the bad thing about it, too. Crime is down in New York City, but as with any major urban destination the world over, you don't want to go around carrying a lot of money on your person. In any case, you have no need to: At some intersections in New York, you'll find a bank on almost every corner, allowing you the security of withdrawing only as much cash as you'll need for a day or two at a time.

The big players—Chase, Citibank, and similar institutions—have lots of locations, and the various ATM networks are well represented. For example, Chase is hooked into the Cirrus, NYCE, Plus, Pulse, Visa, MasterCard, and MAC systems. If you *really* don't want to go looking, though, the **Cirrus** (☎ 800/424-7787 or 800/4CIRRUS) and **Plus** (☎ 800/843-7587) phone services will give you specific locations of ATMs where you can withdraw your money. Big banks usually don't charge any extra fee above what your own bank charges for transactions. The fees depend on what your bank is, of course. Smaller banks, like Apple and NatWest will charge you. A message should warn you that you're going to be charged before you proceed with the transaction.

Check It Out

If you feel you need the security of traveler's checks and don't mind the hassle of showing identification every time you want to cash a check, you'll be happy to know that you can get them at almost any bank. **American Express** offers checks in denominations of $10, $20, $50, $100, $500, and $1,000. You'll pay a service charge ranging from 1%–4%, though AAA members can obtain checks without a fee at most AAA offices. You can also get American Express traveler's checks over the phone by calling ☎ **800/ 221-7282;** Amex gold and platinum cardholders who call this number are exempt from the 1% fee.

Visa also offers traveler's checks, available at Citibank locations across the country and at several other banks. The service charge ranges from 1.5%–2%; checks come in denominations of $20, $50, $100, $500, and $1,000. **MasterCard** also offers traveler's checks; call ☎ **800/223-9920** for a location near you.

Dollars & Sense

Though you'll be able to get in touch with your money through ATMs, you may have to pay a price for the privilege, particularly at non-bank locations. There are cash machines in such out-of-the-way places as supermarkets and indoor arcades, which is convenient if you've been forgetful, but they may clip you $1 or more for the transaction.

Time-Savers

There are so many ATMs, it's easier to say where they are *not*. The far West Village has a dearth of machines; if you find yourself going there for dinner, remember that just about the only machines are the Chase and Citibank branches at Sheridan Square, and the Chase at Hudson and 12th streets. In Soho, unbelievably, there are no banks west of Broadway except for the rather remote Chase at Hudson Street and Canal. The East Village is also a little short on cash machines, and the lines are always long at the ones that are available.

Plastic Money

Credit cards are invaluable when traveling. They're a safe way to carry money and they provide a convenient record of all your travel expenses when you arrive home. Plus, if you run short of the green stuff, you can get **cash advances** off your cards at any bank. Keep in mind, though, that you'll start paying interest on the advance the moment you receive the cash, and you won't receive frequent-flyer miles on an airline credit card. At most banks, you don't even need to go to a teller; you can get a cash advance at the ATM if you know your personal identification number (PIN). If you've forgotten your PIN or didn't even know you had one, call the phone number on the back of your credit card and ask the bank to send it to you. It usually takes 5–7 business days, though some banks will do it over the phone if you give them your mother's maiden name or offer some other form of ID.

Stop, Thief! (What to Do If Your Money Gets Stolen)

Almost every credit card company has an emergency 800 number you can call if your wallet or purse is stolen. They may be able to wire you a cash advance off your credit card immediately, and in many places they can get you an emergency credit card in a day or two. The issuing bank's 800 number is usually on the back of the credit card, but that doesn't help you much if the card was stolen, does it? **Citicorp Visa's** U.S. emergency number is ☎ **800/645-6556. American Express** cardholders and traveler's check holders should call ☎ **800/221-7282** for all money emergencies. **MasterCard** holders should call ☎ **800/307-7309.** Or, you can call **800 information** at ☎ **800/555-1212** to find out your card's 800 number.

If you opt to carry traveler's checks, be sure to keep a record of their serial numbers in a safe place so that you can handle just such an emergency.

Odds are that if your wallet is gone, you've seen the last of it, and the police aren't likely to recover it for you. After you realize that it's gone and you cancel your credit cards, however, it's still worth a call to inform the police. You may need the police report number for credit card or insurance purposes later.

Extra! Extra!

A few money tips for ya...

➤ Avoid outdoor ATMs. Use an indoor machine instead.

➤ Remember that some hotels have individual safes in rooms in which you can stash some cash.

➤ Many merchants are now set up to debit your account directly (through your ATM money card), which can help you cut down on cash purchases without running up your credit cards.

So What's This Trip Gonna Cost?

Budgeting a trip to New York will be different from planning a trip to Europe or a visit to the Grand Canyon, or even a journey to another American city that's spread out over more square miles. Some things, like hotels, will cost more than you want to believe; other things, like transportation, are relatively cheap. There's an incredible number of restaurants, and they are inexpensive relative to what you would spend, for example, dining out in a European capital (and they offer a lot more variety). The budget worksheets at the end of this chapter will help you figure out where your money's going to go.

Lodging

This is the least elastic part of your budget. As you'll learn in chapter 5, if you can find a hotel room (a *decent* hotel room, that is) in New York for under $100, you're doing great. If you can find one for $150, you're still doing well (and, incidentally, still under the average).

Transportation

The main function of a rental car in New York is to have a central place from which to have your belongings stolen. You just don't need one, and the last thing we *all* need is yet another car on the road to snarl the traffic flow. (Besides, you'd either have to pay through the nose for a garage or spend hours hunting for a parking space—parking in NYC is *not* for the weak of heart.) Manhattan is a small island, and most of the major sights are within 30 minutes of each other by subway, bus, or cab. Even sights located outside of Manhattan, such as the Bronx Zoo, are easily reached by subway. So, assuming you'd normally spend $40–$50 per day on car rental, figure that this money is now going into your lodging budget.

Restaurants

Dining options in Manhattan range from the very inexpensive to the astronomical and cover every possible cuisine. Since finding great food for high prices is never a problem, think about your bottom line. If you're really trying to eat cheap, you can get a full breakfast for $3 to $5, a soup-and-salad lunch for a little more, an early-bird dinner for $10 to $15, or a burrito for $5 to $7. If you can live on hot dogs, street vendors sell them for $1 apiece—and, of course, they *are* the best anywhere. With a bagel here and a sandwich there, you can trim a few daytime meals and splurge for a great dinner.

Attractions

Your budget for entrance fees and admissions will depend, of course, on what you want to see. Refer to chapter 13 and make a list of your "must sees." Unfortunately, the admission at one museum is not good at another (as is the case in some other cities).

Dollars & Sense

Read the fine print when you're buying tickets to an attraction. Sometimes, if you look carefully, you'll see that the admission price listed on the sign is the *suggested* contribution. But be fair. "From each according to his ability" is a good rule. Or choose the free admission night. (See individual museum listings for details.)

Shopping

Again, this is a flexible part of your budget, and you don't have to buy anything at all if that's your style. But New York is a shopping mecca, particularly before and after the holidays, and has some of the most famous stores in the world, so you might find self-restraint a bit of a challenge. There are great bargains to be had, but if all of your 52 cousins want a $15 souvenir tee shirt, you have a problem.

Entertainment

Your evening entertainment is going to be your biggest expense in this category. A ticket to a Broadway show—a good orchestra seat, not a high altitude perch—will run you about $75. Take a look at the chart below for a general idea of what you'll be paying.

What Things Cost

1 subway or city bus ride	$1.50
Can of soda	$1.00
Pay phone call	$.25
Movie ticket	$8–$8.50
Coffee (your standard cuppa joe)	50¢–60¢
Decaf macciato with yak milk (or something similar)	$2–$3
Ticket to top of Empire State Building	$6
Ticket to top of World Trade Center	$11
Cover charge at a Village Jazz club (excluding 1- or 2-drink minimum)	$15–$30
Boat ride around Manhattan on the Circle Line, adult	$20
Boat ride on the Circle Line, children	$10
Adult admission to MOMA	$8.50
Bar-brand martini at the Rainbow Room	$8
Gallon of gasoline	$1.35–$1.60

Taxis will cost you $2 just for stepping in the door, plus 30¢ per 1/5 mile or 20¢ per min. when stuck in traffic, plus a 50¢ afterhours surcharge. The average fare in Manhattan is $5.25.

Tipping

The golden rule for tipping always used to be a minimum of 15%, but almost everybody in Manhattan (at least those who don't carry calculators) follows this easy formula: Take the tax on your bill (8.25%) and double it. Often restaurants will add the tip (15%–20%) to the bill for parties of six or more. If you're just drinking at a bar, 10%–15% is typical. Taxi drivers also should get the 15% minimum. Everybody else generally gets a buck: Bellhops get $1 or $2 per bag, maids $1 per day, coat check people $1 per garment, automobile valets $1.

What Are All Those Dollar Signs?

In certain places in the book—for example, in the hotel and restaurant listings—you'll see one or more dollar symbols attached to each item. These symbols are neither decorative nor arbitrary; they're keyed to a scale at the beginning of the chapter and help you tell at a glance what particular bracket that item falls into. For example, a hotel prefaced by "$$" will cost $100–$200, and one marked "$$$" will cost $200–$300.

New York Stories

If you think the city's 13.25% hotel tax seems ridiculous, be glad you didn't plan your trip a few years ago, when it was 19.25%. (Occasionally, some things in New York get cheaper.)

What If I'm Worried I Can't Afford It?

If you're now thoroughly frightened that you'll be washing dishes to pay for your meals, relax. Carefully go over the worksheet at the end of this chapter. If the number comes out too high, think about where you can, or are willing to, economize.

There are plenty of ways, some little and some big, to cut down on costs. Note the "Dollars & Sense" boxes scattered throughout this book, which offer hints on places to trim your budget. Up front, here are a few ways to save money in the Apple:

➤ **Go in the off-season.** If you can travel at non-peak times, you'll find hotel prices that are as low as half what they are during peak months. Check with a hotel reservation bureau that offers lodging discounts of 10%–60%, but check the rate with the hotel yourself to see if the discount is real.

➤ **Travel on off days of the week.** Airfares vary depending on the day of the week. If you can travel on a Tuesday, Wednesday, or Thursday, you may find cheaper flights to your destination. When you inquire about airfares, ask if you can obtain a cheaper rate by flying on a different day. Also remember that staying over a Saturday night can cut your airfare by more than half.

➤ **Reserve your flight well in advance,** taking advantage of APEX—"Advance Purchase Excursion"—fares, or watch the last-minute "e" fares on-line for bargains. (See "Surfing the Web to Fly the Skies" in chapter 3 for a discussion of on-line strategies.)

➤ **Try a package tour.** For many destinations, one call to a travel agent or packager can net you airfare, hotel reservations, ground transportation, and even some sightseeing, all for a lot less than if you tried to put the trip together yourself. (See the section on package tours in chapter 3 for specific suggestions of companies to call.)

➤ **Pack light.** That way, you can carry your own bags (don't forget to tip yourself) and take a bus rather than a cab from the airport.

➤ **Reserve a hotel room with a kitchenette** and do your own cooking. It may not feel as vacation-like as snapping your fingers for service in a fine restaurant, but you'll save a heckuva lot of money this way. Even if you only make breakfast and an occasional bag lunch in the kitchen, you'll still save in the long run. Plus, you'll never be shocked by a hefty room service bill.

➤ **Always ask for discount rates.** Always ask for corporate, weekend, or other discount rates. Membership in AAA, frequent flyer plans, trade unions, AARP, or other groups may qualify you for discounted rates on plane tickets, hotel rooms, car rentals (though like we said, it's still a bad idea to drive a car in New York), and even meals. Ask about everything—you could be pleasantly surprised.

➤ **Ask if your kids can stay in your room with you.** A room with two double beds usually doesn't cost any more than one with a queen-size bed, and many hotels won't charge the additional-person rate if the additional person is pint-sized and related to you. Even if you have to pay $10 or $15 for a rollaway bed, you'll save hundreds by not taking two rooms.

➤ **Try expensive restaurants at lunch instead of dinner.** Lunch tabs are usually a fraction of what dinner would cost at most top restaurants, and the menu often boasts many of the same specialties.

➤ **Don't rent a car!** They're more trouble than they're worth.

➤ **Study up on the public transit system.** And try to do it in advance—we've included a subway map in the front of this book to get you started. Relying on cabs is a quick way to break your budget. Remember that New York is pretty small and its farthest fringes are little-visited anyway, so you can actually walk almost anywhere you need to go. You'll save money, get your exercise for the day, and get to know the city more intimately.

➤ **Buy a daily or weekly MetroCard pass.** The $4 daily pass and $17 weekly pass (are available after July 1998) are great for visitors, allowing unlimited travel on public transportation for a fraction of the per-ride fare.

➤ **Skip the souvenirs.** Your photographs and your memories are the best mementos of your trip. If you're worried about money, you can do without the t-shirts, key chains, salt-and-pepper shakers, Statue of Liberty crowns, and other trinkets. (OK, so maybe you can splurge on one good snow-globe.)

Convenience Costs

Remember that convenience always comes with a price tag—and not just in New York. Doing things at the last minute, forgetting where you'll be at meal times, and taking whatever's closest to hand will cost you money. The main antidote to spending more than you want is *planning*. Here are a few more suggestions to use on the ground:

➤ Avoid sit-down lunches; alternatively, have a gourmet prix fixe or buffet lunch and make dinner a light snack.

➤ Find the small local restaurant, not the big, famous factory.

➤ Don't pay for amenities you don't think you'll use.

➤ Visit museums on the nights that are free or suggested admission.

➤ Don't eat in most museum cafeterias—they're P-R-I-C-E-Y.

➤ Don't drink in hotel bars. (Ditto.)

➤ Carry some kind of snacks with you, bought at a supermarket if possible; the delis and bodegas will often mark them up.

➤ Keep an eye on the time. Breakfast may double in price at 10:01am and the early-bird dinner menu may end at 6:35pm, just when you realize you're hungry.

➤ Avoid tourist traps. For help, see the hints throughout this book.

➤ Buy a MetroCard (see the section "Going Undergroung—Using the Subway" section in chapter 8). Its free-transfer feature is almost a two-for-one deal on transportation.

➤ It may seem obvious, but count your change.

Dollars & Sense

Question: How many times a day can you stop to buy a soda or bottled water ($1 or more a pop) when it's 99 degrees and 90% humidity? Answer: a lot. Carry your own bottle and refill it at your various stops. A dumb way to save? It could be your lunch money.

Budget Worksheet: You Can Afford This Trip

Expense	Amount
Airfare (multiplied by number of people traveling)	
Car Rental (if applicable)	
Lodging (multiplied by number of nights)	
Parking (multiplied by number of nights)	
Breakfast (multiplied by number of nights) *Note: May be included in your room rate*	
Lunch (multiplied by number of nights)	
Dinner (multiplied by number of nights)	
Baby-sitting	
Attractions (admission charges to museums, monuments, tours, theaters, nightclubs)	
Transportation (cabs, subway, buses)	
Souvenirs (t-shirts, postcards, that thingie you just gotta have)	
Tips (think 15% of your meal total plus $1 a bag every time a bellhop moves your luggage)	
The cost of getting to and from the airport in your hometown, plus long-term parking (multiplied by number of nights)	
Grand Total	

Chapter 3

How Will I Get There?

In This Chapter

➤ Planes, trains, and automobiles: figuring out the vehicle for you

➤ Advice on whether to take a tour or design your trip yourself

➤ How to fly smart, where to fly to

Getting there may not *really* be half the fun, but you certainly have a lot of choices. Are you going to wrangle through them yourself or get a travel agent to help you? And when you arrive, will you feel comfortable working the town on your own or will you want the kind of guidance you get with a group tour?

Travel Agent—Friend or Foe?

A good travel agent is like a good mechanic or a good plumber: hard to find, but invaluable once you've found the right person. And the best way to find a good travel agent is the same way you find a good plumber or mechanic or doctor—word of mouth.

Any travel agent can help you find a bargain airfare, hotel, or rental car, but a good travel agent will stop you from ruining your vacation by trying to save a few dollars. The best agents can tell you how much time you should budget in a destination, find a cheap flight that doesn't require you to change planes in Atlanta and Chicago, get you a better hotel room for about the same price, arrange for a competitively priced rental car, and even give recommendations on restaurants.

Travel agents work on commission. The good news is that *you* don't pay the commission; the airlines, accommodations, and tour companies do. The bad news is that unscrupulous travel agents will try to persuade you to book the vacations that net them the most money in commissions.

To make sure you get the most out of your travel agent, do a little homework. Read about your destination (you've already made a sound decision by buying this book) and pick out some accommodations and attractions you think you'd like. If necessary, get a really comprehensive travel guide, such as *Frommer's*. If you have access to the Internet, check prices on the Web yourself in advance so that you can do a little prodding. (See "Fighting the Airfare Wars" later in this chapter for more information on how to do that.) Then take your guidebook and Web information to the travel agent and ask him or her to make the arrangements for you. Because agents have access to more resources than even the most complete Web travel site, they should be able to get you a better price than you could get by yourself. And they can issue your tickets and vouchers right in their office. If they can't get you into the hotel of your choice, they can recommend an alternative, and you can look for an objective review in your guidebook right there and then.

In the past two years, some airlines and resorts have begun limiting or eliminating travel agent commissions. The immediate result has been that travel agents don't bother booking these services unless the customer specifically requests them. But some travel industry analysts predict that if other airlines and accommodations throughout the industry follow suit, travel agents may have to start charging customers for their services. When that day arrives, the best agents should prove even harder to find.

Should I Join an Escorted Tour or Travel on My Own?

Do you like to let your bus driver worry about traffic while you sit in comfort and listen to a tour guide explain everything you see? Or do you prefer going out and following your nose, even if you don't catch all the highlights? Do you like to have lots of events planned for each day, or would you rather improvise as you go along? The answers to these questions will determine whether you should choose the guided tour or travel *à la carte*.

Some people love escorted tours. They free travelers from spending lots of time behind the wheel; they take care of all the details; and they tell you what to expect at each attraction. You know your costs up front, and there aren't many surprises. Escorted tours can take you to the maximum number of sights in the minimum amount of time with the least amount of hassle.

Other people need more freedom and spontaneity—and they can't *stand* guided tours. They prefer to discover a destination by themselves, and don't mind getting caught in a thunderstorm without an umbrella or finding that a recommended restaurant is no longer in business—that's just the adventure of travel.

Hey, Mister Bus Driver!

If you do choose an escorted tour, ask a few simple questions before you buy:

1. **What's the cancellation policy?** Do you have to put a deposit down? Can they cancel the trip if they don't get enough people? How late can you cancel if you are unable to go? When do you pay? Do you get a refund if you cancel? If *they* cancel?

2. **How jam-packed is the schedule?** Do they try to fit 25 hours into a 24-hour day, or is there ample time for relaxing and shopping? If you don't enjoy getting up at 7 am every day and not returning to your hotel until 6 or 7 pm, certain escorted tours may not be for you.

3. **How big is the group?** The smaller the group, the more flexible it'll be and the less time you'll spend waiting for people to get on and off the bus. Tour operators may be evasive about this, because they may not know the exact size of the group until everybody has made their reservations, but they should be able to give you a rough estimate. Some tours have a minimum group size and may cancel the tour if they don't book enough people.

4. **What's included?** Don't assume anything. You may have to pay to get yourself to and from the airport. Or a box lunch may be included in an excursion but drinks might cost extra. Or beer might be included but wine might not. How much choice do you have? Can you opt out of certain activities, or does the bus leave once a day, with no exceptions? Are all your meals planned in advance? Can you choose your entree at dinner, or does everybody get the same chicken cutlet?

Plush Bus or Busted Buggy?

If you do decide to join an escorted tour, there are several different levels to choose from. **Maupintour,** Box 807, Lawrence, KS 66044 (☎ **800/468-2825** or 913/843-1211), operates deluxe escorted tours of New York by motor coach at the busiest times of the year: Thanksgiving and Christmas. The 7-day Thanksgiving tour includes accommodation at the Hilton Towers, most meals (including a Thanksgiving dinner at Tavern on the Green), two Broadway shows, a Rockettes show, a trip to the Statue of Liberty and Ellis Island, and a 1-day excursion to the Hudson Valley. Cost is $1,940 per person, plus airfare. The Christmas tour (6 days) includes basically the same accommodations, dining, and sightseeing, except that the shows are *The Nutcracker* and the Rockettes. Cost is $1,730 per person, plus airfare.

Globus, 5301 South Federal Circle, Littleton, CO 80123 (☎ **800/221-0090** or 303/797-2800), runs first-class "independent tours" of New York, which means that a "host" is on hand to answer questions but doesn't take you around the city (except on a designated day). The package ($569 per person, plus airfare) includes hotel, local transportation, welcome drink and American breakfast each day, and a Statue of Liberty tour.

Cosmos offers economy tours for $389 per person plus airfare; this is a downscale version of the Globus tour. Cosmos and Globus have teamed up and can be reached at the same number, or at their Web site **www.globus andcosmos.com**.

If you choose an escorted tour, think strongly about purchasing travel insurance, especially if the tour operator asks to you pay up front. But don't buy insurance from the tour operator! If they don't fulfill their obligation to provide you with the vacation you've paid for, there's no reason to think they'll fulfill their insurance obligations either. Get travel insurance through an independent agency. (See the section "What About Travel Insurance?" in chapter 4 for some tips.)

The Pros & Cons of Package Tours

Package tours are not the same thing as escorted tours. They are simply a way of buying your airfare and accommodations at the same time, and for popular destinations like New York, they're really the smart way to go because they save you a ton of money. In many cases, a package that includes airfare, hotel, and transportation to and from the airport will cost you less than just the hotel alone if you booked it yourself. That's because packages are sold in bulk to tour operators who resell them to the public. It's kind of like buying your vacation at Sam's Club, except that it's the tour operator who buys the 1,000-count box of garbage bags and resells them ten at a time at a cost that undercuts what you'd pay at your neighborhood supermarket.

Tour packages vary as much as garbage bags, too. Some packages offer a better class of hotels than others. Some offer the same hotels for lower prices. Some offer flights on scheduled airlines while others book charters. In some packages, your choices of accommodations and travel days may be limited. Some packages let you choose between escorted vacations and independent vacations; others will allow you to add on just a few excursions or escorted day trips (also at prices lower than if you booked them yourself) without booking an entirely escorted tour.

Each destination usually has one or two packagers that are better than the rest because they buy in even bigger bulk. The time you spend shopping around for a package will be well rewarded.

Pick a Peck of Pickled Packages

The best place to start looking is the travel section of your local Sunday newspaper. Also check the ads in the back of national travel magazines like *Travel & Leisure, National Geographic Traveler,* and *Condé Nast Traveler.*
Liberty Travel (many locations; check your local directory since there's not a central 800 number) is one of the biggest packagers in the Northeast, and usually boasts a full-page ad in Sunday papers. You won't get much in the way of service, but you will get a good deal: For a 5-night stay at the Sheraton Towers, including airfare but with no extras, the cost would be

$1,100–$1,200 from Chicago. The price with airfare from Los Angeles would be about $100 less.

Another good resource is the airlines themselves, which often package their flights together with accommodations. When you pick the airline, you can choose one that has frequent service to your hometown and/or one on which you accumulate frequent flyer miles. Disreputable packagers are uncommon, but they do exist, so buying your package through the airline is a bit safer bet—you can be pretty sure the company will still be in business when your departure date arrives. Among the airline packages, your options include **American Airlines FlyAway Vacations** (☎ 800/321-2121), which offers a 5-night stay at the Drake Swisshotel, with tickets to a Broadway matinee, a two-day bus pass for a double-decker tour bus, and a helicopter tour of the city, including airfare from Chicago, for $924 per person. **Continental Airlines Grand Destinations** (☎ 800/634-5555), offers packages for two people sharing a double room (Loews New York Hotel), 5 nights, with airfare from Chicago but no extras, for $1,459. The same package from Los Angeles costs $1,939. **Delta Dream Vacations** (☎ 800/872-7786), and **US Airways Vacations** (☎ 800/455-0123) are also good bets.

Extra! Extra!

Through the Web site **www.vacationpackager. com**, you can link up with many different operators and design your own package.

The biggest hotel chains, casinos, and resorts also offer packages. If you already know where you want to stay, call the resort itself and ask if they can offer land/air packages.

Some other packagers you might try include **TWA Getaway Vacations** (☎ 800/438-2929), **New Frontiers** (☎ 800/366-6387), **New Frontiers West** (☎ 800/677-4277), and **American Express Vacations** (☎ 800/241-1700).

Fighting the Airfare Wars

Airfares are capitalism at its purest, to the point that passengers in the same cabin on the same airplane rarely pay the same fare as each other; rather, they each pay what the market will bear.

Business travelers who need the flexibility to purchase their tickets at the last minute, change their itinerary at a moment's notice, or get home before the weekend pay the premium rate or full fare. Passengers who can book their ticket long in advance, who don't mind staying over Saturday night, or who are willing to travel on a Tuesday, Wednesday, or Thursday pay the least, usually a fraction of the full fare. On most flights, even the shortest hops, the full fare is close to $1,000 or more, but a 7-day or 14-day advance purchase ticket is closer to $200–$300. Obviously, it pays to plan ahead.

The airlines also periodically hold sales in which they lower the prices on their most popular routes. These fares have advance-purchase requirements and date-of-travel restrictions, but you can't beat the price: usually no more than $400 for a cross-country flight. Keep your eyes open for these sales as you're planning your vacation, then pounce on them. The sales tend to take place in seasons of low travel volume. You'll almost never see a sale around the peak summer vacation months of July and August, or around Thanksgiving or Christmas, when people have to fly regardless of the fare.

Consolidators, also known as bucket shops, are a good place to check for the lowest fares. Their prices are much better than the fares you could get yourself, and are often even lower than what your travel agent can get you. You see their ads in the small boxes at the bottom of the page in your Sunday travel section. Some of the most reliable consolidators include **1-800-FLY-4-LESS** or **1-800-FLY-CHEAP.** Another good choice, **Council Travel (☎ 800/226-8624),** caters especially to young travelers, but their bargain-basement prices are available to people of all ages.

Surfing the Web to Fly the Skies
Another way to find the cheapest fare is by using the Internet to do your searching for you. After all, that's what computers do best: search through millions of pieces of data and return information in rank order. The number of virtual travel agents on the Internet has increased exponentially in recent years, and agencies now compete the way locksmiths do in the yellow pages for the first alphabetical listing. At this writing, 007Travel, 1st Choice Travel, and 1Travel.com all preceded A Plus Travel in an alphabetical listing of on-line travel agents.

There are too many companies now to mention, but a few of the better-respected ones are **Travelocity (www.travelocity.com), Microsoft Expedia (www.expedia.com),** and **Yahoo's Flifo Global (http://travel.yahoo.com/travel/).** Each has its own little quirks—Travelocity, for example, requires you to register with them—but they all provide variations of the same service. Just enter the dates you want to fly and the cities you want to visit, and the computer looks for the lowest fares. The Yahoo site has a feature called "Fare Beater," which will check flights on other airlines or at different times or dates in hopes of finding an even cheaper fare. Expedia's site will e-mail you the best airfare deal once a week if you so choose. Travelocity uses the SABRE computer reservations system that most travel agents use, and has a "Last Minute Deals" database that advertises really cheap fares for those who can get away at a moment's notice.

Great last-minute deals are also available directly from the airlines themselves through a free e-mail service called **E-savers.** Each week, the airline sends you a list of discounted flights, usually leaving the upcoming Friday or Saturday, and returning the following Monday or Tuesday. You can sign up for all the major airlines at once by logging on to **Epicurious Travel (http://travel.epicurious.com/travel/c_planning/02_airfares/email/signup.html),** or go to each individual airline's Web site:

➤ **American Airlines:** www.aa.com

➤ **Continental Airlines:** www.flycontinental.com

➤ **TWA:** www.twa.com

➤ **Northwest Airlines:** www.nwa.com

➤ **US Airways:** www.usairways.com

Happy Landings

Connections between the airports in the New York area and the city are good, though the options may seem confusing at first. The closest airport to Manhattan (ergo, the cheapest to come from and go to) is **La Guardia Airport** in northern Queens. You can then take a cab or a bus from there into Manhattan. (The M60 city bus will also take you into Manhattan, but it only runs to 104th St. on the West Side, about 60 blocks from Midtown. If you're looking to save money, this is an option, although it's time-consuming and can be confusing.) Taxi and bus fares into the city from **Kennedy Airport** in southern Queens are a couple of dollars higher. (To save money from there, you can take the A train, but it takes forever to get into Midtown.)

Even though **Newark International Airport** is in New Jersey, it's still relatively convenient, especially if your hotel is on the West Side or Downtown. It also offers the most ways of getting into the city (including a public bus-train combo, a two-hour odyssey you shouldn't try). There are buses to several locations in Manhattan.

The Inside Scoop on the Comfort Zone

The seats in the front row of each airplane cabin, called the **bulkhead seats,** usually have the most leg room. They have some drawbacks, however. Because there's no seat in front of you, there's no place except the overhead bin in which to put your carry-on luggage. The front row also may not be the best place to see the in-flight movie. And lately, airlines have started putting passengers with young children in the bulkhead row so the kids can sleep on the floor. This is terrific if you have kids, but a nightmare if you have a headache.

Emergency-exit row seats also have extra leg room. They are assigned at the airport, usually on a first-come, first-served basis. Ask when you check in whether you can be seated in one of these rows. In the unlikely event of an emergency, you'll be expected to open the emergency exit door and help direct traffic.

Ask for a seat toward the front of the plane. The minute the captain turns off the "Fasten Seat Belts" sign after landing, people jump up out of their seats as though Ken Griffey, Jr. just hit a home run. They then stand in the aisles and wait for 5 to 10 minutes while the ground crew puts the gangway in place. The closer to the front of the plane you are, the less hurry-up-and-waiting you'll have to do. Why do you think they put first class in the front?

If you have special dietary needs, be sure to order a special meal. Most airlines offer vegetarian meals, macrobiotic meals, kosher meals, meals for the lactose intolerant, and several other meals in a large variety of categories. Ask when you make your reservation if the airline can accommodate your dietary restrictions. Some people without any special dietary needs order special meals anyway, because they are made to order, unlike the mass-produced dinners served to the rest of the passengers.

Wear comfortable clothes. The days of getting dressed up in a coat and tie to ride an airplane went out with Nehru jackets and poodle skirts. And dress in layers; the supposedly controlled climate in airplane cabins is anything but predictable. You'll be glad to have a sweater or jacket that you can put on or take off as the temperature on board dictates.

Bring some toiletries aboard on long flights. Airplane cabins are notoriously dry places. Take a travel-size bottle of moisturizer or lotion to refresh your face and hands at the end of the flight. If you're taking an overnight flight (a.k.a."the red eye"), don't forget to pack a toothbrush to combat that feeling upon waking that you've been sucking on your seat cushion for six hours. If you wear contact lenses, take them out before you get on board and wear glasses instead. Or at least bring eye drops.

Jet lag is not usually a problem for flights within the United States, but some people are affected by three-hour time zone changes. The best advice is to get acclimated to local time as quickly as possible. Stay up as long as you can the first day, and then try to wake up at a normal time the second day. Drink plenty of water both days, as well as on the plane, to avoid dehydration.

If you're flying with kids, don't forget chewing gum for ear pressure problems, a deck of cards or favorite (preferably *quiet*) toys to keep them entertained, extra bottles or pacifiers, and a bag of diapers.

Getting There by Car

As we've already stressed several times, having a car in New York is one big smelly albatross. If you do insist on driving to the city, plan on treating your car to indoor lodging to the tune of up to $35 per day. There are some long-term outdoor lots for about half that much along the West Side Highway, one of them being run by the city (at Houston Street and West Side Highway, in the SoHo/Village area), and several in the Fifties.

From the west and south, you cross into the city at the Holland Tunnel (around Canal Street), the Lincoln Tunnel (Midtown), or the George Washington Bridge (far, far Uptown), depending on your destination. The inbound toll is $4, and the outbound is free (in case you're broke when you leave). From the north, it's the Deegan Expressway (I-87), the Taconic Parkway to the Sawmill River Parkway to the Henry Hudson Parkway, or the

New England Thruway (I-95). The Henry Hudson turns into the West Side Highway, which runs along the Hudson on the West Side of the island; on the other side, the FDR Drive runs along the East River. To get to the East Side when coming from the north, follow the signs to the Triborough Bridge. The Cross Bronx Expressway runs east-west and connects to the George Washington Bridge; you can use it to get to whichever side of the island you want.

Alternatively, if you're wedded to your car but want to avoid all this confusion (not to mention traffic), you can park at a commuter train station in New York, New Jersey, or Connecticut and take the commuter rail into the city, but you'll still have to find parking.

Getting There by Train

Amtrak (☎ **800-USA-RAIL**) trains arrive at Penn Station on the West side, a major hub for all forms of transportation. Be sure to book well in advance. From Boston (a 4-hour journey), the average round-trip fare to New York is around $100; from Chicago, $140–$282 (and 16–18 hours); from Washington, D.C. (about 3½ hours), $53 round trip.

The train is much more comfortable than a plane or bus, but probably only works if you're traveling along the Northeast Corridor. The amount of luggage you carry could also be a factor. Be sure to bring food, since what is sold on the train is virtually inedible.

Getting There by Bus

Given that a bus journey of more than about 4 hours is fatiguing if not downright painful (though buses are roomier now and some show movies), you probably won't be arriving in New York by bus. If you come from New England, however, note that there are three bus lines operating between Boston and New York that charge about half what Amtrak does for a trip of the same duration. New York buses arrive at the Port Authority Bus Terminal, near Times Square.

Fare Game—Choosing an Airline

Arranging and booking flights is a complicated business—that's why a whole industry has grown up to handle it for you. If you're searching around for a deal, though, it helps to leave a trail of breadcrumbs through the maze so you can easily find your way to your destination and back. You can use this worksheet to do just that.

There's a chance that you won't be able to get a direct flight, especially if you're looking to save money, so we've included space for you to map out any connections you'll have to make. If a connection is involved in the fares you're quoted, make sure to ask how much of a layover you'll have between flights, 'cause *nobody* likes hanging around the airport for eight or ten hours. Be sure to mark the layover times in the appropriate spot on the worksheet, so you can compare them easily when you go back over everything to make your decision.

1   Schedule & Flight Information Worksheets

Travel Agency: _____ **Phone #:** _____

Agent's Name: _____ **Quoted Fare:** _____

Departure Schedule & Flight Information

Airline: _____ Airport: _____

Flight #: _____ Date: _____ Time: _____am/pm

Arrives in _____ Time: _____ am/pm

Connecting Flight (if any)

Amount of time between flights: _____ hours/mins.

Airline:_____ Flight #:_____ Time: _____am/pm

Arrives in _____ Time: _____ am/pm

Return Trip Schedule & Flight Information

Airline:_____ Airport: _____

Flight #: _____ Date: _____ Time: _____am/pm

Arrives in _____ Time: _____ am/pm

Connecting Flight (if any)

Amount of time between flights: _____ hours/mins.

Airline:_____ Flight #:_____ Time: _____am/pm

Arrives in _____ Time: _____ am/pm

2   Schedule & Flight Information Worksheets

Travel Agency: _____ **Phone #:** _____

Agent's Name: _____ **Quoted Fare:** _____

Departure Schedule & Flight Information

Airline: _____ **Airport:** _____

Flight #: _____ **Date:** _____ **Time:** _____am/pm

Arrives in _____ **Time:** _____ am/pm

Connecting Flight (if any)

Amount of time between flights: _____ hours/mins.

Airline: _____ **Flight #:** _____ **Time:** _____am/pm

Arrives in _____ **Time:** _____ am/pm

Return Trip Schedule & Flight Information

Airline: _____ **Airport:** _____

Flight #: _____ **Date:** _____ **Time:** _____am/pm

Arrives in _____ **Time:** _____ am/pm

Connecting Flight (if any)

Amount of time between flights: _____ hours/mins.

Airline: _____ **Flight #:** _____ **Time:** _____am/pm

Arrives in _____ **Time:** _____ am/pm

3   Schedule & Flight Information Worksheets

Travel Agency: _____ **Phone #:** _____

Agent's Name: _____ **Quoted Fare:** _____

Departure Schedule & Flight Information

Airline: _____ Airport: _____

Flight #: _____ Date: _____ Time: _____am/pm

Arrives in _____ Time: _____ am/pm

Connecting Flight (if any)

Amount of time between flights: _____ hours/mins.

Airline:_____ Flight #:_____ Time: _____am/pm

Arrives in _____ Time: _____ am/pm

Return Trip Schedule & Flight Information

Airline:_____ Airport: _____

Flight #: _____ Date: _____ Time: _____am/pm

Arrives in _____ Time: _____ am/pm

Connecting Flight (if any)

Amount of time between flights: _____ hours/mins.

Airline:_____ Flight #:_____ Time: _____am/pm

Arrives in _____ Time: _____ am/pm

4   Schedule & Flight Information Worksheets

Travel Agency: _____   **Phone #:** _____

Agent's Name: _____   **Quoted Fare:** _____

Departure Schedule & Flight Information

Airline: _____   Airport: _____

Flight #: _____ Date: _____ Time: _____am/pm

Arrives in _____ Time: _____ am/pm

Connecting Flight (if any)

Amount of time between flights: _____ hours/mins.

Airline:_____ Flight #:_____ Time: _____am/pm

Arrives in _____ Time: _____ am/pm

Return Trip Schedule & Flight Information

Airline:_____   Airport: _____

Flight #: _____ Date: _____ Time: _____am/pm

Arrives in _____ Time: _____ am/pm

Connecting Flight (if any)

Amount of time between flights: _____ hours/mins.

Airline:_____ Flight #:_____ Time: _____am/pm

Arrives in _____ Time: _____ am/pm

Chapter 4

Tying Up the Loose Ends

In This Chapter

➤ Insurance

➤ What to do in case of illness

➤ Gathering information

➤ Making entertainment reservations

➤ Packing up

So, you have a flight to get you to New York. Now all you need to do is decide where you're going to stay (we'll deal with that question in chapters 5 and 6), determine what you're going to do there, make the reservations, put the dog in the kennel, pack your bags, and do 50 other last-minute things. Organizing these "details" coherently and thoroughly ahead of time will save you precious New York minutes waiting in line, trying to get tickets, calling around town, being miserable, buying the underwear you forgot to bring, and dealing with all the other annoyances that plague the unprepared traveler. In this chapter, we'll help you make sure you've got everything covered, from getting travel insurance to packing comfortable walking shoes. The worksheet at the end of the chapter will help you keep track.

Do I Need to Rent a Car in New York?

No, you don't. Not only that, but we'll be mad at you if you do. (See the discussion on this subject under "Transportation" in chapter 2.)

What About Travel Insurance?

There are three kinds of travel insurance: trip cancellation insurance, medical insurance, and lost luggage insurance.

Trip cancellation insurance is a good idea if you've paid a large portion of your vacation expenses up front and would lose out if your trip was cancelled or if you or someone in your family got sick and you couldn't go. But the other two types of insurance don't make sense for most travelers. Your existing health insurance should cover you if you get sick while on vacation—though if you belong to an HMO you should check to see whether you're fully covered when away from home. And your homeowner's insurance should cover stolen luggage if you have off-premises theft. Check your existing policies before you buy any additional coverage. The airlines are responsible for $1,250 on domestic flights if they lose your luggage; if you plan to carry anything more valuable than that, keep it in your carry-on bag.

Some credit cards (American Express and certain gold and platinum Visas and Mastercards, for example) offer automatic flight insurance against death or dismemberment in case of an airplane crash. If you still feel you need more insurance, try one of the companies listed below, but don't pay for more insurance than you need. For example, if you only need trip cancellation insurance, don't purchase coverage for lost or stolen property. Trip cancellation insurance costs approximately 6%–8% of the total value of your vacation. The following are among the reputable issuers of travel insurance:

➤ **Access America,** 6600 W. Broad St., Richmond, VA 23230 (☎ 800/284-8300)

➤ **Mutual of Omaha,** Mutual of Omaha Plaza, Omaha, NE 68175 (☎ 800/228-9792)

➤ **Travel Guard International,** 1145 Clark St., Stevens Point, WI 54481 (☎ 800/826-1300)

➤ **Travel Insured International, Inc.,** P.O. Box 280568, East Hartford, CT 06128 (☎ 800/243-3174)

What If I Get Sick away from Home?

It can be hard to find a doctor you trust when you're away from home, or to get in touch with your doctor back home if you need a prescription phoned in. Bring all your medications with you, as well as a prescription for more if you worry that you'll run out. If you have health insurance, be sure to carry your identification card in your wallet. Bring an extra pair of contact lenses in case you lose one. And don't forget over-the-counter medications for common travelers' ailments like upset stomach or diarrhea.

If you suffer from a chronic illness, talk to your doctor before taking the trip. For such conditions as epilepsy, diabetes, or a heart condition, wear a **Medic Alert Identification Tag,** which will immediately alert any doctor to your condition and give him or her access to your medical records through Medic

Alert's 24-hour hotline. Membership is $35 plus a $15 annual fee. Contact the Medic Alert Foundation, P.O. Box 1009, Turlock, CA 95381-1009 (☎ **800/825-3785**).

If you worry about getting sick away from home, purchase medical insurance (see the section "What About Travel Insurance?" earlier in this chapter). It will cover you more completely than your existing health insurance.

If you do get sick, ask the concierge at your hotel to recommend a local doctor—even his or her own doctor. This is probably a better recommendation than any national consortium of doctors available through an 800 number. If you can't get a doctor to help you right away, try the emergency room at the local hospital (see Appendix A for a listing of hospital addresses and phone numbers). Many hospital emergency rooms have walk-in clinics for emergency cases that are not life-threatening. You may not get immediate attention, but you won't pay the high price of an emergency room visit—usually a minimum of $300 just for signing your name, on top of whatever treatment you receive.

Making Reservations & Getting Tickets Ahead of Time

In New York's subways, hotels, and restaurants—and even in Central Park on a really nice summer day—you can get the feeling you're competing for space with millions of people. You are. For this reason, it's a good idea to get tickets in advance for Broadway shows, concerts, some exhibitions, and even some restaurants. Waiting in line, or going to the discount ticket booths, is hit-or-miss. If there's a particular show you want to see, definitely get your tickets before you arrive in New York City, or you may find yourself singing the blues.

So What's Goin' on Here?—New York Entertainment

You'll probably have gathered some information about current entertainment events in New York from the general sources listed in chapter 1. In addition, check these printed and virtual info-spots:

NEWSPAPERS & MAGAZINES
To find out what's going on in the city before you get here, consult your nearest newsstand. The easiest place to look for information is in nationally distributed newspapers and magazines that list cultural and other events in New York City. Listings are given in the Friday and Sunday *New York Times,* and the magazines *The New Yorker* and *New York* also give a thorough rundown of events. You may also find *TimeOut*

Time-Savers

If you really don't have time, or just can't face the chore of reserving your entertainment agenda in advance, consider booking your trip through a **packager** (see chapter 3) who can take care of some of these details for you.

New York and the *Village Voice* in your neighborhood. Incidentally, the latter is distributed free from streetside bins in Manhattan (as is the *New York Press,* another listing source, but you'll only find that once you're in the city).

WEB SITES Several of the above publications (and other organizations) have Web sites you can access for info:

➤ **The *New York Times,*** at **www.nytimes.com**, is a prime site for gathering information, reading theater and restaurant reviews, and checking out the Sunday "Arts & Leisure" section. The only drawback is that you have to register and may have to pay for access to certain sections.

➤ ***TimeOut New York*** has a Web site at **www.timeoutny.com**.

➤ **Sidewalk.com** has a New York site at **www.newyork.sidewalk.com** where you'll find listings for entertainment, dining, and more.

➤ ***Gallery Guide,*** the monthly bible for art lovers, lists exhibitions around the city and beyond and is reachable at **www.galleryguide.com**. Every month they update the listing of what's going on at galleries and museums; you can also access the previous month's list. Using this site is much easier than consulting each museum individually.

➤ **The American Museum of Natural History** (at **www.amnh.org**) allows you to get information about the museum's exhibitions, as well as to link up with other scientific and informational sites.

➤ A lot of information is also available through search engines such as WebCrawler. Try **http://webcrawler.city.net/countries/united_states/ new_york/travel_and_attractions**.

New York Stories

New York has more than 400 art galleries and more than 150 museums.

TELEPHONE In addition to all of the preceding resources, you can get information on current theater from **NYC/On Stage** (☎ 212/768-1818) and **Broadway Line** (☎ 212/302-4111), either of which will transfer you to a ticket vendor or booking agency after you've listened to dates and schedules.

New York Stories

New York has 17,000 restaurants. That's about 1 restaurant per 1,000 people. There are 35 theaters on Broadway, with 42,000 seats.

You Make the Call

Once you know what you're dying to see, you can use tons of other companies that will help you make the reservations and get the tickets before you leave. Many are listed on the Web at **www.vacationpackager.com**. Here are some of the major ones:

➤ **Telecharge,** P.O. Box 998, Times Square Station, New York, NY 10108-0998 (☎ **212/239-6200**).

➤ **TicketMaster** (☎ **212/307-4100**).

➤ **Tickets and Travel/Tickets Up Front USA,** 1099 N. Meridian St., Suite 150, Indianapolis, IN 46204 (☎ **800/876-8497** or 317/633-6406, fax 317/633-6409).

➤ **New York Concierge,** 1350 Broadway, Suite 1203, New York, NY 10018 (☎ **800/NYS-HOWS** or 212/239-2570).

➤ **Showtix,** 1501 Broadway, Suite 1915, New York, NY 10036 (☎ **800/677-1164** or 212/302-7000, fax 212/302-7069).

Time-Savers

Common sense should tell you that when you read about a great new restaurant written up in *Gourmet, Bon Appetit, Food and Wine,* or a travel magazine, thousands of other people have, too. Take the extra time before your trip to line up a reservation.

Pack It Up

Start your packing by taking everything you think you'll need and laying it out on the bed. Then get rid of half of it.

Men in Black

New Yorkers are a little like Henry Ford: They like any color as long as it's black. If you're feeling a little intimidated about visiting the city and want to blend in (with the people *and* the buildings), remember when you're packing that somber colors are always appropriate, and certainly stand out less than fuschia sport coats and wild stripes.

It's not that the airlines won't let you take it all—they will, with some limits—it's just that you don't want to get a hernia from lugging half your house around with you.

One necessity is comfortable walking shoes, 'cause your feets is your car in the Apple. Also, it's better to dress in layers; that way, you can peel off or put on pieces as the temperature demands. Because buildings are often excessively air conditioned, it's helpful to have a light sweater even in warm weather. (By the way, weather in New York can be full of surprises. As you can see from the chart in chapter 1, you'd better be prepared for rain. For the daily temperature and the following day's **weather forecast** you can call ☎ 212/976-1212. You should also check the national weather trends in your paper before you leave.) Some other essentials: a camera, toiletries and medications (pack these in your carry-on bag so that you'll have them if the airline loses your luggage), and something to sleep in. (See the packing list later in this chapter for other essential packing suggestions.)

As far as formal wear is concerned, things are more flexible than they used to be. In particular, there's no need for formal evening clothes for Broadway shows. For men, a jacket and tie will serve in any situation, and even these are unnecessary in all but the fanciest restaurants. For women, you might want to bring one nice dress (what about the basic black one?) to shine in the most elegant outings.

When choosing your suitcase, think about the kind of traveling you'll be doing. Wheels help, but you'll be hard pressed to keep one of those suitcases-on-casters upright on a rough New York sidewalk. A wheeled carry-on type of bag with collapsible handle is a better idea. A foldover garment bag will help keep dressy clothes wrinkle-free, but they're kinda big and unwieldy. Hard-sided luggage protects breakable items well but weighs more than soft-sided bags.

When packing, start with the biggest, hardest items (usually shoes), and then fit smaller items in and around them. Pack breakable items in between several layers of clothes, or keep them in your carry-on bag. Put things that could leak, like shampoos and suntan lotions, in zip-seal bags. Lock your suitcase with a small padlock (available at most luggage stores, if your bag doesn't already have one), and put an identification tag on the outside.

Airlines allow either one or two pieces of carry-on luggage on planes—call for the latest policy—and it must fit in the overhead compartment or under the seat in front of you. Carry on any breakable items, a book or something else for you to do on the plane, a snack in case you don't like the airline food, and any vital documents you don't want to lose in your luggage (like your return tickets, passport, and wallet).

Packing Checklist—Don't Forget Your Toothbrush

- ☐ Socks
- ☐ Underwear
- ☐ Shoes (try to keep this to two or three pair; don't forget a good pair of walking shoes)
- ☐ Pants and/or skirts
- ☐ Shirts or blouses
- ☐ Sweaters and/or jackets
- ☐ Umbrella (the folding kind, so you can carry it with you)
- ☐ A belt
- ☐ A jacket and tie or a dress (only if you plan to go someplace fancy in the evening)
- ☐ Shorts (in warm weather)
- ☐ Coat, hat, scarf, and gloves (in cold weather)
- ☐ Bathing suit (if your hotel has a swimming pool or if you'll be trekking to the beach)
- ☐ Workout clothes (if you plan to use the hotel gym)
- ☐ Toiletries (don't forget a razor, toothbrush, comb, deodorant, makeup, contact lens solutions, hairdryer, extra pair of glasses, sewing kit)
- ☐ Camera and film (if you buy film in New York, buy it at a drugstore, NOT at one of the overpriced streetside tourist shops)
- ☐ Medications (pack these in a carry-on bag so that you'll have them even if you lose your luggage)

Part 2

Finding the Hotel That's Right for You

When you go to rent a room, the three things you'll be looking for are space, amenities, and location (put them in the order that suits you). And, oh yeah, price.

Prepare yourself for the fact that hotels in New York are notoriously expensive, with the average price tag around 175 clams. Consequently, accommodation may take up a much larger portion of your total travel budget than it would in another city. Don't be scared off, though; there are offsetting advantages to New York: You won't need a car, for instance, and there are literally thousands of cheap restaurants.

You can have it all—a large, beautifully decorated room on an attractive street, close to the things you want to see and with someone around to peel you a grape—as long as you leave out that nagging fourth variable: price. Once you start thinking about what it's going to cost, you'll probably also have to start considering compromises in the other three factors. That's reality. Welcome to New York.

The compromises don't have to be painful, however. For example, you won't need to pay for a lot of amenities you won't use if you'll only be returning to your hotel to rest. They may sound nice, but if you don't use them it's money down the drain, and the drain in New York can be very large indeed. On the other hand, if you see your hotel as a temporary home, where you'll want to relax, entertain, work out, or spend some time reading, space and amenities will matter more.

Chapter 5

Pillow Talk—The Lowdown on the New York Hotel Scene

In This Chapter

➤ How to choose a neighborhood

➤ How to choose a hotel

➤ How to choose a room

Of the four factors you need to consider—price, location, roominess, and amenities—you already know the first, since you worked out your budget with the worksheet at the end of chapter 2. If you see this as a once-in-a-lifetime trip and plan to pull out all the stops, you may want to go ahead and splurge on the Trump International, if only for the Trump Attaché (hint: this isn't something you put papers in), or some other luxurious hotel. Now, on to the second consideration: location.

Location! Location! Location!

New York wasn't built in a day. In fact, it started out as a series of independent cities and small neighborhoods that over time came together to form the Apple as we know it. Each of these neighborhoods has its own distinctive style and character, which will affect the kind of New York experience you have, should you choose a hotel there. In the sections following, we'll run through all the major Manhattan neighborhoods you have to choose from.

Midtown

Midtown is the place where most of the skyscrapers are located, the other bunch being down at the southern tip of the island. It is roughly defined by

21st Street to the south, where it borders Gramercy Park on the east side and Chelsea on the west, and by Central Park's 59th Street border to the north. During the day, Midtown is a hectic place of business, seething with serious-looking people on their way to or from work. After dark, much of Midtown is quiet (except Times Square and the Theater District, of course), and some of it is positively dull. But Midtown is huge, and such generalizations are generally inaccurate. Let's look more closely at the parts that make up the whole.

Central Park South—59th Street between Fifth and Eighth avenues—is one of the most glamorous views in the city. At one end (west) you have Columbus Circle, and at the other you have the Plaza Hotel. Subway stops are located at both ends, the area is safe, and it's quieter than Times Square. The park is just across the street, Fifth Avenue's most tony stretch of shops is at the corner, and Lincoln Center is not far. The downside is that the area is pricey.

At the intersection of 34th Street, Broadway, and Sixth Avenue (also called the Avenue of the Americas) is **Herald Square,** a bustling area known primarily for shopping. This is the home of Macy's, and with ongoing development, more national chain stores are appearing all the time. The Empire State Building is nearby, and you can get almost anywhere except the Upper East Side without changing trains. The area is safe, though as in any heavy shopping district, there are pickpockets. If you go as far west as Penn Station (between Seventh and Eighth avenues at 32nd Street), things get more grungy.

Murray Hill/Midtown East lies east of Fifth Avenue and below 42nd Street. It's a mixture of business and residential property where a 40-story slab may rub up against a 5-story apartment building. The area is safe and quiet—*very* quiet at night, so you'll probably have to find your entertainment elsewhere. There are few sightseeing stops located here, but many blocks of beautiful brownstones and a number of hotels. Above 42nd Street is Midtown East, which is more commercial in character and includes a number of famous shops that line 57th Street between Fifth and Lexington. The main attractions are the United Nations and the newly renovated and once-again breathtaking Grand Central Station. The subway network on this side of Fifth Avenue is not as dense and it is somewhat less convenient.

New York Stories

New York has 230 hotels—not counting bed-and-breakfasts and other alternative options—and 59,000 hotel rooms.

Times Square in Midtown West used to be a nasty—some would say colorful—place full of peep shows and sex shops, but an ambitious improvement campaign put a stop to that, and it's now safer and more wholesome, with renovated theaters, the Walt Disney Store, and a less threatening atmosphere. (You're still advised to be alert, however.) The neon is bigger, brighter, and more spectacular than ever (including the largest TV screen in the world), and just up Broadway is the theater district, making the many hotels in this area perfect for theatergoers. The density of hotels means strong competition and fairly reasonable prices. Shop around. The area churns with activity, so don't expect it to be quiet; the scale is grand, so it's not the kind of place where you step out for a casual stroll under the trees (there aren't any). Restaurant Row is close by on 46th Street, and transportation is plentiful.

In a nutshell:

☺ You'll be close to the theaters.

☺ You'll be close to Central Park.

☺ You're never more than a block or two from transportation, and it's an easy trip downtown.

But...

☹ It can get pretty hectic.

☹ Parts of it lack for nightlife.

☹ You'll never be lulled to sleep by crickets here. (The reputed one in Times Square is a myth.)

Upper West Side

A gentrified neighborhood of quaint brownstones and majestic prewar apartment buildings (and some nondescript new ones), the Upper West Side has plenty of restaurants and shops catering to the yuppie inhabitants, as well as attractions that include Lincoln Center and the American Museum of Natural History at the southern end, Central Park to the east, and Riverside Park to the west. The hotels are cheaper here, though the selection is thinner and they lack the high-end strength of the Upper East Side; however, the atmosphere is livelier and the spirit less dour and perhaps less weighed down by a superfluity of cash.

In a nutshell:

☺ You'll be close to Lincoln Center and Central Park.

☺ You'll be close to the Museum of Natural History.

☺ You'll be in a neighborhood with some great architecture—perfect for an evening stroll.

But...

☹ You'll probably have to take transportation to the theaters.

☹ There aren't a lot of hotels to choose.

☹ It's a pretty long schlep downtown, especially if you're going to the East Village.

Upper East Side

Appropriately, for one of the wealthiest communities anywhere, the Upper East Side also has some of the most luxurious and expensive hotels. Most of the major art museums in New York City are here, so it's a logical choice for travelers for whom museum-going will be a primary activity. (And there are even a few lower-priced choices, so non-millionaires can afford to stay here, too.) The most touristed areas are eminently safe, quiet, and rather staid (unless you head *far* east). Only one subway line runs through the neighborhood, though (buses are a better choice), so it's a little cut off and less convenient to the theater district and certain downtown sights than are Midtown or the Upper West Side.

In a nutshell:

☺ You'll be close to Museum Mile and Central Park.

☺ Your neighbors will probably be millionaires.

☺ You'll be in one of the safest and quietest neighborhoods in Manhattan.

But...

☹ Transportation is a problem—unless you want to take taxis everywhere.

☹ The hotels are generally very pricey.

☹ It can get pretty drowsy at night—though some people might want that.

Downtown

"Downtown" actually covers a lot of neighborhoods: the Financial District, SoHo, Greenwich Village (East and West), Tribeca, Little Italy, Chinatown—but, for the purposes of choosing a hotel, you'll find your options focused in a few spots. The big downtown hotels are at the end of the island, which brings you close to the hustle and bustle of **Wall Street** and to attractions such as the World Trade Center, Brooklyn Bridge, South Street Seaport, and Battery Park. On the down side, you're far from the main nightlife and the area is fairly deserted at night. There are a few hotel options in **SoHo** and **Greenwich Village,** in the heart of one of New York's most beautiful historic areas and a center for alternative culture, nightlife (especially jazz), and fine dining.

In a nutshell:

☺ You'll be in the oldest and most historic part of New York.

☺ You'll be closest to the arts and music scenes.

☺ You'll be close to a lot of major attractions, like South Street Seaport, the Statue of Liberty, and the World Trade Center.

But...

⊗ There aren't a lot of good hotels to choose.

⊗ You'll be pretty far from the theaters and the museums.

⊗ You're far from Central Park and other large patches of greenery.

The Price Is Right

The **rack rate** is the maximum rate that a hotel charges for a room. It's the rate you'd get if you walked in off the street and asked for a room for the night. You sometimes see the rate printed on the fire/emergency exit diagrams posted on the back of your door. Hotels are happy to charge you the rack rate, but you don't have to pay it—hardly anybody does. Perhaps the best way to avoid paying the rack rate is surprisingly simple: Ask for a cheaper or discounted rate. You may be pleasantly surprised. Remember, though, that you have to take the initiative and ask, because no one in New York is going to help you save money.

In all but the smallest accommodations, the rate you pay for a room depends on many factors, not the least of which is how you make your reservation. A travel agent may be able to negotiate a better price with certain hotels than you could get by yourself. (That's because the hotel gives the agent a discount in exchange for steering his or her business toward the hotel.) Reserving a room through the hotel's 800 number may also result in a lower rate than if you called the hotel directly. On the other hand, the attendant at the central reservations number may not know about discount rates at specific locations. For example, local franchises may offer a special group rate for a wedding or family reunion, but they may neglect to tell the central booking line. Your best bet is to call both the local number and the 800 number and see which one gives you a better deal.

Here's a few other ways to save money on your room:

➤ **Weekend packages:** The most commonly offered package is for a weekend. Hotels with many business clients, for example, discount their weekend rates to keep their volume up. If you can't find one at your first-choice hotel, try another. Look in the Sunday travel section of the *New York Times* for hotels advertising package deals.

➤ **Holiday rates:** If you're thinking of traveling on a holiday, ask if there's a special holiday rate.

➤ **Corporate rates:** Many hotels, particularly those in the mid- to upper-range, have corporate rates. Find out if these apply to you.

➤ **Senior citizen rates:** If you're 65 or older, there's a good chance you may be able to get a senior discount.

➤ **All-in-one/inclusive packages:** Sometimes a package is offered that includes meals, tours, and tickets to the theater. If you were planning on doing these things anyway, the package may result in a savings.

➤ **Family rates:** Packages and discounts for families vary a great deal from hotel to hotel. Ask what's available, and be sure to find out exactly how many kids of what age can stay in the parents' room for free. Ask how much you'll pay for an extra bed in a room or for accommodations for an extra child. For more about families, see the "Hotel Strategies for Families Traveling with Kids" section, later in the chapter.

Room rates also change depending on whether a hotel is empty or close to full. If close to full, managers may be less likely to extend discount rates; if close to empty, managers may be willing to negotiate. Room prices are subject to change without notice, so even the rates quoted in this book may be different from the actual rate you receive when you make your reservation. Be sure to mention membership in AAA, AARP, frequent flyer programs, and any other corporate rewards program when you make your reservation. You never know when it might be worth a few dollars off your room rate.

What Off Season?

Notice that nothing has been said about saving money by traveling in the off season, as you would expect to be able to do visiting another location. Tourism in New York City is not as seasonally sensitive as it is in other places. It may be more helpful to talk about when the high season is, and go from there. The period around Thanksgiving and Christmas is a very popular time to visit New York—what with the parades, shopping, festivities, and all. After the New Year, tourism sags around February and March, when the weather is at its most rotten. Tourism can also be slow in the summer months; the heat and humidity can be numbing, and the art world and some theater (specifically opera) take a holiday. Summer is therefore another period in which to look for a seasonal package.

Taxes & Service Charges

As you proceed with the selection process, don't forget that there will be other fees on top of the basic rate you pay. The hotel tax in New York City is 13.25%, and there's also a room charge of $2 per night. When you reserve, make sure you find out whether or not the price you're being quoted includes taxes. Ditto for packages.

Tourist Traps

Hotel telephones and mini-bars are a perennial source of nasty misunderstandings. Many of the hotels in the moderate to expensive range now have free local calling from rooms, but don't count on it. Ask when you reserve, or you may wind up with a whopping service charge for those 30 restaurants you called on Saturday night, trying to get a reservation for six people and a dog. Minibars in rooms are also a potential rude surprise: Just because it's stocked, that don't mean it's free. Prices can often be two or three times higher than in a local store. The cost-conscious will want to bring their own.

What's in It for Me?—What You Get for Your Money

In the next chapter, you'll see that each hotel listing is prefixed by a number of dollar signs, ranging from one to five ($$$$$). Each represents a range, with the number of dollar symbols indicating the upper end: two symbols ($$) for rooms that cost $100–$200, three symbols ($$$) for those from $200–$300, and so on. Remember that each hotel also has its own range of prices, which may be narrow ($140–$155 for the Hotel Beacon, for example) or wide ($189–$360 for the Marriott Marquis). Prices quoted are for a double room with private bath.

Don't waste time trying to figure out which of these hotels are dumps; the places listed in this book are all decent and reputable, and we've screened out those in dire need of renovation. Of course, the amenities in a $500 room are a bit more substantial than those in a $75 one. (Remember the old joke about the room so small you had to step outside to change your mind?)

Extra! Extra!

In terms of data access and new technologies, it seems that most hotels (except for the least expensive) now have two-line phones with a **data port** as a standard feature in all rooms. If you want to make extra sure of this feature, ask when inquiring about reservations. At the same time, you can check and see whether there have been any recent additions such as a business center—or even fax capabilities in the rooms, which is becoming more common. Always ask if there's a fee for these services, and remember that if you're not a heavy business user, you might as easily pick up your e-mail from one of the many "cybercafes" that have recently opened.

The first category—the low end of the scale—represents true bargains. Don't expect a lot of space or extras: You won't get room service; fitness equipment will be minimal or nil; there will be a TV, but not movies and cable; and there are probably no bellhops. If you're really looking to save money, check out several of these hotels in which you can have a room with a shared bath for as little as $50.

Moving up one level **($$),** the rooms are a little larger, the decor is less spartan, and the degree of overall comfort is higher. There will probably be a fitness center, though in some cases you may have to pay extra for it. (The same holds for business facilities.) Some of the hotels in this category have complimentary continental breakfast. Generally, this is a better quality cheap room with a few amenities to take the edge off.

The middle-range hotels **($$$)** can be expected to provide you with the big hotel feeling at a reasonable cost. They give you room service; a phone with a data port; probably a refrigerator and perhaps some kind of cooking facility (though not always a full kitchenette); cable TV and/or VCR; and free access to a health club, whether on-site or off. Many provide complimentary breakfast or beverages (afternoon wine and cheese), and there's usually a restaurant located within the hotel. The variables become so many that trying to compare them can be bewildering; make a list of what *you* want, and look for that spectrum of amenities.

The next level **($$$$)** is confusing: Is it the top of the middle or the bottom of the top? The previously mentioned amenities are pretty much standard; on top of those, the decor tends toward luxury—these are some of the most famous hotels in the city, or in the world. You'll have plenty of space, fine furnishings (sometimes even antiques), and that oft-touted Old World charm. Service is excellent, and, because these hotels often cater to business people during the week, they offer special amenities like complimentary car service to the Financial District. There are usually several on-site dining and drinking options.

At the money-is-no-object level **($$$$$),** you get more than a place to stay: You get an experience. These are hotels with style, fame, elegance, and a reputation for impeccable service. If you can afford it, you'll get everything you need (and probably many things you don't).

Extra! Extra!

Most hotels in the moderate and upper brackets have **room service,** but it's not always of the 24-hour variety. If this is important to you, be sure to inquire when you call to reserve. Keep in mind that you're not staying in a lonesome vale where the coyotes howl; New York really is open all night, and if you choose a high-traffic neighborhood, you're likely to find all-night bars and restaurants close to your hotel. Many eateries will deliver, too.

What Kind of Place Is Right for You?

The variety of accommodations in New York can be bewildering. There are small hotels with a few rooms and big ones with a thousand, trendy "boutique" hotels and national or worldwide chains. New York has a lot of small bed-and-breakfasts (B&Bs), too.

Among our criteria for listing a hotel is that it has sufficient capacity—'cause there's not much point in directing you and a million other readers to a place that only has three rooms. This, of course, immediately rules out listing individual B&Bs; instead, we'll deal with them collectively (see the following section, "Bed-and-Breakfasts").

Other criteria are that the hotel is in a reasonably safe area. The hotels listed offer a good value for their price category, and they're either renovated or well-maintained, even if the decor is spartan.

Extra! Extra!

Some hotels offer **"free Continental breakfast"** as an enticement, but this may be a far cry from the bacon-and-eggs you're used to. Considering how many diners, bagel depots, and coffee shops are in town (some with breakfast specials before 10 or 11am), this amenity may not be much of savings, though it may help you catch up on your sleep.

Bed & Breakfasts

New York is not really a place to go the B&B route unless you're patient and adventurous. A few very nice homes have been turned into inns—for example, some historic houses in the West Village—but they have only a few rooms and are off the beaten track. Often what you get through B&B associations is a room in an apartment where someone lives, not a professional B&B. They can range from enormous loft spaces to cozy brownstones, and the prices go from ridiculously cheap to ridiculously expensive. If you're traveling by yourself and really want to save money, a B&B could work. Here are some organizations that will help you:

➤ **At Home In New York Inc.,** P.O. Box 407, New York, NY 10185, ☎ **212/956-3125,** fax 212/247-3294.

➤ **Manhattan Home Stays,** P.O. Box 20684, Cherokee Station, New York, NY 10021, ☎ **212/737-3868,** fax 212/265-3561.

➤ **Manhattan Lodgings,** 70 E. 10th St., Suite 18C, New York, NY 10003, ☎ **212/475-2090,** fax 212/477-0420.

➤ **New York Bed and Breakfast Reservation Center,** 331 W. 57th St., Suite 221, New York, NY 10019, ☎ **212/977-3512.**

Getting the Best Room

Somebody has to get the best room in the house, and it might as well be you.

Always ask for a corner room. They're usually larger and quieter, have more windows and light than standard rooms, and don't always cost any more.

When you make your reservation, ask whether the hotel is renovating; if it is, request a room away from the renovation work. Many hotels now offer non-smoking rooms; by all means ask for one if smoke bothers you. Inquire, too, about the location of the restaurants, bars, and discos in the hotel: These could all be a source of irritating noise. Lastly, ask for an inside room if you're a light sleeper, otherwise you might be disturbed by the street noise.

If you aren't happy with your room when you arrive, talk to the attendant at the front desk. If another room is available, the attendant should be happy to accommodate you, within reason.

Extra! Extra!

It used to be that the burden was upon the non-smoker to find the no-smoking areas of public places, but this is the '90s, babe. New York has cracked down on smoking in a big way, and the situation has been reversed: It's the smoker who must now inquire about designated places to pursue the habit. If you want to smoke in your room, ask for "a smoker."

Hotel Strategies for Families Traveling with Kids

If you've got the rugrats along, you're fortunate that New York hotels are now courting families with special amenities that vary from playrooms to "childproof" suites to theme restaurants. (Especially good family choices are starred with a "kid-friendly" icon in the next chapter.) Ask what facilities are available when you reserve. In terms of amusement, consider a location close to Central Park for some breathing room (Times Square is exciting, but not exactly a place to play Catch). In terms of economy, look for a hotel that will let your child/children stay for free in your room. Another option is to get a suite with a kitchenette in order to cut down on restaurant expenses and to have some "at home" time together.

Hotel Strategies for Travelers with Disabilities

Not all hotels, especially the old ones, have been brought up to date with access regulations. Small hotels, B&Bs, and budget hotels are unlikely to be very advanced in this respect. Some hotels, however, have special facilities for folks that need 'em, such as roll-in showers to accommodate wheelchairs, lower sinks, and extra space to move around, but in any case you'll have to ask for one of these accessible rooms when you reserve. Also, some chains (like Hilton), have specially accessible rooms in all their hotels. You can call **Hospital Audiences** (Hotline ☎ **888/424-4585;** local 212/575-7676; TDD 212/575-7673) for more details about hotels and accessibility. (And see chapter 6 for our recommendations.)

What If I Didn't Plan Ahead?

If you for some reason arrive in New York without a reservation, don't panic. Reservation bureaus buy up rooms in bulk and resell them, so you may be able to get a room by placing a phone call. (Hint: It's easier to do this from the airport than from a street corner with your baggage piled around you.) Here are a few bureaus to try if you're in a jam:

➤ **Accommodations Express** (☎ **800/950-4685**). 80% of hotels participate in this service; discounts 10%–40% off rack rates.

➤ **Hotel Reservations Network** (☎ **800/96-HOTEL**). 65 hotels participate; discounts 20%–50% off rack rates.

➤ **Quickbook** (☎ **800/789-9887**). Covers 50 hotels; discounts up to 60%.

It is possible to schlep around inquiring in person at hotels, but why would you want to? If that's your style, though, concentrate on Midtown, where the density of hotels is the greatest; a huge hotel like the Sheraton that caters to conventions is obviously more likely to have a room—unless there's a convention.

Chapter 6

New York Hotels from A to Z

In This Chapter

➤ Quick indexes of hotels by location and price

➤ Reviews of all the best hotels in the city

➤ A worksheet to help you make your choice

OK, here's where the rubber hits the road: It's time to choose your place to snooze. We've started this chapter with some handy-dandy lists that break down our favorite hotels by neighborhood and price, and then we reviewed them all, giving you the information you'll need to make your decision.

The reviews are arranged alphabetically so that they're easier to refer back to, and the neighborhood each hotel is located in appears right beneath its name; check them against the maps to give yourself a better idea of where they are in relation to what you want to see. If you want to be near the theaters, for example, Midtown West is your part of town; if you want to be near Central Park, it's either the Upper West Side or Upper East Side; for a young and funky scene, try the Village or Chelsea; for Museum Mile, the Upper East; for Lincoln Center, the Upper West.

As far as price goes, we've noted rack rates in the listings and also preceded each with a dollar-sign icon to make quick reference easier. The more $$$ signs under the name, the more you pay. (Dollar sign icons reflect the average of a hotel's high- and low-end rack rates.) It runs like this:

$$\begin{aligned}
\$ &= \$75\text{--}\$100 \\
\$\$ &= \$100\text{--}\$200 \\
\$\$\$ &= \$200\text{--}\$300 \\
\$\$\$\$ &= \$300\text{--}\$400 \\
\$\$\$\$\$ &= \$400 \text{ and up}
\end{aligned}$$

In instances where the rack rates hovered within about $10 of an even hundred (say, $210), we've been kind and assigned it the lower of the dollar sign designations (in this case, we'd give it $$) rather than jumping all the way up to the next hundred.

Kids We've also added a "Kid-Friendly" icon to those hotels that are especially good for families, and included special features throughout that will direct you to the best hotels for those of you with special considerations in mind—the best for romance, the best for business travelers, and so on.

Hint: As you read through the reviews, keep track of the ones that appeal to you. We've included a chart at the end of this chapter where you can rank your preferences, but to make matters easier on yourself now, why don't you just put a little checkmark next to the ones you like. Remember how your teachers used to tell you not to write in your books? Now's the time to rebel. Scrawl away.

Quick Picks—New York's Hotels at a Glance
Hotel Index by Location

Upper West Side

Hotel Beacon $$

Mayflower Hotel on the Park $$

Radisson Empire Hotel $$$

Trump International Hotel and Tower $$$$

Upper East Side

The Barbizon $$

The Carlyle $$$$$

The Lowell $$$$

The Mark $$$$

The Pierre $$$$$

Surrey Hotel $$$

Midtown East

Drake Swissôtel $$$

Grand Hyatt New York $$$

Hotel Elysee $$$$

Jolly Madison Towers Hotel $$

The Kimberly $$$

Morgans $$$

The Pickwick Arms Hotel $

Quality Hotel Fifth Avenue $$

The Waldorf Astoria and Waldorf Towers $$$

Midtown West

The Ameritania $$

Casablanca $$$

Crowne Plaza Manhattan $$$

Doubletree Guest Suites $$$

Herald Square Hotel $

Hotel Metro $$

The Michelangelo $$$$$

New York Marriott Marquis $$$

Novotel New York $$

The Plaza Hotel $$$$$

Portland Square Hotel $

Quality Hotel and Suites Rockefeller Center $$

The Royalton $$$$

Salisbury Hotel $$$

Sheraton New York Hotel $$$

58

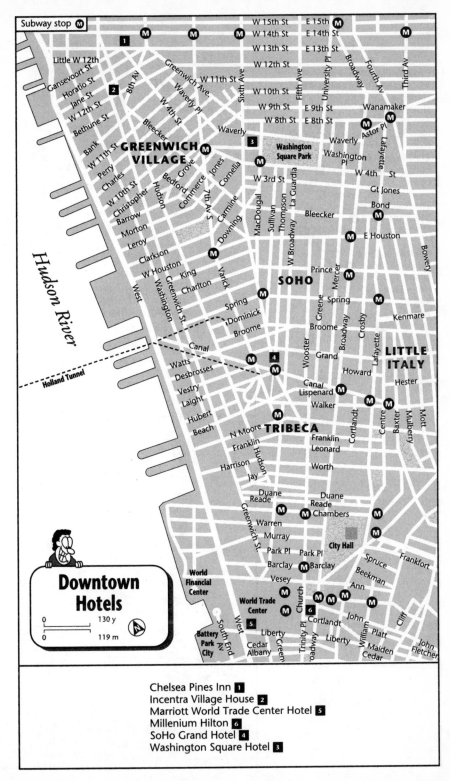

Downtown Hotels

0	130 y
0	119 m

Chelsea Pines Inn **1**
Incentra Village House **2**
Marriott World Trade Center Hotel **5**
Millenium Hilton **6**
SoHo Grand Hotel **4**
Washington Square Hotel **3**

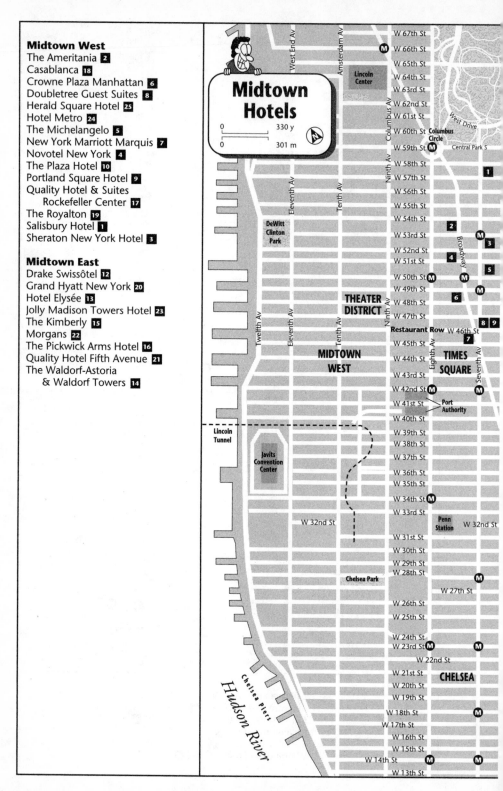

Midtown West
The Ameritania **2**
Casablanca **18**
Crowne Plaza Manhattan **6**
Doubletree Guest Suites **8**
Herald Square Hotel **25**
Hotel Metro **24**
The Michelangelo **5**
New York Marriott Marquis **7**
Novotel New York **4**
The Plaza Hotel **10**
Portland Square Hotel **9**
Quality Hotel & Suites
   Rockefeller Center **17**
The Royalton **19**
Salisbury Hotel **1**
Sheraton New York Hotel **3**

Midtown East
Drake Swissôtel **12**
Grand Hyatt New York **20**
Hotel Elysée **13**
Jolly Madison Towers Hotel **23**
The Kimberly **15**
Morgans **22**
The Pickwick Arms Hotel **16**
Quality Hotel Fifth Avenue **21**
The Waldorf-Astoria
   & Waldorf Towers **14**

Chelsea/Greenwich Village/SoHo

Chelsea Pines Inn $

Incentra Village House $$

Washington Square Hotel $$

SoHo Grand Hotel $$$

Downtown

Marriott World Trade Center $$$$

The Millenium Hilton $$$$

Hotel Index by Price

$$$$$

The Carlyle (Upper East Side)

The Michaelangelo (Midtown West)

The Pierre (Upper East Side)

The Plaza (Midtown East)

$$$$

Hotel Elysee (Midtown East)
The Lowell (Upper East Side)

The Mark (Upper East Side)

Marriott World Trade Center (Downtown)

The Millenium Hilton (Downtown)

The Royalton (Midtown West)

Trump International Hotel and Tower (Upper West Side)

$$$

Casablanca (Midtown West)

Crowne Plaza Manhattan (Midtown West)

Doubletree Guest Suites (Midtown West)

Drake Swissôtel (Midtown East)

Grand Hyatt New York (Midtown East)

The Kimberly (Midtown East)

Morgans (Midtown East)

New York Marriott Marquis (Midtown West)

Novotel New York (Midtown West)

Radisson Empire Hotel (Upper West Side)

The Salisbury (Midtown West)

Sheraton New York Hotel and Towers (Midtown West)

SoHo Grand Hotel (SoHo)

Surrey Hotel (Upper East Side)

The Waldorf-Astoria and Waldorf Towers (Midtown East)

$$

The Ameritania (Midtown West)

The Barbizon (Upper East Side)

Hotel Beacon (Upper West Side)

Hotel Metro (Midtown West)

Incentra Village House (Chelsea/West Village)

Jolly Madison Towers Hotel (Midtown East)

Mayflower Hotel on the Park (Upper West Side)

Quality Hotel and Suites Rockefeller Center (Midtown West)

Quality Hotel Fifth Avenue (Midtown East)

Washington Square Hotel (West Village/NYU area)

$

Chelsea Pines Inn (Chelsea/West Village)

Herald Square Hotel (Midtown West)

The Pickwick Arms Hotel (Midtown East)

Portland Square Hotel (Midtown West)

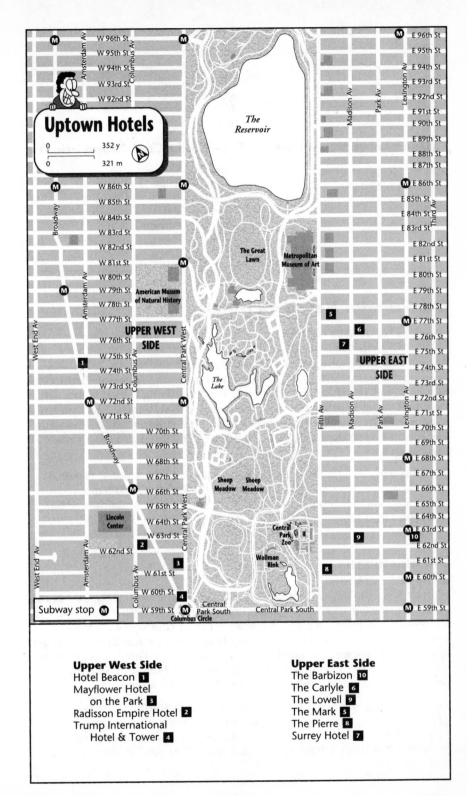

Uptown Hotels

0 ——————— 352 y
0 ——————— 321 m

The Reservoir

The Great Lawn

Metropolitan Museum of Art

American Musum of Natural History

UPPER WEST SIDE

The Lake

UPPER EAST SIDE

Lincoln Center

Sheep Meadow **Sheep Meadow**

Central Park Zoo

Wollman Rink

Subway stop Ⓜ

Central Park South

Columbus Circle

Streets and avenues

W 96th St / E 96th St
E 95th St
W 95th St
W 94th St / E 94th St
E 93rd St
W 93rd St
E 92nd St
W 92nd St
E 91st St
E 90th St
E 89th St
E 88th St
E 87th St
W 86th St / E 86th St
E 85th St
W 85th St
W 84th St / E 84th St
W 83rd St / E 83rd St
W 82nd St / E 82nd St
W 81st St / E 81st St
W 80th St / E 80th St
W 79th St / E 79th St
W 78th St / E 78th St
W 77th St / E 77th St
W 76th St / E 76th St
W 75th St / E 75th St
W 74th St / E 74th St
W 73rd St / E 73rd St
W 72nd St / E 72nd St
W 71st St / E 71st St
W 70th St / E 70th St
W 69th St / E 69th St
W 68th St / E 68th St
W 67th St / E 67th St
W 66th St / E 66th St
W 65th St / E 65th St
W 64th St / E 64th St
W 63rd St / E 63rd St
W 62nd St / E 62nd St
W 61st St / E 61st St
W 60th St / E 60th St
W 59th St / E 59th St

Amsterdam Av, Columbus Av, Broadway, West End Av, Central Park West, Fifth Av, Madison Av, Park Av, Lexington Av, Third Av

---

Upper West Side
Hotel Beacon **1**
Mayflower Hotel
on the Park **3**
Radisson Empire Hotel **2**
Trump International
Hotel & Tower **4**

Upper East Side
The Barbizon **10**
The Carlyle **6**
The Lowell **9**
The Mark **5**
The Pierre **8**
Surrey Hotel **7**

Don't Leave Home Without This—Credit Card Abbreviations

AE	American Express
CB	Carte Blanche
DC	Diners Club
DISC	Discover Card
JCB	Japan Credit Bank
MC	MasterCard
V	Visa

Our Favorite New York Hotels

The Ameritania
$$. Midtown West.

As an all-around choice, the Ameritania has much to offer. It's reasonably priced, convenient, and well appointed, with niceties like marble bathrooms (the hotel was renovated not long ago). The Ameritania is located just outside the Theater District and close to Restaurant Row. Central Park and Fifth Avenue are within walking distance. For families, children under 16 stay for free if they stay in the room with the parents. The hotel also has a small exercise room.

1701 Broadway at 54th Street (half a block west of Seventh Avenue). ☎ *800/ 922-0330 or 212/247-5000. Fax 212/247-3316.* **Subway:** *B/D/E to Seventh Avenue stop, and then walk one block west on 53rd Street to Broadway and turn right.* **Parking:** *$20 per day.* **Rack rates:** *$165–$225 double. AE, DC, JCB, MC, V.*

The Barbizon
$$. Upper East Side.

With its Spanish Gothic front and art deco lobby, the Barbizon speaks of elegance but also whispers of economy. Recently renovated, this former residential hotel for women is a good, moderately priced choice in a convenient neighborhood. Some of the improvements include new furniture and stereo systems in the rooms (the hotel also has a CD library). Guests have complimentary access to the Equinox Fitness Club (in the building), which has a pool and spa. Children under 12 stay free in parents' rooms.

140 E. 63rd St. (three blocks from Bloomingdale's). ☎ *800/223-1020 or 212/838-5700. Fax 212/888-4271.* **Subway:** *B/Q train to Lexington Avenue stop; N/R train to Lexington Avenue stop, and then walk north three blocks on Lexington.* **Parking:** *$29 per day.* **Rack rates:** *$190–$225 double. AE, DC, DISC, EU, MC, V.*

🌟Kids **The Carlyle**
$$$$$. *Upper East Side.*

This is that great hotel Jack Nicholson may have mentioned to you—or was it David Bowie? A favorite with stars and dignitaries (including JFK), The Carlyle is renowned for its fine service (rated tops by *Frommer's*), and no wonder: The hotel has more staff than guests—about *twice* as many. Traditionally decorated and English in flavor, The Carlyle is elegant, to say the least. Some of the rooms have Steinway grand pianos, and all of them have marble baths with whirlpools, Givenchy toiletries, and plush towels and terrycloth robes. Rooms on upper floors have a view of Central Park, and major museums are a stone's throw away. Baby sitting is available, and there's a state-of-the-art fitness center with saunas and massage available. Downstairs is the famous Cafe Carlyle where Bobby Short plays, and the restaurant serves a renowned Sunday brunch. Also, the place is pet friendly.

35 E. 76th Street at Madison Avenue (one block north of the Whitney Museum). ☎ ***800/227-5737*** *or 212/744-1600. Fax 212/717-4682.* **Subway:** *6 train to 77th Street stop, and then walk one block west on 76th Street to Madison Avenue.* **Parking:** *Valet, $39 per day.* **Rack rates:** *$355–$525 double. AE, DC, MC, V.*

Casablanca Hotel
$$$. *Midtown West.*

Why would you want to stay at a theme hotel? If it offered good value, it might be the start of a beautiful friendship. The Casablanca, opened in 1997 and sporting potted palm trees and Moroccan mosaic tiles, has the Moroccan theme *down*. There really is a Rick's Cafe, a guests-only restaurant with fire-place, bar, piano, and cappuccino when you want (and also something Bogey didn't have: Internet access). The rooms have carved wooden headboards, ceiling fans like in the movie (don't worry, there's A/C as well), and gold-trimmed mirrors. Some of the rooms are small, but the hotel is altogether very pleasant, with high-quality service and plenty of amenities, including fine chocolates in the room, Caswell-Massey toiletries, complimentary conti-nental breakfast and tea and cookies throughout the day, and complimentary wine and cheese on weekday evenings. Videos are available for viewing in your room, and you have free access to the New York Sports Club (with pool and sauna).

147 W 43rd St. between Sixth Avenue and Broadway (half a block from Times Square). ☎ ***888/922-7225*** *or 212/869-1212. Fax 212/391-7585.* **Subway:** *1/2/3/9/7/N/R/S trains to Times Square stop, and then walk half a block east on 43rd Street.* **Parking:** *$18 per day.* **Rack rates:** *$225–$245 double. AE, DC, JCB, MC, V.*

Chelsea Pines Inn
$. *Chelsea/West Village.*

Recently renovated, this is one of the better gay-oriented hotels in the city and is close to Chelsea and the West Village. Its low price, greenhouse, backyard garden (seasonal), and understanding staff make it a good choice for the gay traveler.

317 W. 14th St. between Eighth and Ninth avenues. ☎ *212/929-1023. Fax 212/620-5646.* **Subway:** *A/C/E/L trains to 14th Street/Eighth Avenue stop, and then walk half a block west on 14th Street.* **Parking:** *On street.* **Rack rates:** *$75–$99 double. AE, CB, DC, DISC, MC, V.*

Crowne Plaza Manhattan
$$$$. Midtown West.

Right in Times Square, within a stone's throw of the theaters and Restaurant Row and a five-minute walk from Central Park, this is the flagship of Holiday Inn Worldwide's upscale Crowne Plaza line. Rooms have contemporary furnishings, marble baths, coffeemakers, hairdryers, irons, safes, and pay-per-view movies. The lobby contains a nice bar, there are a couple of restaurants on the premises, and guests have use of the New York Sports Club on the 15th floor. Children under 19 stay free in room with parents.

1605 Broadway between 48th & 49th streets. ☎ *800/227-6963 or 212/ 977-4000. Fax 212/333-7393.* **Subway:** *N/R trains to 49th Street stop, and then walk one block west; 1/9 trains to 50th Street stop, and then walk one block south.* **Parking:** *Valet Parking $34.* **Rack Rates:** *$199–$389 double. AE, CB, DC, DISC, JCB, MC, V.*

 ## Doubletree Guest Suites
$$$. Midtown West.

You might not think of Times Square as the best place for your kids, but the Doubletree is perhaps the leading family-oriented hotel in the city. Walking distance from theaters, Central Park, Rockefeller Center, and Fifth Avenue,

Best Hotels for Families

Ameritania	$$
Hotel Beacon	$$
Carlyle	$$$$$
Doubletree Guest Suites	$$$
Mayflower Hotel on the Park	$$
Novotel New York	$$$
Salisbury	$$$
Surrey	$$$

it's centrally located and offers a good value. The hotel only has suites, which have two rooms (separate bedroom and living room, with a sofa bed). Guests choose between a king-size bed or two double beds. There's no charge for cribs. The suites have no kitchenette, but there is a microwave, coffeemaker, and refrigerator. Other family-oriented features are two floors of "childproofed" suites for those with small children, a playroom, an arts-and-crafts center, and electronic amusements. Children under 15 stay free in the parents' suites. Complimentary tea and coffee.

1568 Broadway at 47th Street and Seventh Avenue. ☎ *800/325-9033 or 212/ 719-1600. Fax 212/921-5215.*

Subway: N/R to 49th Street stop, and then walk two blocks south on Seventh Avenue; 1/2/3/7/9/S to Times Square stop, and then walk four blocks north on Seventh Avenue. *Parking:* $30 per day. *Rack rates:* $225–$325 suite. AE, DC, DISC, JCB, MC, V.

Drake Swissôtel
$$$$. Midtown East.
One of the traditional top-drawer New York hotels, the Drake, now owned by Swiss Air, is a favorite for business travelers. Even if you aren't on business, this may be the hotel for you if you appreciate large rooms and big closets (with safes, no less). A recent renovation has kept the old hotel up with the times and improved the rooms. Amenities include desks and refrigerators in the rooms, a new business center with all the equipment (your first 2 hours of meeting room use is complimentary), and a brand-new fitness center. Children under 15 stay free in the parents' rooms. There's a complimentary car service to Wall Street on weekday mornings.

440 Park Ave. at 56th Street. ☎ *800/DRAKENY or 212/421-0900. Fax 212/565-9930. Subway: E/F trains to Lexington/Third Avenue stop, and then walk one block west on 53rd, turn right and walk three blocks north on Park Avenue; 6 train to 51st Street stop, and then walk one block west to Park Avenue, turn right and walk five blocks north. Parking: $30 per day. Rack rates: $245–$355 double. AE, CB, DC, DISC, EU, JCB, MC, V.*

Grand Hyatt New York
$$$$. Midtown East.
Another Donald Trump production, the Grand Hyatt is next door to Grand Central Terminal and offers several layers of accommodation. While the standard rooms are not large, the Business Plan rooms have up-to-date technology including fax and access to photocopiers and printers at all hours. The Regency Club rooms, at the top of the scale, have a private concierge. Both Business Plan and Regency Club guests receive a complimentary continental breakfast. The hotel has a new fitness center and a business center. Two children under 18 can stay for free in the parents' room.

109 E. 42nd St. at Park Avenue. ☎ *800/233-1234 or 212/883-1234. Fax 212/661-8256. Subway: 4/5/6/7/S to Grand Central stop; exit at 42nd Street and turn left. Parking: Valet, $34 per day. Rack rates: $300–$325 double. AE, CB, DC, DISC, JCB, MC, V.*

Herald Square Hotel
$. Midtown West.
The price of this hotel is its selling point. Formerly the headquarters of *Life* magazine, the building is near the Empire State Building and Macy's and has comfortable but small rooms with air conditioning, TV, and in-room safes. The hotel is owned by the same family that runs the Portland Square Hotel.

19 W. 31st St. between Fifth Avenue and Broadway (two blocks south of the Empire State Building). ☎ *800/727-1888 or 212/279-4017. Fax 212/643-9208.*

Subway: B/D/F/Q/N/R to 34th Street stop, and then walk south two blocks on Broadway to 31st Street and turn left. *Parking:* $21 per day. *Rack rates:* $95–$105 double. AE, DISC, JCB, MC, V.

Kids Hotel Beacon
$$. Upper West Side.

If you don't mind roughing it (no room service) or are traveling with children, the Hotel Beacon is a good choice: The rooms are good-sized and have kitchenettes, and there's a coin-op laundry (or valet service, if you don't want to rough it that much). Suites are available, which have an additional room and a pull-out couch. The location is good for families, too: near Lincoln Center, Central Park, the Museum of Natural History, and the Children's Museum. Coffee and in-room movies are complimentary. Children under 17 stay free in the parents' room.

2130 Broadway at 75th Street (three blocks from the American Museum of Natural History). ☎ *800/572-4969 or 212/724-0839. Fax 212/724-0839. Subway: 1/2/3/9 train to 72nd Street stop, and then walk three blocks north on Broadway. Parking: $20 per day. Rack rates: $145–$155 double. AE, CB, DC, DISC, MC, V.*

Hotel Elysee
$$$$. Midtown East.

The Elysee is a chic, "boutique" hotel with a European flair, both in the clientele and the furnishings. The baths have Italian marble, the rooms are good sized but not huge, and complimentary continental breakfast, afternoon tea, and evening wine and cheese are served. The Monkey Bar is a popular nightspot, from which you can also order room service during lunch and dinner hours. Guests enjoy free access to the New York Sports Club nearby.

60 E. 54th St. between Madison and Park avenues. ☎ *800/535-9733 or 212/753-1066. Fax 212/980-9278. Subway: E/F train to Fifth Avenue stop, and then walk one and a half blocks east on 54th Street. Parking: Valet, $24 per day. Rack rates: $265–$375 double. AE, CB, DC, JCB, MC, V.*

Hotel Metro
$$. Midtown West.

The art deco Hotel Metro is a good buy for the budget traveler; for slightly more than you'd pay for the cheapest of the cheap, you get a number of amenities: complimentary continental breakfast; room service from the Metro Grill; European-style decor; marble baths equipped with hair dryers; and a fitness room. You even get a nice view of the Empire State Building from the roof terrace.

45 W. 35th St. between Fifth and Sixth avenues (just east of Herald Square, one block from the Empire State Building). ☎ *800/356-3870 or 212/947-2500. Fax 212/279-1310. Subway: B/D/F/Q/N/R to 34th Street stop, and then walk north on Sixth Avenue to 35th Street and turn right.* **Parking:** *$18 per day.* **Rack rates:** *$165–$250 double. AE, DC, MC, V.*

Incentra Village House
$$. Chelsea/West Village.
Made up of two 19th-century historic townhouses, Incentra is smaller than Chelsea Pines (see above)—only 12 rooms here—but it also caters to gay visitors. Decorated with antiques, most of the rooms have kitchenettes and functioning fireplaces. It's conveniently located to the nightlife of the West Village and Chelsea, and with the M10 bus just across the street, you can also easily get to the Theater District and other Uptown attractions.

32 Eighth Ave. between 12th and Jane streets, just north of Abingdon Square. ☎ *212/ 206-0007. Fax 212/604-0625.* **Subway:** *A/C/E/L to 14th Street/Eighth Avenue stop, and then walk two blocks south on Eighth Avenue.* **Parking:** *On street.* **Rack rates:** *$149–$179 double. AE, MC, V.*

**Best Hotels for
Gay Travelers**

Chelsea Pines Inn	$
Incentra Village House	$$

Jolly Madison Towers Hotel
$$. Midtown East.
Despite the name, the Jolly Madison is an Italian hotel, and is tastefully decorated and clean, though the rooms are small. There's an Italian restaurant and the Whaler Bar on the premises, and the neighborhood is residential and quiet. One child under 13 can stay for free in the parents' room.

22 E. 38th St. at Madison Avenue (one block north of the Pierpont Morgan Library). ☎ *800/225-4340 or 212/802-0600. Fax 212/447-0747.* **Subway:** *4/6/7/S to Grand Central stop, exit at 42nd Street, walk west to Madison Avenue, turn left, and walk four blocks south.* **Parking:** *$15 per day.* **Rack rates:** *$190–$220 double. AE, DC, JCB, MC, V.*

The Kimberly
$$$. Midtown East.
With attractive, comfortable standard rooms as well as huge suites (dining and living rooms, kitchens, marble baths, and balconies), the Kimberly is a good value in its price range and offers summer and weekend rates. What really makes the hotel different is its affiliation with the New York Health & Racket Club: Guests receive a complimentary 3-hour cruise on the club's boat (May–Oct only) and can use any of its facilities in the city. That means you have access to pools, tennis courts, gyms, and even indoor golf. The rooms are technologically with it, including fax machines. Children under 17 stay free in the parents' room.

145 E. 50th St. between Lexington and Third avenues. ☎ ***800/683-0400*** *or 212/755-0400. Fax 212/750-0113.* **Subway:** *6 train to 51st Street stop, and then walk one block south on Lexington and turn left on 50th Street.* **Parking:** *Valet, $23 per day.* **Rack rates:** *$265–$365 double. AE, DC, DISC, JCB, MC, V.*

The Lowell
$$$$. Upper East Side.

How many hotels have a suite with a private gym? The Lowell does. (It also has 43 other suites and 21 rooms.) Located in an art deco historic landmark building, the suites are elegant, individually appointed, and furnished with fine antiques, and the bathrooms are done in marble and brass. The fitness center offers spa treatments. A quiet location that is nonetheless convenient to many attractions rounds out The Lowell's appeal.

28 E. 63rd St. between Park and Madison avenues. ☎ ***800/221-4444*** *or 212/838-1400. Fax 212/319-4230.* **Subway:** *B/Q to Lexington Avenue stop, and then walk west one and a half blocks on 63rd Street.* **Parking:** *Valet, $45 per day.* **Rack rates:** *$315–$515 double. AE, DC, DISC, ER, JCB, MC, V.*

The Mark
$$$$$. Upper East Side.

In luxury, the Mark vies with the Carlyle, only a block and a half away, matching the latter's English gentility with Italian neoclassicism. Owned by a Monaco company, the Mark attracts Europeans and a strong business clientele, but ask about the weekend and summer packages. Connecting doubles are available, and the executive suite with a queen-size and a sofa bed does as well for a family as for a CEO. The dazzling bathrooms with oversized tubs and heated towel racks get rave reviews, as do the fresh flowers in every room. There's complimentary car service to Wall Street (weekdays) or the Theater District (Friday and Saturday evenings), a small health club, and a first-class restaurant (Mark's; see Chapter 10). Children under 16 stay free in the parents' room.

25 E. 77th St. between Fifth and Madison avenues (a couple of blocks from the Whitney Museum). ☎ ***800/THEMARK*** *or 212/744-4300. Fax 212/744-2749.* **Subway:** *6 train to 77th Street stop, and then walk west two and a half blocks on 77th to Madison.* **Parking:** *Valet, $35 per day.* **Rack rates:** *$375–$420 double. AE, CB, DC, DISC, ER, EU, JCB, MC, V.*

Marriott World Trade Center Hotel
$$$$. Downtown.

Formerly the New York Vista, the Marriott feels like a new hotel thanks to a multi-million-dollar renovation. You couldn't ask for a better Downtown location: It's located between the twin towers of the World Trade Center. The waterfall in the three-story atrium is impressive, and the rooms aren't too shabby either, with marble baths, full-length windows, and a decent amount of space. Because of its business center, its proximity to Wall Street, and an

Executive Floor with complimentary breakfast and other amenities, the hotel is appealing to business travelers (though everyone gets to enjoy such features as the rooftop health club, swimming pool, indoor track, and saunas).

#3 World Trade Center between Liberty and Vesey streets (the building between the Twin Towers). ☎ ***800/228-9290*** *or 212/ 938-9100. Fax 212/444-4094.* **Subway:** *1/9/N/R train to Cortland Street stop, and then up the internal passage to the World Trade Center; C/E trains to World Trade Center stop.* **Parking:** *Valet parking $28 per day.* **Rack rates:** *$309–$329 double. AE, DC, DISC, EU, JCB, MC, V.*

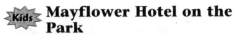 Mayflower Hotel on the Park

$$. Upper West Side.
If you want to see Central Park from your room but don't want to pay through the nose for the privilege, the Mayflower is the hotel for you. Old-fashioned and proud of it, the hotel is well kept, though you may want to specify that you don't want a floor where renovation is underway. The rooms are large, with plenty of storage space, though sometimes the bathrooms are not big. Rooms have a refrigerator and sink in a pantry alcove, but no cooking facilities. Families may want to take advantage of the available connecting doubles or suites. There's an exercise room, as well as a restaurant (The Conservatory) that serves three meals per day. *Note:* The Mayflower is much in demand at Thanksgiving because it's an optimal viewing point for the Macy's Parade.

Best Hotels for Business Travelers	
Drake Swissôtel	$$$
Grand Hyatt New York	$$$
The Mark	$$$$
Marriott World Trade Center	$$$$
The Michelangelo	$$$$$
Millenium Hilton	$$$$
The Pierre	$$$$$
Sheraton New York	$$$
Trump International	$$$$

15 Central Park West between 61st and 62nd streets. ☎ ***800/223-4164*** *or 212/265-0060. Fax 212/265-0227.* **Subway:** *A/C/1/9/B/D to Columbus Circle stop, and then walk north two blocks on Central Park West.* **Parking:** *$28 per day.* **Rack rates:** *$170–$210 double. AE, CB, DC, DISC, ER, JCB, MC, V.*

The Michelangelo
$$$$$. Midtown West.
Sometimes, big bucks really do translate into big advantages, as in the case of this elegant European-owned hotel. It offers a very central location, with Times Square, Broadway's Theater District, Central Park, Rockefeller Center, and Fifth Avenue at walking distance, though it's somewhat secluded from the most crowded spots. The hotel has an atmospheric and tasteful lobby, very large rooms with king-size beds, Italian marble bathrooms with large tubs, terry-cloth robes, and even Baci chocolates on your pillow—we're talking real luxury in soft tones. Continental breakfast is complimentary, as is weekday car service to Wall Street and use of a small fitness center (to really

keep in shape, you can pay a small fee for use of the Equitable Health and Swim Club across the street). If you're not traveling by mobile command post, for a little extra you can get a "smart desk" room with computer, fax, and modem.

152 W 51st St., at the corner of Seventh Avenue (one block east of Broadway).
☎ *800/237-0990 or 212/765-1900. Fax 212/541-6604.* **Subway:** *1/9 train to 50th Street stop, and then walk half a block east on 51st. Street; N/R train to 49th Street stop, and then walk one block north on Seventh Avenue; B/D/E train to Seventh Avenue stop, and then walk two blocks south on Seventh Avenue.* **Parking:** *Valet parking $18 per day.* **Rack rates:** *$295–$750 double. AE, CB, DC, DISC, JCB, MC, V.*

The Millenium Hilton
$$$$. Downtown.
An enormous (58 stories) glass slab facing the World Trade Center, the Millenium is a favorite for business visitors to the city. The technological amenities include faxes in the rooms and a 24-hour business center. The rooms themselves are large and snazzily appointed, with marble baths, attractive wooden furniture, and other niceties. And the higher the floor, the better the view. The Hilton makes an effort to court the tourist visitor, too, and has a weekend planning service to help guests with ideas for everything from dining out to sightseeing. There's a fitness center and pool, and free car service to Midtown.

55 Church St. between Fulton and Dey streets (across the street from the World Trade Center). ☎ *800/835-2220 or 212/693-2001. Fax 212/571-2316.* **Subway:** *1/9/N/R train to Cortland Street stop, and then cross the street; C/E trains to World Trade Center stop, and then cross the street.* **Parking:** *$35 per day.* **Rack rates:** *$299–$380 double. AE, CB, DC, DISC, JCB, MC, V.*

Morgans
$$$. Midtown East.
If you want to pretend you're not staying in a hotel, Morgans is the place. This "boutique" hotel has no sign outside and a sleek, minimalist feel inside, with maple furniture and subdued colors. The bathrooms (not large) are classic black and white. Features include a fax in each room, 24-hour room service, a low-key breakfast room for guests, and complimentary access to the New York Sports Club close by.

237 Madison Ave. at 37th Street (near the Morgan Library). ☎ *800/334-3408 or 212/686-0300. Fax 212/779-8352.* **Subway:** *4/5/6/7/S to Grand Central stop, exit at 42nd Street, turn right, walk west to Madison Avenue, turn left, walk five blocks south.* **Parking:** *$32 per day.* **Rack rates:** *$265–$290 double. AE, DC, DISC, MC, V.*

New York Marriott Marquis
$$$. Midtown West.
Relatively inexpensive for what it offers, and with a world record–holding 37-story atrium, the Marriott Marquis is right smack in the middle of the Theater District. (Two theaters were destroyed to make room for it.) Built in 1985, it was redecorated in 1997 to include—among other things—workstations in the rooms. It offers a health club with whirlpool and sauna. After your workout, check out the view from The View, the three-story revolving restaurant on top of the building.

1535 Broadway between 45th and 46th streets (just north of Times Square).
☎ **800/228-9290** *or 212/398-1900. Fax 212/704-8930.* **Subway:**
1/2/3/7/9/N/R/S to Times Square stop, and then walk two blocks north on Broadway. **Parking:** *$30 per day.* **Rack rates:** *$189–$360 double. AE, CB, DC, DISC, JCB, MC, V.*

215
E

Novotel New York
Kids
$$$. Midtown West.
This French hotel is convenient to the Theater District (the views from the upper floors are fabulous) and also a good choice for families. The furnishings are simple but the rooms are relatively large, as are the baths. Two children under 17 stay for free in the parents' room, and you receive a complimentary continental breakfast. Rooms have either a king-size bed or two double beds and a sofa bed. There's a business center (computers and cellular phones can also be rented), a fitness room, and a Children's Corner.

226 W. 52nd St. at Broadway. ☎ **800/221-3185** *or 212/315-0100. Fax 212/765-5369.* **Subway:** *B/D/E trains to Seventh Avenue stop, and then walk west on 53rd Street to Broadway and turn left.* **Parking:** *$16 per day.* **Rack rates:** *$179–$269 double. AE, DC, JCB, MC, V.*

Pickwick Arms Hotel
$. Midtown East.
Like the Washington Square Hotel Downtown, the Pickwick offers small rooms for a small price. It does, however, have some nice features, like a roof garden and a cocktail lounge. If you're looking for a cheap place to stay in an expensive neighborhood and don't particularly care about amenities, the Pickwick is your best pick.

230 E. 51st St. between Second and Third avenues. ☎ **800/749-5945** *or 212/355-0300. Fax 212/755-5029.* **Subway:** *6 train to 51st Street stop, and then walk one block east on 51st to Third Avenue; E/F train to Lexington Avenue stop, and then walk south two blocks on Third Avenue and turn left.* **Parking:** *$20 per day.* **Rack rates:** *$105 double. AE, MC, V.*

The Pierre
$$$$$. Upper East Side.

Overlooking Central Park, the Pierre is one of the most luxurious hotels in New York, with elegant public spaces and a diverse variety of accommodations (28 different kinds), as well as little extras like a packing and unpacking service available upon request. It's hard to beat the location, and there's a complimentary car service to the Theater District. Traditional elegance is complimented by up-to-date technology. Among the facilities are a business center and a fitness center.

Most Intimate, Quiet Hotels

Drake Swissôtel	$$$
Jolly Madison	$$
Morgans	$$$
The Lowell	$$$$

Fifth Avenue at 61st Street. ☎ *800/ 332-3442 or 212/838-8000. Fax 212/ 940-8109.* **Subway:** *N/R train to Fifth Avenue stop, and then walk two blocks north on Fifth Avenue.* **Parking:** *Valet, $33 per day.* **Rack rates:** *$445–$645 double. AE, CB, DC, ER, EU, JCB, MC, V.*

The Plaza Hotel
$$$$$. Midtown East.

This hotel needs no introduction: It's a famous New York and national historic landmark familiar from many films. Don't assume that you'll get the same room as your favorite movie star, however; some rooms are small, though the amenities are first-rate throughout. What you pay for is the location and the feeling of Old New York. The best deals are for the more expensive rooms; those overlooking Central Park have gorgeous views. Although the fitness facilities are limited, you have free access to the nearby Atrium Health Club and pool.

768 Fifth Ave. between 58th and 59th streets (just on Central Park South). ☎ *800/527-4727 or 212/759-3000. Fax 212/546-5324.* **Subway:** *B/Q train to 57th Street, and then walk one block east on 58th Street; E/F train to Fifth Avenue stop, and then walk five blocks north on Fifth Avenue.* **Parking:** *Valet parking $35 per day.* **Rack rates:** *$335–$475 double. AE, DC, DISC, JCB, MC, V.*

Portland Square Hotel
$. Midtown West.

The Portland Square, owned by the same family that operates the Herald Square Hotel, has a few more amenities than its sibling and is convenient to the Theater District—some famous actors used to stay here. The rooms are small and spartan, but clean, and there's a business center with faxes and computers, as well as a small exercise room.

132 W. 47th St. between Sixth and Seventh avenues (one block from Rockefeller Center). ☎ *800/388-8988 or 212/382-0600. Fax 212/382-0684.* **Subway:** *B/D/F/Q to Rockefeller Center stop, and then walk west on 47th Street; 1/9 to N/R* to 49th Street stop, and then walk two blocks south on Seventh Avenue and turn left; 1/9 trains to 50th Street stop, and then walk three blocks south on Seventh Avenue and turn left. **Parking:** $24 per day. **Rack rates:** $94–$104 double. AE, MC, V.

Quality Hotel and Suites Rockefeller Center
$$. Midtown West.
Looks can be deceiving: Behind the elegant beaux arts facade of this place lies a reasonably priced hotel, centrally located. That said, it may be a surprise that the Quality Hotel has such up-scale amenities as complimentary continental breakfast, fitness and business centers, free local phone calls (phones have voice mail and a data port, too), and coffeemakers and irons in the rooms. Children under 19 stay for free in the parents' rooms.

59 W. 46th St. between Fifth and Sixth avenues (two blocks from Rockefeller Center). ☎ *800/848-0020 or 212/719-2300.* **Subway:** *B/D/F/Q to Rockefeller Center stop, and then walk three blocks south on Sixth Avenue and turn left on 46th Street.* **Parking:** *$25 per day.* **Rack rates:** *$119–$169 double. AE, CB, DC, DISC, EU, JCB, MC, V.*

Quality Hotel Fifth Avenue
$$. Midtown East.
A bargain, no matter how you look at it. This hotel is on Fifth Avenue and is convenient to most Midtown sights, offers a low price (as well as discounts and specials), and is simple but tidy. Rooms have either a queen-size bed or double beds. Two children under 19 stay free in the parents' room. Free coffee and newspapers in the morning. Rooms on the upper stories may have views. A health club and pool (not on the premises) are available for a $15 fee.

3 E. 40th St. at Fifth Avenue (just south of the main Public Library). ☎ *800/ 228-5151 or 212/447-1500. Fax 212/213-0972.* **Subway:** *7 train to Fifth Avenue stop, and then walk two blocks south on Fifth Avenue, turn right on 40th Street; 4/5/6/S to Grand Central stop, exit at 42nd Street, walk two blocks south on Park Avenue, turn right on 40th Street, and walk two blocks west.* **Parking:** *$18 per day.* **Rack rates:** *$195–$210 double. AE, CB, DC, DISC, EU, JCB, MC, V.*

Radisson Empire Hotel
$$$. Upper West Side.
Located only a block from Central Park and across the street from Lincoln Center, the Radisson is a natural for people who plan to take in the opera. The feeling is intimate and the furnishings traditional (two-poster beds), though the rooms are not excessively large—the building used to be the old Empire Hotel but was renovated by Radisson. Guests may use the New York Sports Club for free. The decor may be less trendy and the accommodations less pampering than at more upscale hotels, but the Radisson is generally what you would expect for a standard mid-range hotel. For families, the message is mixed: With the park nearby, there's plenty of safe room to play

during the day, yet you will also be close to nightlife. Being an older building, the rooms and closets are smaller than what you might like.

44 W. 63rd St. at Broadway. ☎ ***800/333-3333*** *or 212/265-7400. Fax 212/245-3382.* **Subway:** *A/B/C/D/1/9 to Columbus Circle stop, and then walk four blocks north on Broadway, turn left on 63rd Street.* **Parking:** *$25 per day.* **Rack rates:** *$250 double. AE, CB, DC, DISC, JCB, MC, V.*

Hotels with the Best Service

The Carlyle	$$$$$
The Waldorf Astoria	$$$

The Royalton
$$$$. Midtown West.

Chic and design-conscious, the Royalton was created by the same people who brought you Morgans (see earlier in this chapter). It's showier, though, and closer to the action (the Theater District), and it draws a hip crowd. All the rooms are spacious, with separate living and working areas, the latter equipped for the electronic rather than the Gilded Age. The beds are either queen- or king-size, and some of the rooms have special features; if you want a tub the size of a frog pond or a working fireplace, stay at the Royalton.

44 W 44th St. between Fifth and Sixth avenues (two blocks from the New York Public Library and four blocks from the Rockefeller Center). ☎ ***800/635-9013*** *or 212/869-4400. Fax 212/869-8965.* **Subway:** *B/D/F/Q train to 42nd Street stop, and then walk two blocks north on Sixth Avenue; 7 train to Fifth Avenue stop, and then walk two blocks north on Fifth Avenue.* **Parking:** *Valet parking $30 per day.* **Rack rates:** *$305–$330 double. AE, DC, EU, MC, V.*

Salisbury Hotel
$$$. Midtown West.

Affordable, centrally located, and roomy, the Salisbury is a good choice for families or for anyone who wants space and doesn't mind not being waited on hand and foot. Housed in a former residential hotel across from Carnegie Hall, the Salisbury has apartment-size rooms, most of which have a kitchenette, sink, and small refrigerator. The regular rooms have walk-in closets, living space, and cable TV; the suites (one- or two-bedroom) include business centers. Children under 16 stay free in the parents' rooms. Guests can order from local restaurants 24 hours per day, and (for a small extra fee) have access to the health club at the Parker Meridien.

123 W. 57th St. between Sixth and Seventh avenues. ☎ ***800/NYC-5757*** *or 212/246-1300. Fax 212/977-7752.* **Subway:** *B/Q to 57th Street stop, and then walk half a block west on 57th Street; N/R train to 57th Street stop, and then walk half a block east on 57th Street.* **Parking:** *$18 per day.* **Rack rates:** *$219–$239 double. AE, CB, DC, JCB, MC, V.*

Sheraton New York Hotel and Towers
$$$. Midtown West.

A huge hotel catering to conferences and business travelers, the Sheraton New York has been recently renovated. It has the anonymity of a big hotel on one hand and numerous conveniences on the other (a large desk with a voicemail– and data port–equipped phone in every room; business center; health club; complimentary use of the pool at the Sheraton Manhattan across the street; 24-hour room service). The Club Level, and above it The Towers, offer further amenities, more technology, and more pampering—for more money. Two children under 18 stay free in the parents' room.

811 Seventh Ave. at 53rd Street (one block west of MOMA). ☎ *800/223-6550 or 212/581-1000. Fax 212/315-4265.* **Subway:** *B/D/E to 49th Street stop.* **Parking:** *$30 per day.* **Rack rates:** *$189–$275 double. AE, CB, DC, DISC, ER, JCB, MC, V.*

SoHo Grand Hotel
$$$. SoHo.

The SoHo Grand Hotel is a new addition to the ranks of tony New York hotels—for those who prefer the chic SoHo atmosphere to Midtown or Uptown. The rooms are small, but everything in the hotel is custom designed and stylish, with the designs reflecting the area's industrial past and artistic present. The baths have pedestal sinks and traditional tiles, and amenities include interactive TV and in-room movies as well as a fitness room.

310 W. Broadway between Grand and Canal streets. ☎ *800/965-3000 or 212/965-3000. Fax 212/965-3244.* **Subway:** *A/C/E to Canal Street stop, and then walk one block east on Canal to West Broadway and turn left.* **Parking:** *Valet parking $25 per day.* **Rack rates:** *$229–$369 double. AE, CB, DC, DISC, EU, JCB, MC, V.*

Kids Surrey Hotel
$$$. Upper East Side.

If you don't mind reproductions instead of antiques, and if you'd like to stay at a hotel similar to the nearby Carlyle or Mark but don't want to mortgage your house to do it, the Surrey is a sweet deal: The one-bedrooms have two doubles and a roll-away sofa bed, making this a good hotel for families. Weekly and monthly discount rates are also available. Not only are the rooms (including the bathrooms) clean and large; they also have kitchenettes with a refrigerator, sink, and stove, as well as dining areas. If you don't have time to shop for food, the staff will take care of

Best Hotels for Travelers with Disabilities

Doubletree Guest Suites	$$$
New York Marriott Marquis	$$$
SoHo Grand Hotel	$$$
Millenium Hilton	$$$$

that detail for $5. This all-suite hotel is also close to restaurants (with the Daniel, under chef Daniel Boulud, downstairs), Museum Mile, and Central Park.

20 East 76th St. at Madison Avenue (one block north of the Whitney Museum). ☎ *800/ME-SUITE or 212/288-3700. Fax 212/628-1549.* **Subway:** *6 train to 77th Street stop, and then walk two blocks west to Madison Avenue.* **Parking:** *Valet parking $35 per day.* **Rack rates:** *$250–$365 suite. AE, CB, DC, DISC, JCB, MC, V.*

Kids Trump International Hotel and Tower
$$$$. Upper West Side.

A brand-new luxury hotel, Trump International goes overboard with amenities, starting with your own personal Trump Attaché, who will help you with everything from business matters to provisioning your refrigerator (while you gaze out over the park through a telescope—another standard feature). You can have a chef from the hotel's restaurant come to your room and prepare a gourmet meal (each suite has a full kitchen). The hotel is perfect for hyperactive executives, with a fax machine, two-line phone with data port, and entertainment center in every room, and a 6,000-square foot fitness center and spa with a 55-foot pool. On the other hand, Trump International might work well for your family. There are children's programs, and children stay free in the parents' room—but leave your car at home.

1 Central Park West at 60th Street. ☎ *888/44-TRUMP or 212/299-1000. Fax 212/299-1150.* **Subway:** *A/B/C/D/1/9 train to Columbus Circle stop.* **Parking:** *Valet parking $42 per day.* **Rack rates:** *$395 suite. AE, CB, DC, DISC, JCB, MC, V.*

Best Facilities for Health and Fitness

The Barbizon	$$
The Carlyle	$$$$$
The Kimberly	$$$
Marriott World Trade Center	$$$$
Millenium Hilton	$$$$
Trump International	$$$$

The Waldorf-Astoria and Waldorf Towers
$$$. Midtown East.

Home of the Waldorf Salad, this is one of the most famous of the grand old hotels of this or any other city. The Waldorf is now part of the Hilton chain, which has spent millions to refurbish it. The lobby is tasteful and elegant, and, with an ongoing restoration, most of the rooms are elegant, too. In terms of size, the rooms are spacious enough though not well suited to families unless you get a connecting double. All the baths are marble. The Waldorf Towers, though more expensive and lavish, has a complimentary continental breakfast and hors d'oeuvre, as well as butler service. The hotel has a variety of restaurants and bars, from Japanese to French. There's health club, but a $30 charge is attached. The Waldorf offers weekend packages. Children stay for free in the parents' rooms.

301 Park Ave. between 49th and 50th streets. ☎ ***800/WALDORF*** *or 212/355-3000. Fax 212/872-4784.* ***Subway:*** *6 train to 51st Street stop, and then walk one block west to Park Avenue.* ***Parking:*** *Valet parking $37 per day.* ***Rack rates:*** *$287–$324 double. AE, CB, DC, DISC, EU, JCB, MC, V.*

Washington Square Hotel
$$. West Village/NYU.

Some years ago, the Washington Square Hotel, a family-run hotel overlooking historic Washington Square, was a dingy little place with drab, tiny rooms. Now it's a renovated place with an attractive lobby and redecorated tiny rooms. What you get for being away from Midtown is a much lower rate; what you lose is space and amenities. (There's no room service.) But with the West Fourth Street subway close at hand and the Union Square Station 10 blocks away, you can get pretty much anywhere in Manhattan from here without too much trouble. Another plus is that breakfast is included, and the hotel organizes jazz packages and tours of Greenwich Village.

103 Waverly Place between Fifth and Sixth avenues. ☎ ***800/222-0418*** *or 212/777-9515. Fax 212/979-8373.* ***Subway:*** *A/B/C/D/E/F/Q trains to West 4th Street/Washington Square stop, walk one block east on West 4th Street to Washington Square, turn left, and walk along the park to the hotel at the northwest corner.* ***Parking:*** *$19 per day.* ***Rack rates:*** *$115–$140 double. AE, JCB, MC, V.*

Help! I'm So Confused!

For some of you the decision may be easy. Maybe your grandfather always told you about the time he stayed at the Waldorf and you've always wanted to stay there yourself. Or maybe your big ambition in the city is to attend the opera at Lincoln Center, so choosing the hotel across the street is a no-brainer. Some others among you, though, might not have a clear preference, and that's where organization comes into the picture. Some people charge lots of money for getting other people organized, but we'll throw it in free, just because we like you.

On the next page, then, is a chart. You probably read through the reviews in this chapter and said, at least a few times, "Hey, that one sounds good." If you put a little red check next to those, you're ahead of the game (if not, we hope you have a good memory), but it would still be a royal pain in the butt to flip around among a few dozen pages comparing and contrasting hotels. So, what you want to do is jot down the names and vital statistics of those places in the chart following, get everything lined up and orderly, then scan the lines to see how they stack up against each other. As you rank them in your mind, rank them in the column on the right, too; that way you can have your preferences all ready when making reservations, and if there's no room at the inn for choice number 1, just move right on to number 2.

Hotel Preferences Worksheet

Hotel	Location	Price per night

Advantages	Disadvantages	Your Ranking (1–10)

Part 3

Learning Your Way Around New York

Once you arrive in New York, you need to get a feel quickly for your surroundings and learn the ropes of transportation—beginning with getting from the airport to your hotel intact.

New York is one of the oldest cities in the country, but it's nowhere near as confusing as some other old cities. For the most part it's laid out in a logical grid, though the oldest part of the city, down at the tip of the island, has the usual European format: an "artistic" arrangement of streets rather than a logical grid. Greenwich Village, which originally really was a village located some miles outside of the town proper, also is notoriously arbitrary in its street plan and is full of crooked but picturesque streets—some of which used to be farmer's paths.

Fortunately for you, Midtown and Uptown are easy to figure out—except for Broadway, which does some pretty strange things between the bottom of the island and the top. First, you should master the basics: the neighborhoods and what to find in each one. Then you can go on to the finer points, like being able to tell Park Avenue from Park Avenue South, West 12th Street from Little West 12th, Broadway from West Broadway, and Seventh Avenue from Varrick Street. Then you won't be surprised when West 4th Street intersects West 10th.

Getting Your Bearings

In This Chapter

➤ Point A to point B (From the <u>A</u>irport to your <u>B</u>ed)

➤ Key to the city: Learning the lay of the land

➤ How to get unlost

When your plane touches down and the captain says "Welcome to New York City, folks!" don't think you're going to step out of the terminal and see Radio City Music Hall right across the street. No such luck.

The thing is, though New York City is made up of five boroughs (Manhattan, Brooklyn, Queens, the Bronx, and Staten Island), most of what you'll be doing and seeing on your visit will be in Manhattan, a 13-mile-long island that measures only about 2.5 miles across at its widest point and is so full of life that there's no room for an airport. Instead, the airports are located away from the center of things—La Guardia and Kennedy airports in Queens and Newark Airport across the Hudson in New Jersey.

Here's how you'll get across the water.

Fly Me to the Moon...or New York...whichever...

The three New York airports serve almost 80 million passengers per year, and they are crowded, sprawling, permanently under construction, and busy. The best thing to do is to get in and out as fast as possible. Air-Ride (☎ **800/ 247-7433**) is a service that provides recorded information about ground transportation from all the airports. You can also go to the information desk

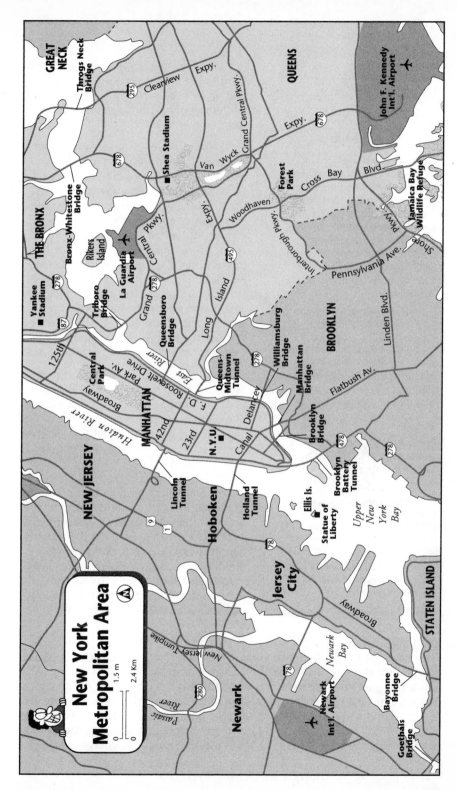

New York Metropolitan Area

0   1.5 m
0   2.4 Km

GREAT NECK

QUEENS

THE BRONX

MANHATTAN

BROOKLYN

NEW JERSEY

STATEN ISLAND

Throgs Neck Bridge

Clearview Expy.

295

John F. Kennedy Int'l. Airport

Grand Central Pkwy.

Shea Stadium

678

Expy.

678

Van Wyck

Forest Park

Cross Bay Blvd.

Jamaica Bay Wildlife Refuge

Bronx-Whitestone Bridge

Rikers Island

La Guardia Airport

Central Pkwy.

Grand

Expy.

Woodhaven

Interborough Pkwy.

Shore Pkwy.

Yankee Stadium

Triboro Bridge

278

87

278

Queensboro Bridge

495

Long Island

Pennsylvania Ave.

Linden Blvd.

125th

Central Park

Park Av.

Broadway

East River

F.D. Roosevelt Drive

Queens-Midtown Tunnel

278

Williamsburg Bridge

Manhattan Bridge

Flatbush Ave.

Hudson River

42nd

23rd

N.Y.U.

Canal

Delancey

Brooklyn Bridge

478

278

Lincoln Tunnel

Holland Tunnel

Ellis Is.

Statue of Liberty

Brooklyn Battery Tunnel

Upper New York Bay

Hoboken

9

1

78

Jersey City

Broadway

New Jersey Turnpike

Passaic River

280

78

Newark

Newark Int'l. Airport

Newark Bay

Bayonne Bridge

Goethals Bridge

85

Time-Savers

One of the few places in New York where you don't find yourself bumping into cash machines at every turn is at the airports. When you realize you have no money, you may have to hike a while to find some, bags and all. So make sure you have some bucks when you board your plane.

in the arrival area if you're feeling lost or want to get a private car service to pick you up (see the section "May I Call You a Limousine, Ma'am?" later in this chapter).

A cab from JFK to Manhattan will take about an hour, unless you're unlucky enough to arrive at rush hour. From La Guardia and Newark, allow slightly less time: around 45 minutes. (Ditto on the way back, of course.) A private bus will take about half an hour longer, if you factor in the time spent waiting for the bus and for all the passengers' tickets to be taken. The bus may also make other stops before yours. The main points in Manhattan where the bus companies stop are the World Trade Center, Penn Station, the Port Authority, and Grand Central Station.

On the way to Manhattan from La Guardia or Kennedy, you'll pass through Brooklyn and/or Queens. Although Manhattan is glamorous and a magnet for the rich, the famous, and the lucky, most New Yorkers are in fact middle class, lower middle class, or outright poor, and parts of the outer boroughs are pretty grim; this is one reason people tend to avoid the public transportation from the airports. Don't get us wrong: Many, many parts of the outer boroughs are beautiful, historic, and fascinating—some of the very ethnic neighborhoods look like they were plopped there right out of the old country, and parts of Brooklyn are as beautiful as Paris—but you'd need a guidebook the size of Rushmore and more time than the average visitor has to adequately cover them.

New York Stories

New York was the capital of the United States from George Washington's inauguration in 1789 until 1790, when the capital was moved to Philadelphia.

Yo, Taxi!

The easiest way to get into Manhattan is by taxi. After collecting your luggage, follow the signs for "Ground Transportation" or "Taxi." There should be a uniformed taxi dispatcher on duty, and a railed or chained-off area for customers to line up in. The dispatcher will probably ask you how many are in your party; consider that cabs only take four people, so if you have a larger group you'll have to take two cabs, thereby doubling the cost. You have to pay the bridge or tunnel tolls ($3.50–$4), and the night surcharge (50¢) if you're in a New York City yellow cab. Your bags ride free, so don't let anyone try to charge you for them, even if the driver hoisted them into the trunk. You should tip at least 15%, however.

The following taxi prices are without tolls:

➤ From La Guardia, the fare to Midtown should run around $25, a little less if you have no traffic.

➤ From JFK, it'll run you about $30–$40. Ask the dispatcher if you can get the flat rate of $30.

➤ From Newark, you take a New Jersey cab on the way in and a New York cab on the way back, and neither is allowed to poach on the other's territory. The airport taxi dispatcher sets the price based on your destination ($30–$43, plus toll and tip).

The Magic Bus

Several private bus companies serve the three airports:

➤ **Carey Transportation** (☎ **800/ 678-1569** or 718/632-0500) serves La Guardia and JFK. Their buses pick up and drop off passengers across from Grand Central Terminal on 42nd Street/Park Avenue, and also at the Port Authority Bus Terminal at 42nd Street and Eighth Avenue. They have free shuttle buses to Penn Station and many of the Midtown hotels; check when you reserve. You have to call the shuttle to come pick you up when you leave.

➤ **Gray Line Air Shuttle** (☎ **800/ 451-0455** or 212/315-3006) serves La Guardia, JFK, and Newark. Buses to La Guardia and JFK pick up and drop off passengers inside the Port Authority Bus Terminal at 42nd Street and Eighth Avenue and from a streetside stop on 41st Street between

Time-Savers

Both La Guardia and JFK offer a circuitous route to the city via public bus and/or subway (the A train from Kennedy, the no. M60 bus from La Guardia). This way is cheap, but is to be avoided. It will take up to a couple of hours; you'll spend those hours confused, anxious, and possibly uncomfortable; and you won't get the best first impression of New York.

New York Stories

The number of languages spoken by the taxi driver community in New York is an astounding 60. Speak slowly and clearly; you had to learn English, too, remember.

Tourist Traps

Don't let anyone other than a uniformed official taxi dispatcher get you a cab. The folks who hang out at the airport and ask, "need a cab?" prey on tourists and are unofficial as well as illegal.

Park and Lexington Avenues (near Grand Central Terminal). Buses to and from Newark pick up and drop off passengers at their hotels and must be reserved in advance.

➤ **Olympia Trails** (☎ 212/964-6233) serves Newark only. They pick up and drop off passengers from their office at 120 E. 41st Street between Park and Lexington avenues, a block from Grand Central; from street-side at the corner of 34th Street and Eighth Avenue (near Penn Station); from inside the Port Authority Bus Terminal; and in front of the Marriott Hotel at the World Trade Center.

Consult the chart below for schedules and fares.

Airport Bus Schedule

Carey	
Departs JFK	Every 20–30 mins., 6am–11pm
Departs La Guardia	Every 20–30 mins., 6:30am–11pm
Departs Grand Central and Port Aurhority	Every 20–30 mins., 5am–10pm
Fare	$10 La Guardia (round trip $15, seniors $3; $13 JFK (round trip $20, seniors $4)
Gray Line	
Departs JFK	Every 20 mins., 5am–midnight
Departs La Guardia	Every 20 mins., 5am–midnight
Departs Grand Central and Port Aurhority	Every 20 mins.,5am–midnight
Fare	$10 La Guardia; $12 JFK; $18.50 Newark (by reservation only)
Olympia (to/from Newark only)	
To Penn Station a & Grand Central	Every 15–30 mins.,6:15am–12:30am;
To World Trade Center	Every 30 mins., 7:45am–8:15pm
To Port Authority	24-hour service: Every 20–30 mins., 6am–12:30am and at 1am, 2am, 3:45am, and 5am
Departs Penn Station & Grand Central	Every 15–30 mins., 5am–11pm
Departs World Trade Center	Every 30 mins., 6:15am–8pm Mon–Fri (7:30am–7:30pm Sat–Sun)
Departs Port Authority	Every 15–30 mins., 5am–12:40am and at 1am, 2am, and 3:30am
Fare	$10

May I Call You a Limousine, Ma'am?

"Car service" is a New York term for "limousine," but is more accurate because a car is exactly what you get (a Lincoln Town Car, most probably).

A number of companies operate them and the competition is strong enough to keep the price in the same ballpark as a taxi fare. But, because you reserve them in advance (a day or half-day), you don't have to worry about hailing a cab if you're running late. Some of the companies are **Allstate** (☎ **800/453-4099** or 212/741-7440), **Sabra** (☎ **212/777-7171**), and **Tel Aviv** (☎ **800\222-9888**). It's a good idea to have the driver meet you in the baggage claim area, rather than outside the airport.

Taking the Sea Route

Delta Airlines has a **Water Shuttle** from La Guardia Airport that cruises down the East River to Midtown and then to Pier 40 at Wall Street. The fare is $20. Ask for details when you book a flight with Delta.

The Bronx Is Up & the Battery's Down (and All the Other Directions You'll Need)

New York is not a hard city in which to orient yourself (geographically, at least), except that its crampedness makes it look deceptively small on the map.

Manhattan runs slightly northeast by southwest, but don't try to tell that to anyone—as far as New Yorkers are concerned, everything is straight north or straight south. Avenues run north-south, streets east-west, though there have to be a few exceptions, of course, primarily downtown.

The history of New York in the postwar period can be read in the transformations of the neighborhoods. The death of Manhattan as a port in the 1960s—except for passenger ships, most shipping has moved to Staten Island and New Jersey—the flight of industry to cheaper areas, and gentrification of the abandoned areas have all brought major upheavals.

Downtown

The downtown area is actually a collection of neighborhoods. **Wall Street** and the Financial District are the world capital of capitalism. Being the oldest part of the city, there are some important historical landmarks like Trinity Church. South Street Seaport and the Brooklyn Bridge are to the north, on the East River; on the Hudson side stands the World Trade Center. Exciting by day, at night you could hear a Krugerrand drop.

TriBeCa (more typically written just as "Tribeca"), formerly just a warehouse area with some impressive industrial architecture, is now extremely trendy. The name stands for "triangle below Canal." Canal Street runs straight across the island, going through the heart of **Chinatown,** which lies to the east of Tribeca. Chinatown is booming, constantly expanding, and gradually swallowing **Little Italy** (directly to the north), which is truly little at this point. There are still some Italian shops and restaurants here, and even some people who speak Italian. Even further east is the **Lower East Side,** a funky, historic area that was once the Jewish ghetto, and is now split between boho trendy and fairly dangerous; the farther east you go, the worse it gets. To the west is **SoHo,** famed for its cast iron architecture. Fifteen years ago it was the center of the art scene (now in the process of moving to Chelsea); today, it's a major shopping and entertainment area.

New York Stories

At the turn of the century, the Lower East Side was one of the most densely populated areas on earth.

Greenwich Village (East and West)

At the turn of the century, **Greenwich Village** (now regularly referred to as the West Village) was, in that hoary old cliche, a hotbed of radicalism, where Max Eastman and Emma Goldman tried to change the world. (She got deported.) It was not always as affluent as it is today. In the 1950s, it was still the home of longshoremen. Now it's a center of art, dining, shopping, and gay life. The architecture of the Village is worth a visit all by itself. It has the shortest street in the city (Weehawken), and the narrowest house (where Edna St. Vincent Millay lived). The **East Village** is a younger, more alternative area, the focus of rock music as the West Village is the focus of jazz. More raw and less polished, it has a seedier and more intense energy. **NoHo** is a small, fashionable area just east of Broadway and just north of Houston Street.

Chelsea

Chelsea extends from 14th Street to 34th Street and from the Hudson east to Fifth Avenue. It's a booming area, with a large gay community, lots of cultural activities (art galleries in particular), and many restaurants. When you head east from Chelsea and cross Fifth Avenue—which is the spine of New York; house numbers, East and West, branch out from here—you reach the **Gramercy Park** area, a quiet, elegant, moneyed neighborhood known for some very fine restaurants (and the asbestos explosion, but that's been cleaned up).

Midtown

Roughly bounded by 34th Street on the south and 59th Street to the north (the lower limit of Central Park), Midtown is New York's other major business area after Wall Street, but also includes such landmarks as the Empire State Building, the Chrysler Building, Grand Central Terminal, Rockefeller Center and Radio City Music Hall, Times Square, and the United Nations. The theater district is in Midtown West; many of the major hotels and stores are also in Midtown.

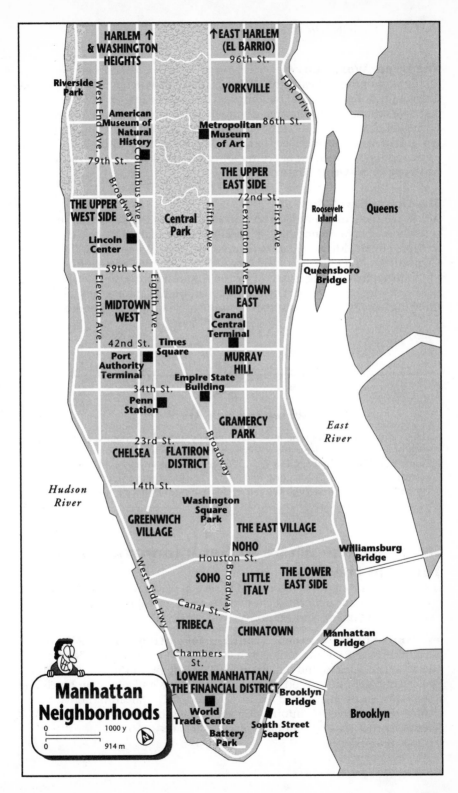

Manhattan Neighborhoods

0   1000 y
0   914 m

91

The Upper West Side

To the west of Central Park, the UWS has Lincoln Center at its southern end, a slew of historic residential buildings such as the Dakota and the Ansonia scattered around its middle, and Columbia University and the glorious Cathedral of St. John the Divine clinging to its northern end, just at the border of Harlem. It's a gentrified, residential neighborhood with a lot of restaurants and shops and a few big cultural institutions, like the **American Museum of Natural History.**

The Upper East Side

Across Central Park from the UWS and stretching to the East River, the UES is the home of "Museum Mile," a treasure chest stretch of Fifth Avenue anchored by the Metropolitan Museum of Art and also including the Guggenheim, the Museum of the City of New York, the International Center of Photography, and the Jewish Museum. Also residential, the UES has an old-money feel and lots of starch in its collar. It's elegant and beautiful, though generally less vibrant than most other New York neighborhoods.

Where the Hell Are We?

Hell's Kitchen, probably the most picturesquely named neighborhood in NYC, was once a rough-and-tumble immigrant community and the home turf of some notorious Irish gangs, but it's not quite like that anymore. It's located west of the Theater District, and real estate developers have been making inroads there lately—though they've avoided using the place's nickname.

Street Smarts—Where to Get Information once You're in the City

Once you're in New York, you can go to several places for further information. Most of them are located close to the main arrival points (Grand Central, Penn Station, Port Authority).

The **Times Square Visitor & Transit Information Center** (229 W. 42nd St. between Seventh and Eighth avenues; hours: 9am–6pm daily; no phone) is the place to find out about what's going on in the Theater District. You can also get information about discount tickets and advice on hotels and restaurants. Partly maintained by the New York City Transit Authority, the Center will also give you information about the subway and bus system. A Theater District walking tour takes place on Fridays at noon.

The **Grand Central Partnership** (Grand Central Terminal, E. 42nd St. and Vanderbilt Avenue; hours: Mon–Fri, 8:30am–6:30pm; Sat–Sun, 9am–6pm; ☎ **212/818-1777**) maintains both an information window inside Grand Central Terminal and a cart outside.

In addition to a window inside Penn Station, the **34th Street Partnership** (Pennsylvania Station, Seventh Avenue between 31st and 33rd streets; hours: Mon–Fri, 8:30am–5:30pm; Sat–Sun, 9am–6pm; ☎ **212/868-0521**) has a cart at the Empire State Building at Fifth Avenue and 32nd Street. There are seasonal carts at Greeley Square (32nd Street at Broadway and Sixth Avenue) in the summer and at Madison Square Garden (above Penn Station at Seventh Avenue and 32nd Street) in above-freezing weather. The carts open a little later and close a little earlier than the indoor window.

The **Manhattan Mall** (Sixth Avenue and 32nd Street; hours: Mon–Sat, 10am–8pm; Sun 11am–6pm; ☎ **212/465-0500**) has traveler information available on the first floor.

For information about current events, look for the publications listed in chapter 4, some of which are distributed free and can be found at newsstands, coffee shops, and in vending boxes around the city. You can get information on current theater over the phone through **NYC/On Stage** (☎ **212/768-1818**) and **Broadway Line** (☎ **212/563-2929**).

Chapter 8

Getting Around the Apple

In This Chapter

➤ Using mass transit

➤ Getting around on foot

New York has a very extensive public transportation system to help you get around: 722 miles of subway track, 3,500 buses, and 14,000 bus stops. The only problem is you have to share the subway with 3.5 million weekly subway riders.

After you've organized your transportation from the airport to the city (see the last chapter), in all likelihood you'll take a cab or courtesy bus to your hotel. After that, you can start exploring the city by one of the following means—and don't forget the tear-out subway and bus map included in this book!

For all transit information, call the **Transit Information Center** (☎ 718/330-1234). Also, call ☎ 718/330-3322 for a copy of *Token Trips Travel Guide,* a brochure that gives you instructions on how to get to the main attractions via mass transit.

Going Underground—Using the Subway System

The New York City subway system may not be as picturesque as it once was (the last graffiti-covered car was taken out of service in 1989), but it is cleaner, safer, and better than ever before. Many of the stations have been renovated, though construction is ongoing, and at $1.50 per ride, it's been called the biggest bargain in New York City. Unlike other systems (Washington,

D.C., for example) you don't pay more for longer rides; you can ride from the Cloisters at the very top of Manhattan all the way to Coney Island at the very bottom of Brooklyn for a buck and a half. Seniors and travelers with disabilities pay half price; children under 3 feet, 8 inches tall ride for free.

On the other hand, the subway is still dirty and noisy, home to thousands of rats (they mostly stay down on the tracks where they belong), and, in the summer, incredibly hot. The 4-5-6 platform under Grand Central is like a blast furnace in July and August. Luckily, there's always the bus.

Dollars & Sense

In 1997, New York finally made **transfers between buses and subways** free, and vice versa. That means if you take the no. 4 train from Fulton Street to Grand Central and then an M42 to Times Square, it still costs you only $1.50—as long as you make the transfer within two hours of your initial boarding.

Subway stops are easy to find—just look for the stairs heading underground, with the subway routes identified on top. Many stops also have picturesque lighted balls on top that—in theory—are supposed to tell you from a distance if the entrance is open (some close late at night): If they're green, it's open; if they're red, it's not. The lights don't always work, though.

Check the **subway map** at the front of this book to familiarize yourself with the routes, and also note that subway stops are marked on all the maps we've included throughout, marked with a little "M" dot. ("M" for "Metropolitan Transit Authority"—official sounding, ain't it?)

Extra! Extra!

On the web, check out **www.nycsubway.org/map s.html** for maps of the entire New York City subway system.

The subways do run on a **schedule,** more or less, but we don't know anyone who considers this in their daily lives. In fact, it's likely that the only person in New York who knows what the schedule is is the person who writes it. What you do is just go down to the platform and wait. If it takes a while before the train comes along, just grumble about it like everybody else—it's part of the subway ritual.

Most subway systems in the world use either **tokens** or **farecards.** New York uses both, but tokens are gradually being phased out. You can no longer buy 10-packs of tokens at token booths, but only individual loose tokens.

The new MetroCard farecard is a high-tech system that encodes a certain number of rides on a magnetic strip. Cards are sold at pre-coded values of $6 or $15, but when one is used up you can have it "refilled" by a booth attendant for any value between $3 and $80. Also, you automatically get one free ride added to your card for each $15 you put on it.

The card has one corner snipped off and a small hole in one side. In the subway, you swipe the card horizontally through the reader in the same direction you're traveling with the cut-off corner on top and at the back (and between your fingers) and the little hole leading the way. Swipe fast (but not *too* fast), or the machine won't read it and you'll get the breath knocked out of you when you hit the unmoving turnstile.

If these instructions seem overly minute and idiotic, wait until you see the way some people bend, twist, and mishandle their cards, then complain loudly that the system doesn't work. At some point, you will get stuck behind one of these people; move to another turnstile.

Dollars & Sense

If two people travel on one card (person A uses the card, and then hands it to person B to pass through the turn-stile), the card remembers. When A and B transfer to the bus, A has only to insert the card *once*, and two transfers will automatically be registered. If A and B both put the card in the bus's machine, they will have wasted a fare.

The MetroCard system is especially welcome for subway riders because the orientation of the subway system is mainly north-south (or uptown-downtown), and it used to be quite a pain to get across town. (There are only a few points where subways go straight east-west: at 14th Street via the L, at 42nd Street via the shuttle or the 7 train, and, for varying distances, via the N, R, E, B, and Q trains headed into Queens from the mid- to high 50s.) Now, with one free transfer automatically encoded when you swipe for your first ride, you can switch to a bus at any point, as long as you do so within two hours of beginning your trip—otherwise you turn into a pumpkin and another $1.50 is deducted from your card when you board the bus.

MetroCards are sold not only in the subway but by more than 2,000 merchants. Look for the signs in their windows.

Subway Hints

If you lose the map that accompanies this book, you can, in theory at least, get a new one at any token booth for free.

We've never understood why New York Transit locates more wall-mounted subway maps on the outside of the turnstiles (before you've entered the station) than on the platforms themselves, but they do. Sometimes there just *isn't* a map once you get down in the pit, so if you need to refresh your memory, take a look before you enter.

Here are some more hints:

➤ Use the off-hours waiting areas at night. They're clearly marked, and are usually closest to the exits.

➤ Don't display money or valuables on the subway.

➤ Don't try to sneak through a subway door that's closing or stop it with your hand. Subway conductors are quite ruthless and seem to enjoy watching people wriggle like fish in a net. You'll end up with bruises, at the very least.

➤ Keep track of where you are; at a number of stations, it is almost impossible to see the name of the station you're entering from a sitting or standing position inside the car (especially a full one).

Time-Savers

Columbus Circle: where Uptown meets Midtown, close to glamorous Central Park South, Lincoln Center, heavily touristed 57th Street, and the Park itself. Seems like it should be an express stop, right? It isn't. If you're going north on the 2 or 3, the next place to get out is 72nd Street; going south, it's Times Square.

➤ Don't expect the announcements to help much, either. Some conductors tell you where you are and the name of the next stop, some don't, and some are completely incomprehensible. Ask a friendly looking person for the name of the next stop. If you're really worried, get out and see for yourself; all you have to lose is time.

➤ Be aware that uptown/downtown transfer is not available at all stations. If you board going the wrong way, you may have to go outside, cross the street, and pay again.

➤ Learn which are the express trains: the A, 2, 3, 4, and 5. That way, you won't see your stop go by at 40 m.p.h.

Traffic, Schmaffic—Using the City Buses

The city buses form a dense web you should be able to use to get almost anywhere, and though they're slower than the subway most of the time—particularly at rush hour—they're generally a lot more pleasant and allow you the advantage of seeing the sights as you go from place to place. On the downside, they get stuck in traffic just like cars do.

Bus routes are generally easy to figure out: Whatever direction you see a bus going in is the direction it will probably continue to follow. Most north-south routes follow a single avenue for their entire length (or at least for most of it) and most crosstown (east-west) routes follow a single street. (There are exceptions, of course, so do yourself a favor and grab one of the **free city bus maps** that are available right by the front door of every bus. If you want to scan the routes before you get to town, you can access full bus maps via the Internet at **www.mta.ny.us/nyct/manbus97.pdf**.)

Dollars & Sense

As this book was being put together, we learned that special **daily, weekly, and monthly MetroCard fares** will be instituted for city buses and subways in mid–1998, allowing you to buy one card and use it for as many rides as you like during those time periods. The monthly card is probably more than you'll need, but the daily and weekly cards will be a real money–saver.

➤ **The daily card** will costs $4, which means if you take at least three subway rides in 24 hours, you've already saved 50¢ over the standard fare.

➤ **The weekly card** will cost $17, and if you're in town for 7 days and take at least three rides a day, each ride will cost you only 80¢ or less, instead of $1.50. What a bargain!

Bus stops are located every couple of blocks along every route, and are distinguished by either a small, glass-walled shelter or by a simple sign stating the bus numbers. The buses themselves flash their route and terminus (where their route finishes) right on their front ends, above the windshield, so you can see it when the bus pulls up.

The buses all run on a **schedule** that brings one along every 5 to 20 minutes or so, depending on the time of day. Schedules for individual routes are posted at most bus stops, and are relatively reliable. You can pay in any of three ways: change (nickels, dimes, and quarters), tokens (same ones as the subway), or MetroCard. *Be aware that buses never, ever take paper money.* By far the easiest of these payment plans is the MetroCard, and it has the advantage of allowing you to transfer to the subway if you want. On the bus, you insert the card downward into the machine with the snipped-off corner up and to the left, the little hole on the bottom, and the side with the magnetic strip facing you. The machine eats it momentarily, then spits it back out and beeps.

Public Transportation for People with Disabilities

If you require the use of a wheelchair, the buses have lifts and special areas where the seats fold up to make extra room. If you're mobile but have problems with stairs, the buses also "kneel," scrunching down when they stop so the first step is not quite so high up.

As for the subways, some stations have elevators, but not all. Call **MTA Customer Assistance** (☎ 718/330-3322; TTY 718/596-8273) to find out which are accessible.

I'm Walkin' Here!—Getting Around on Foot

There's no better way to get around than on your own two feet. It's free, and you go wherever you want (as long as your legs hold out). Certain neighborhoods, like Greenwich Village and the Upper West Side, are particularly good for strolling.

When you walk in New York, it's best to keep on your toes. In Midtown on a weekday, for example, people walk at breakneck speed, pay no attention to traffic lights, and cut you off without a glance. In short, a lot of people walk the way cab drivers drive. It's best to stay out of their way.

Generally, walkers respect "slow lanes" and passing lanes, as on a highway, and if you're dawdling or looking up at the sky, try to avoid being broadsided by someone with a business appointment to get to. It's also not good to walk more than three abreast, unless you're very fast walkers. (You won't get knocked down, but people will hate you.) Keep an eye out for in-line skaters, bike messengers, and people who shouldn't be behind the wheel of a car but are: There are a lot of those.

Time-Savers

Sometimes walking is faster than taking the bus. Traffic sometimes moves through Midtown at a snail's pace—especially during rush hours—and pedestrians typically outdistance cars and buses by blocks. Keep this in mind if you want to avoid frustration.

If you're a walker, one particularly nice place to stroll is the newly renovated downtown piers area on the west side—a promenade stretching from Battery Park to Midtown. Other good ambling areas include Central Park, the Brooklyn Bridge and the Brooklyn Heights Promenade, Riverside Park on the Upper West Side (enter at 72nd Street and go through the short tunnel to get to the river), and the Cloisters and Fort Tryon Park, way uptown at 190th Street. (See chapter 16 for some suggested itineraries.)

Part 4

New York's Best Restaurants

In New York, people take eating seriously. All New Yorkers cultivate their inner gourmet; can name their top five places for, say, Ethiopian food; and keep up obsessively with the newest hot spots—which, due to the intense competition, may be old news or just plain out of business by this time next week. The good news is that all this interest sparks competition, and competition improves the quality of the food; the bad news is that there's a lot of snobbism and fads and places are sometimes crowded or empty more because of trends than because of their cuisine. So, one hears a lot of contradictory information.

In order to make your way in such a jungle and sort through the more than 17,000 eating establishments in the city, you need to know what to expect, where to go, and what to look for. Then you can appreciate a small selection of real favorites that are among the best bets in the city. The final step, of course, after all this talking, is to go out and chow down.

In chapter 10 we tell you the best spots for lunch and dinner, but since those two meals are only the tip of the culinary iceberg, we share some thoughts on spots for serious snacking in chapter 11.

Chapter 9

The Lowdown on the New York Dining Scene

In This Chapter

➤ Choosing what to eat

➤ Choosing where to eat

➤ Choosing how to eat

New York has some of the best restaurants in the world, notable either for the quality of their food or for just plain being famous (both, more often than not). Prices vary widely, depending on a large number of mysterious factors: looks, presentation, luck, subtlety—basically the same factors as those that determine who becomes a celebrity and who doesn't. For restaurants, the list of key characteristics to look for includes timeliness, neighborhood, cuisine, packaging—that is, decor, service, atmosphere, view, color of chef's shirt, and so on—and, only last, quality of the food. These factors make the difference between a good restaurant and a trendy trap or a real dump.

What's Hot

The latest trend is adding Asian touches to traditional French, American, Continental, or other western cuisines—you know, hot dogs in Lotus sauce, meatloaf with bamboo shoots (OK, OK, so we made those up). We love this trend, which often produces some very interesting and delicious combinations. It is, however, only a fresh branch of the movement that brought about "new" American cuisine, where traditional ingredients are explored in new associations and occasionally enhanced with some exotic flavor. You'll find some of the best examples of this category in the restaurant listing in chapter 10.

The other recent trend involves sandwiches and is the California-originated fad for "wraps." It might be described in many fancy ways, but in reality a wrap is a tortilla filled up with whatever crosses the mind of the cook. Some are actually good, but we still prefer a real sandwich with real bread most of the time. This new fad goes hand in hand with the Seattle-imported craze for java. Coffee shops, Starbucks leading the way, have invaded the city and are still multiplying. Some provide really good brews, others give you sock juice and are way worse than some classic traditional New York coffee spots (see chapter 11).

Other items were once hot and innovative in New York and have stuck around long enough that they've become old favorites. The infatuation for Italian cuisine continues and has now become a classic; so has the love for Japanese sushi and sashimi. Old New York specialties—bagels and pizza—are still the rage for fast food that's not fast food. (For more information, see chapter 11 and the section "Unchain My Lunch" later in this chapter.)

Beating the Brunch Crunch

A trendy thing in Manhattan is to have brunch on Sunday. OK, everybody does that in every corner of America and beyond. But remember: Everything regarding food in New York is a little excessive, so people go to extremes in order to have brunch in what is considered the "best" place in the city. Results? Hour-long lines, dirty looks, and occasional inappropriate Sunday behavior. Brunch should mean leisure, calm, good food, and quiet atmosphere, but this is becoming more and more difficult to find. If you want to enjoy this most important meal in the right way, it's best to go early. Luckily, New Yorkers don't get up too early on Sundays and it's enough to go before 11am—even 11:30am for spots downtown—and about 10am for family spots in upper Manhattan.

Location! Location! Location!

Although restaurants and eateries are everywhere in Manhattan, in some areas where you'll find a more serious concentration. As a rule, the more nightlife is in an area, the more restaurants will be there. The following areas are the biggies.

The West Village

This is the best neighborhood to find a place to eat, all things considered. Not only is it a great place to stroll around, with its tree-lined streets and historic houses (see chapter 13), but it's also very safe at any hour of day or night, any day of the week, and it has an incredible number of restaurants, cafes, bakeries, sandwich places, bars, and coffee shops. The variety of cuisine and the quality of the food make it a great choice. Bleecker Street between Sixth Avenue and Hudson Street is lined with places to eat; the parallel street to the north, West 4th Street, is also a very good bet. The area bordered on the east by Sixth Avenue, on the north by Greenwich Avenue, on the west by Hudson Street, and on the south by Barrow and Bedford streets is a prime location for finding very nice restaurants. The other equally good spot is the small area south of Washington Square between Sixth Avenue to the west, La Guardia Place to the east, and Houston Street to the south.

The East Village & NoHo
The East Village has become very popular with the young and arty crowd and has seen the opening of many nice restaurants that are also quite inexpensive. Like the West Village, it's quite lively at any hour of the day and until late at night any day of the week. You may have heard that Alphabet City (way east, where the avenues have letters instead of numbers) is dangerous. Well, it was, but it's well on its way to gentrification now. Some streets are shabby, with rundown buildings mixed with nicely restored ones. The best bets for a restaurant are Second Avenue and Avenue A between 5th and 12th streets and, particularly, 8th Street (St. Mark's Place). Also within the area is **Little India,** the block of 6th Street between First and Second avenues that is completely lined with Indian Restaurants (see the section "Little India" later in this chapter).

NoHo ("North of Houston Street") refers to the westernmost stretch of the East Village, around Broadway and Lafayette streets and including the area around Astor Place, where you'll find the Joseph Papp Public Theater, some beautiful old architecture, and some mightily trendy restaurants.

Extra! Extra!
If you find yourself turning into a New Yorker and becoming obsessive, consider attending a culinary event sponsored by the **James Beard House** (67 West 12th St., ☎ **800/36-BEARD** or 212/675-4984), where workers organize round tables, lectures, and seminars all about eating and offer some sumptuous meals in which food professionals and food amateurs alike are welcome to participate.

SoHo
SoHo (which stands for "South of Houston Street") stretches north and south between Houston and Canal Streets and east and west between Broadway and West Broadway. If you want a nice and trendy place, head for West Broadway at Prince and Spring streets. It's a perfect area to admire the architecture and to have a nice stroll in safety; there are quite a few cafes, plenty

of nice shops, and, of course, art galleries. With the exception of West Broadway, however, it is a relatively less frequented neighborhood at night during the week.

Tribeca

This area has been an increasingly more active player on the restaurant scene in recent years. It's where Robert De Niro chose to open his trendy restaurants **TriBeCa Grill** (see chapter 10) and **Nobu** (105 Hudson St. at Franklin Street, ☎ **212/219-0500**), the latter an extravagant, exquisite, and *expensive* Japanese restaurant where you need to make reservations weeks in advance. In this strange neighborhood, where the many huge industrial buildings still give a deserted feeling to the occasional passerby, are located many of the most expensive and famous restaurants in New York, such as the two outstanding French restaurants **Chanterelle** (2 Harrison St. between Hudson and Greenwich streets, ☎ **212/966-6960**) and **Montrachet** (239 West Broadway between White and Walker streets, ☎ **212/219-2777**). Although it's perfectly safe during the day, take a taxi if you decide to go there at night.

Gramercy Park & the Union Square Area

Another growing neighborhood is the area of **Gramercy Park** and **Flatiron District/Union Square,** where many elegant, quality restaurants have been opening. Beside the famous **Gramercy Tavern** (see chapter 10), where you need to make reservations weeks in advance, there are other great (and expensive) places, such as **Patria** (250 Park Avenue South at 20th Street, ☎ **212/777-6211**), with its contemporary South American creations.

Midtown

Midtown is huge and globally very safe (avoid Port Authority at night, though). The most active neighborhood at night is the **Theater District.** Some of the avenues (Second on the east side and Seventh, Eighth, and Ninth on the west side) have quite a lot of restaurants and delis, but they're usually pretty dispersed. One exception is **Restaurant Row,** on 46th Street between Eight and Ninth avenues. It's a great spot for pre- and post-theater dining, and some of the good bets are **Orso** (322 West 46th St., ☎ **212/489-7212**) for great Italian food, **Lotfi's** (358 W. 46th, ☎ **212/582-5850**) for Moroccan food, and **Joe Allen** (326 W. 46th St., ☎ **212/581-6464**) for great pub fare. We prefer to explore the streets and avenues around the Theater District (particularly on Ninth Avenue), where a lot of great choices can be found, but you can't argue with success, and Restaurant Row has, on the whole, been pretty darn successful.

The World's Best Falafel

If you find yourself in Midtown at lunchtime (Mon–Fri) and want to experience the world's best Middle Eastern falafel, make your way to the southeast corner of 46th Street and Sixth Avenue and look for the tiny sidewalk stand that is **Moshe's Falafel.** Scrunched inside, half a dozen frantic men pitch fried chick peas, lettuce, and tomato into pita bread, then top it with sauce and a spicy pickle to make the best falafel you've ever had—all at the bargain-basement price of $3 per. (And for $1 more they'll give you extra falafel balls on the side, though the regular falafel is more than enough for most people.) Our advice: Order it spicy and then picnic in the little public area half a block east on the south side of the street.

The Upper West Side

As you'd expect, the neighborhood where Lincoln Center and the Juilliard School of Music meet rampant yuppie-ism harbors some pretty decent dining. Right across from Lincoln Center you'll find the very popular **Saloon** (see chapter 10), where, in nice weather, you should try to get a sidewalk table. A few blocks up and closer to the park is the ultimately classy **Café des Artistes** (1 West 67th St. at Central Park West, ☎ 212/877-3500), where you'll need reservations and very deep pockets. Right across Central Park West and glimmering so bright you won't need to ask directions is the famous **Tavern on the Green** (see chapter 10). If you want something a bit more dress-down, try **John's Pizzeria** (see chapter 10), which serves a nice thin-crust pie in a very congenial setting; **Baluchi's,** for great Indian food (see chapter 10); or **Artepasta** (106 W. 73rd, between Columbus and Amsterdam, ☎ 212/501-7014), where you can get good, inexpensive Italian fare in a fun setting. (*Note:* They serve a very reasonable Sunday brunch as well.)

The Upper East Side

The land of bankers and old money doesn't at first glance look like a food mecca, but there are plenty of nice choices here. Second and Third avenues and the streets in between are where most of the action takes place. If you find yourself wanting a quintessential New York experience, venture no farther into the east side than just inside Central Park at 73rd. Street, where, perched on the side of the rowing lake, you'll find the **Boathouse Cafe** (see chapter 10). A little farther east in location and substantially further east in cuisine, **Persepolis** (1423 Second Ave., between 74th and 75th streets, ☎ 212/535-1100) serves fine Persian cuisine, while **Pamir,** neighborly at 1437 Second Ave. (☎ 212/734-3791), is neighborly in cuisine as well, serving delicious Afghani dishes.

Unchain My Lunch

Quite a few restaurants in New York have multiple locations, but don't believe for a minute that they're third-rate chains; often, they're the result of success due to a great combination of quality and price. If you're hungry and see one of these, please, DO go in!

➤ **Kids** **EJ's Luncheonette** serves American/diner food at great prices and it's great for breakfast. 1271 Third Ave. at 73rd Street (☎ 212/472-0600) or 447 Amsterdam Ave. between 81st and 82nd streets (☎ 212/873-3444) or 432 Sixth Ave. between 9th and 10th streets (☎ 212/473-5555).

➤ **Kids** **Hamburger Harry's** is not really a chain (it has only two locations) but you never know—give it time. It serves—guess what?—great hamburgers! 145 W. 45th St. between Sixth and Seventh avenues (☎ 212/840-0566) or 157 Chambers St. at Greenwich Street, north of the World Trade Center (☎ 212/267-4446).

➤ **Kids** **LemonGrass Grill** offers excellent Thai food for very moderate prices and has locations just about everywhere: 2534 Broadway between 95th and 94th streets (☎ 212/666-0888); 494 Amsterdam Ave. at 84th Street (☎ 212/579-0344); 80 University Place at 11th Street (☎ 212/604-9870); 37 Barrow St. at Seventh Avenue South (☎ 212/242-0606).

➤ **Kids** **Mary Ann's** has really good Mexican food, a pleasant decor, and a nice ambience. They have kid's chairs and some of the branches have a kid's menu. 2452 Broadway at 91st Street (☎ 212/887-0132); 1501 Second Ave. between 78th and 79th streets (☎ 212/249-6165); 116 Eighth Ave. at 16th Street (☎ 212/633-0877); 86 Second Ave. at 5th Street (☎ 212/475-5939).

➤ **Zen Palate** is a strictly vegetarian place where they realized long ago that food doesn't have to taste bad to be good for you. The ambience is very Japanese and the extensive menu includes many imitation meat dishes, so you may be able to sneak wheat gluten by junior without him being any the wiser. 2170 Broadway between 76th and 77th streets (☎ 212/501-7768), 663 Ninth Ave. between 45th and 46th streets (☎ 212/582-1669), and 34 Union Square East at 16th Street (☎ 212/614-9291).

Pizza you don't need to be told about—only that it's one of the ubiquitous good deals in town, it's often quite good, and it's sometimes downright transcendent.

Time-Savers

If you want to stay out of the fast food chains yet eat quick, cheap, and on the go, you need know only two words: **pizza** and **bagels.** Pizza is *everywhere*, though some choices are better than others (see our picks in chapter 10). Bagels are a real traditional food in this city, and once you've tasted them, those frozen supermarket imposters will never seem as good again. The best way to have bagels is toasted with cream cheese, and if you add smoked salmon, that little bagel will bring you two steps closer to heaven. (*Hint:* Three of the best bagel places in town—and thus, anywhere—are **H&H Bagels, Ess-A-Bagel,** and **Bagels on the Square.** See chapter 10 for their addresses.)

Fine Dining in the Melting Pot—Ethnic Eats in NYC

City of 1,001 nationalities, New York has many ethnic neighborhoods in which you can indulge your inner sociologist for the price of dinner. Here's some of the best.

Little India

Although there are other Indian restaurants in the city (and sometimes better ones), if you're in the mood for Indian food, this block of 6th Street between First and Second avenues is a sure thing. Besides **Bombay Dining** (see chapter 10), other good ones include **Gandhi** (344 E. 6th St., ☎ 212/614-9718); **Sonali** (326 E. 6th St., ☎ 212/505-7517); **Mitali East** (334 E. 6th St., ☎ 212/533-2508); and **Royal Indian Cuisine,** which has a lovely back garden and is located right around the corner at 93 First Ave. (☎ 212/674-6209).

Many of these restaurants feature live Indian music on certain days of the week. (The days vary, but the musicians are usually sitting right in the window, so you'll know which restaurants have music and which don't.) Also, most of these places don't have liquor licenses, so if you want a libation with your dinner you should bring it with you. Here's a hint: The shop right at the northwest corner of First Avenue has an unbelievable variety of beer, including such Indian brands as Flying Horse (a big thumbs-up), Golden Eagle, and Taj Mahal. All of these go great with the food. Try one.

Chinatown

The most famous of ethnic neighborhoods in New York, Chinatown is also the largest, where you can find not only Chinese restaurants but also Chinese everything else. Don't get cross at the fact that many people here don't speak English—in this neighborhood, they don't really need to. The heart of Chinatown is Canal and Mott Streets, which are lined with Chinese groceries, Chinese restaurants, and a smattering of places from other Eastern Asian countries. It's safe at night and always very busy, but be aware of pickpockets on Canal Street, where it's almost always really crowded.

The top culinary attraction in Chinatown is **dim sum,** a traditional and festive Chinese breakfast/lunch. You sit at your table and little carts filled up with tiny dishes come along. If you like what you see, you pick one or two and the waiter puts a little stamp on your bill (dim sum prices run from about $1 to $3 according to the kind of food, and each is marked by a different stamp); if you don't like it, you wait for the next round. It's a leisurely lunch and a great way to taste many different specialties. Dumplings are high on our list. Besides the **Golden Unicorn** (see chapter 10), other top places for dim sum are **H.S.F.** (46 Bowery Street, ☎ **212/374-1319**) and **Jing Fong** (20 Elizabeth Street between Bayard and Canal Streets, ☎ **212/964-5256**).

Little Italy

Two steps from SoHo, this historical neighborhood is being progressively swallowed up by Chinatown. The street where most Italian restaurants and shops remain is Mulberry Street, particularly at the crossing with Grand Street. "Typical" Italian restaurants are lined up one after the other, and there are quite a few Italian groceries and a great coffee and dessert place, **Ferrara** (see chapter 11). Unless you go more east, where it gets a little deserted at night, it's a very safe neighborhood. Other good spots besides those listed in chapter 10 are **Luna** (112 Mulberry Street between Hester and Canal Streets, ☎ **212/226-8657**) and **Puglia** (189 Hester Street at Mulberry Street, one block north of Canal Street, ☎ **212/226-8912**).

Koreatown

Just by Herald Square, this block of Korean restaurants and shops situated mainly on 32nd Street between Fifth and Sixth avenues has been slowly developing and growing. There are some great places besides **Won Jo** (see chapter 10) such as **Woo Chon** (8 West 36th St. between Fifth and Sixth avenues, ☎ **212/695-0676**) or the vegetarian **Hangawi** (12 E. 32nd St. between Fifth and Madison avenues, ☎ **212/213-0077**).

The Price Is Right

Naturally, the price of a meal will depend on what you order—if you pig out or order the most expensive dishes on the menu, you'll spend more than if you order moderately. The listings in chapter 10 give you two price elements for each restaurant: a dollar symbol that gives you an idea of what a complete meal will cost, and the price range of the entrees on the menu. The two pieces of information combined should help you choose the place that's right for you and your budget (see chapter 2). One dollar sign ($) means inexpensive and five dollar signs ($$$$$—the maximum) means extravagant. Prices include appetizer, entree, dessert, one drink, taxes, and tip (per person).

One important thing to note is that all the listings are for good (often excellent) restaurants where you get a satisfying meal. We didn't list any crummy places just because they were cheap; neither did we list any outrageously expensive places where you pay an arm and a leg for a leaf of well-arranged lettuce. The selection criteria involved restaurants that offer good quality food for a fair price. The difference between one category and the next has more to do with extras such as location, type of cuisine, interiors, service, atmosphere, view, and, of course, trendiness.

Why Bagels Are Bagels

The special trick about bagels that makes them a bread not like any other is that the dough is boiled for a few minutes after having been shaped into a doughnut. Then they're drained and baked. This treatment gives them their doughy texture and their shiny skin. They've become one of New York's major symbols and one of the typical specialties of the city.

➤ **$ (Dirt Cheap):** These are popular places that have mostly been around for a while and are located in not-too-fancy neighborhoods. They offer plain good food in a simple setting. You might expect to spend between $15 and maximum $20 per person for a really full meal.

➤ **$$ (Inexpensive):** These are great choices. These restaurants are cheaper than they might be because they're either located a little out of the main scene or they offer relatively simple fare. Don't expect designer decor; do expect to pay $25–$35 for your meal.

➤ **$$$ (Medium):** These are probably the best bets for a fine, relatively fancy dinner that doesn't cost you a fortune (say, $35–$45 per person). In most of these restaurants the food is classy, the decor is nice, the service is good, and the location is quite central. In a few cases, the food is plentiful and the place is famous.

➤ **$$$$ (Expensive):** These are among the best restaurants in New York: top food, top chefs, top service, top location, and top decor (and it'll cost you about $45–$60 per person).

➤ **$$$$$ (Where the Stars Dine):** These are the glamorous top of the top restaurants. They have achieved world fame, either for the celebrated skills of the chef or for the atmosphere, view, and location. This is where you'll get a unique experience that you'll remember for the rest of your life (and probably run up a good bill on your credit card, too).

Top Hat, White Tie, & Tails? Dressing to Dine

Going out in New York is not a formal affair, and you'll quickly realize that the unwritten dress code is not strict, even in relatively elegant places. In most restaurants in New York, the crowd is mixed, especially during the week: Office workers in suits grabbing something to eat before going home, stylish people of the fashion world dressed to the latest trends, bohemian artists dressed in old-fashioned or just plain weird clothes, and many people just plainly dressed. On weekends the scene is definitely more dressed up, but still with a lot of margin.

In a few restaurants, however, men are required to wear a jacket (and, more rarely, a tie). In these cases, a note is included in the description of the restaurant.

Mind if I Smoke?

Actually, yes: New York has a strict no-smoking law whereby smoking is permitted only in restaurants with fewer than 35 seats, and then only in specially delimited areas that are provided with ventilation. Smoking is also permitted at the bar of those restaurants that have one, but only if the bar is at least 6 feet from the dining area.

Paying Your Taxes & Giving Your Tip

The tax on food in NYC is 8.25%, and whether you think that's high or low, the fact remains that it's convenient. Why so? Well, because: (1) 15% is considered the average tip for your waiter or waitress, (2) it's a known fact that people lose the ability to compute percentages after a good meal, and (3) two times 8.25% is a generous version of 15%, so just multiply the amount of tax on your check by two and you have your tip.

Because waiters and waitresses are paid little in wages and rely on tips for the bulk of their salary, don't leave less than 15% unless the service was really bad. If the service was all right but there was a problem with the food, call the manager and explain your complaint. They'll usually reduce the bill—but only if your complaint is well founded, of course; this isn't a trick to eat cheap.

Do You Have a Reservation, Sir?

When we say that reservation are recommended we mean for dinner. At lunch, for a party of two, it's relatively easy to find a table without having to wait too long. One of the best bets for finding a table without reservations and avoiding long waits (if you're with a small party) is to arrive early—meaning before 12:30pm for lunch and before 7pm for dinner (except in the Theater District, where you're better off going at about 8pm). The other important consideration is the day of the week. On Fridays and Saturdays you need a reservation practically anywhere, often a few days in advance, especially if you're with a larger party.

Chapter 10

New York Restaurants from A to Z

In This Chapter

➤ Restaurant indexes by location, price, and cuisine

➤ Full reviews of all the best restaurants in town

➤ The best places for kids, vegetarians, romantic couples, and more

---

Loosen your belts and pick up your forks: It's time to eat. We've started this chapter with indexes you can use to figure out which are the best bets for your particular tastes and needs. We've indexed by location, so you can find a good restaurant near the sights you're seeing; by price, so you can budget yourself; and by cuisine, so you can more easily satisfy your cravings. Throughout the chapter, we've also provided various specialized listings so that romantic couples, night-owl snackers, and fans of exotic eats can find their place in the sun.

After that, it's on to our picks of the best restaurants in town, listed alphabetically so that they're easier for you to refer back to, and with each name followed by its price range, what part of town it's in, and the type of cuisine you'll find. As described in the last chapter, the price ranges per person—including appetizer, entree, dessert, one drink, taxes, and tip—run something like this:

$	=	Under $25
$$	=	$25–$35
$$$	=	$35–$45
$$$$	=	$45–$60
$$$$$	=	Over $60

Use these icons to get a rough idea how much a place will cost, but don't rely on them solely; restaurants may offer prix fixe meals or other deals that won't be reflected in their icon rankings.

Quick Picks—New York's Restaurants at a Glance
Restaurant Index by Location

Chinatown
20 Mott Street $$
Golden Unicorn $$

Downtown
Windows on the World $$$$$

East Village
Angelica Kitchen $
Bombay Dining $
Iso $$$
Jules $$$
Second Avenue Deli $
Shabu Tatsu $$
Veselka $

West Village
Baluchi's $$
Brothers BBQ $$
Florent $$
John's Pizzeria $
Gotham Bar and Grill $$$$$
Mi Cocina $$$

Harlem
Sylvia's $$

Lincoln Center
John's Pizzeria $
The Saloon $$$
Picholine $$$$$

Little Italy
Il Cortile $$$
Lombardi $$
Vincent's Clam Bar $$

Midtown East
Hatsuhana $$$$
Diwan Grill $$$
Oyster Bar $$
Sparks Steak House $$$$
Zarela $$$

Midtown West
"21" Club $$$$$
Cabana Carioca $$
Carnegie Delicatessen and Restaurant $
Carmine's $$$
John's Pizzeria $
Rainbow Room $$$$$
Remi $$$$
Won Jo $$$

NoHo
Indochine $$$
NoHo Star $$$

SoHo
Abyssinia $$
Baluchi's $$
Kelley and Ping $
L'Ecole $$
Provence $$$$

Restaurants

20 Mott Street **58**
Abyssinia **18**
Angelica Kitchen **31**
Baluchi's **8 17**
Bombay Dining **43**
Brothers BBQ **15**
Chanterelle **20**
EJ's Luncheonette **6**
Florent **1**
Gandhi **44**
Golden Unicorn **60**
Gotham Bar & Grill **28**
H.S.F. **56**
Hamburger Harry's **22**
Il Cortile **55**
Indochine **42**
Iso **30**
Jing Fong **56**
John's Pizzeria **10**
Jules **40**
Kelley & Ping **48**
L'Ecole **52**
Lemongrass Grill **9 29**
Lombardi **51**
Luna **55**
Mary Ann's **45**
Mi Cocina **2**
Mitali East **44**
Montrachet **57**
NoHo Star **46**
The Odeon **21**
Provence **16**
Puglia **55**
Royal Indian Cuisine **44**
Second Avenue Deli **33**
Shabu Tatsu **35**
Sonali **44**
Tribeca Grill **19**
Veselka **37**
Vincent's Clam Bar **54**
Windows on the World **24**
Zen Palate **26**

Light Bites & Munchies

Anglers & Writers **14**
Bagels on the Square **11**
Barnes & Noble Cafe **41**
California Burrito Co. **23**
California Pizza Oven **27**
Chinatown Ice Cream Factory **59**
Danal **13**
Dean & DeLuca **49**
Ellen's Cafe & Bake Shop **61**
Ferrara **53**
Grassroots **50**
Gray's Papaya **7**
Heartland Brewery **25**
McDonald's (the fancy one) **62**
The Magnolia Bakery **4**
Moishe's Kosher Bake Shop **39**
Moondog Ice Cream **5 13 36**
Porto Rico Importing Company **12**
St. Marks Pizza **38**
Two Boots to Go-Go **3 47**
Veniero's **32**

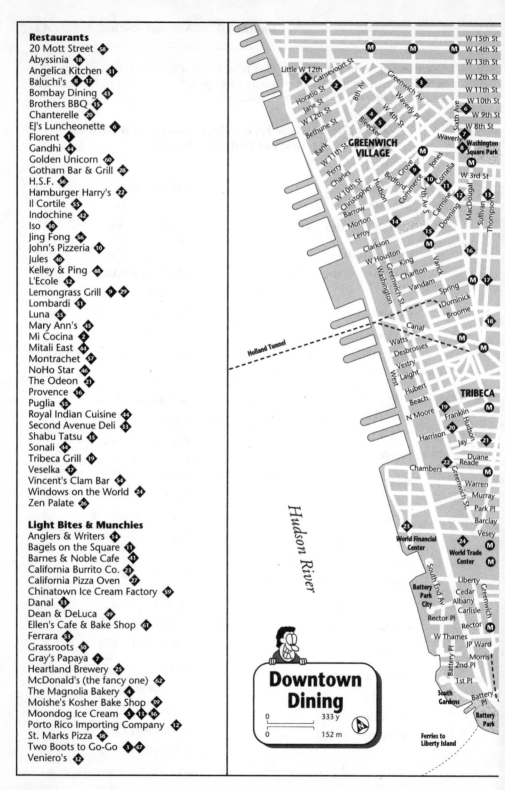

Downtown
Dining

0 _____ 333 y
0 _____ 152 m

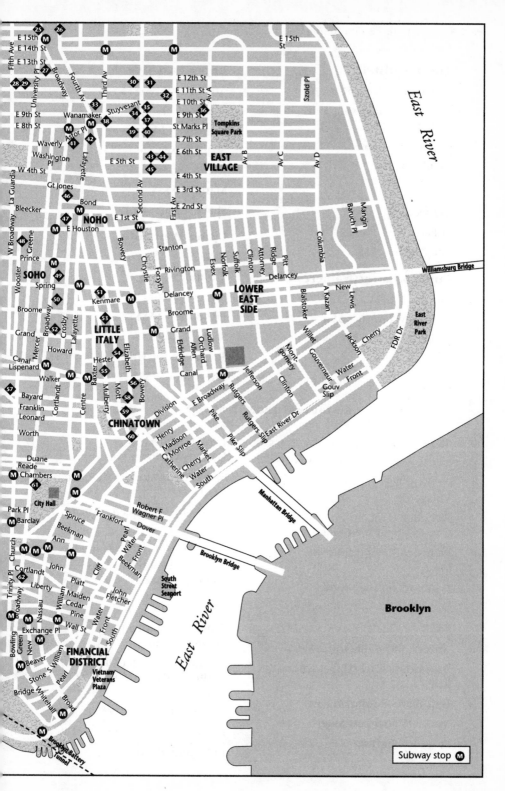

Subway stop Ⓜ

115

Theater District

Cabana Carioca $$

Carnegie Delicatessen and
Restaurant $

Carmine's $$$

John's Pizzeria $

Remi $$$$

Tribeca

TriBeCa Grill $$$$

The Odeon $$$

Union Square/Gramercy

America $$$

Gramercy Tavern $$

Verbena $$$$

Upper East Side

Arizona 206 $$$$

Arizona Café $$

Baluchi's $$

Boat House Café $$$$

John's Pizzeria $

Mark's $$$$

Shabu Tatsu $$

Upper West Side

Baluchi's $$

Carmine's $$$

John's Pizzeria $

Picholine $$$$$

Shabu Tatsu $$

Tavern on the Green $$$$

The Saloon $$$

Restaurant Index by Price

$$$$$

"21" Club (Midtown West)

Gotham Bar and Grill (West
Village/Union Square)

Picholine (Lincoln
Center/Upper West Side)

Rainbow Room (Midtown
West)

Windows on the World
(Downtown)

$$$$

Arizona 206 (Upper East Side)

Boat House Café (Upper East
Side)

Hatsuhana (Midtown East)

Mark's (Upper East Side)

Provence (SoHo)

Remi (Theater
District/Midtown West)

Sparks Steak House (Midtown
East)

Tavern on the Green (Upper
West Side)

TriBeCa Grill (Tribeca)

Verbena (Union Square/
Gramercy Park)

$$$

America (Union Square/
Gramercy Park)

Carmine's (Theater District/
Midtown West, Upper West
Side)

Diwan (Midtown East)

Il Cortile (Little Italy)

Indochine (NoHo)

Iso (East Village)

Jules (East Village)

L'Ecole (SoHo)

Mi Cocina (West Village)

NoHo Star (NoHo)

The Odeon (Tribeca)

The Saloon (Lincoln Center/Upper West Side)

Won Jo (Koreatown/Herald Square/Midtown West)

Zarela (Midtown East)

$$

20 Mott Street (Chinatown)

Abyssinia (SoHo)

Arizona Café (Upper East Side)

Baluchi's (Upper West Side, Upper East Side, West Village, SoHo)

Brothers BBQ (West Village)

Cabana Carioca (Theater District/Midtown West)

Florent (West Village)

Golden Unicorn (Chinatown)

Gramercy Tavern (Union Square/Gramercy)

Lombardi's (Little Italy)

Oyster Bar (Midtown East)

Shabu Tatsu (East Village, Upper East Side, Upper West Side)

Sylvia's (Harlem)

Vincent's Clam Bar (Little Italy)

$

Angelica Kitchen (East Village)

Bombay Dining (Little India/East Village)

Carnegie Delicatessen and Restaurant (Theater District/Midtown West)

John's Pizzeria (West Village, Midtown West, Upper West Side, Upper East Side)

Kelley and Ping (SoHo)

Second Avenue Deli (East Village)

Veselka (East Village)

Restaurant Index by Cuisine

American

"21" Club (Midtown East, $$$$$)

America (Union Square/ Gramercy, $$$)

NoHo Star (NoHo, $$$)

The Odeon (Tribeca, $$$)

The Saloon (Lincoln Center/ Upper West Side, $$$)

Asian

Indochine (NoHo, $$$)

Kelley and Ping (SoHo, $$)

Brazilian

Cabana Carioca (Theater District/Midtown West)

Chinese

20 Mott Street (Chinatown, $$)

Golden Unicorn (Chinatown, $$)

Restaurants

"21" Club 20
America 53
Cabana Carioca 25
Carmine's 9
Carnegie Delicatessen & Restaurant 4
Comedy Nation 5
Diwan Grill 29
Dragon Gold 33
Hamburger Harry's 24
Hangawi 47
Hard Rock Cafe 1
Harley-Davidson Cafe 18
Hatsuhana 28
Jekyll & Hyde Club 15
Joe Allen 8
John's Pizzeria 10
Lotfi's 8
Malika 39
Marichu 36
Mary Ann's 13
Orso 8
Oyster Bar 40
Palm 38
Patria 56
Planet Hollywood 14
Rainbow Room 23
Remi 19
Shaliga 35
Sparks Steak House 35
Verbena 57
Won Jo 46
Woo Chon 45
Zarela 32
Zen Palate 7 60

Light Bites & Munchies

Cafe S.F.A. 27
California Burrito Co. 5
Canova 22
Chelsea Brewing Company 12
Daily Soup 41
Del Monico Gourmet Food Market 42
East 47
Ess-a-Bagel 30 50
Flavors 52
Fresco Tortilla Grill 48 44
Gramercy Tavern 55
H&H Bagels 6
Hansen's Times Square Brewery 11
Le Train Bleu 17
Mariella Pizza 1 2 59
Moshe's Falafel 26
Old Navy Coffee Shop 51
Palm Court 16
Parlour Cafe 54
Regency Gourmet 43
Royal Canadian Pancake House 31 58
Soup Kitchen International 3
Soup Nutsy 34
Typhoon Brewery 21

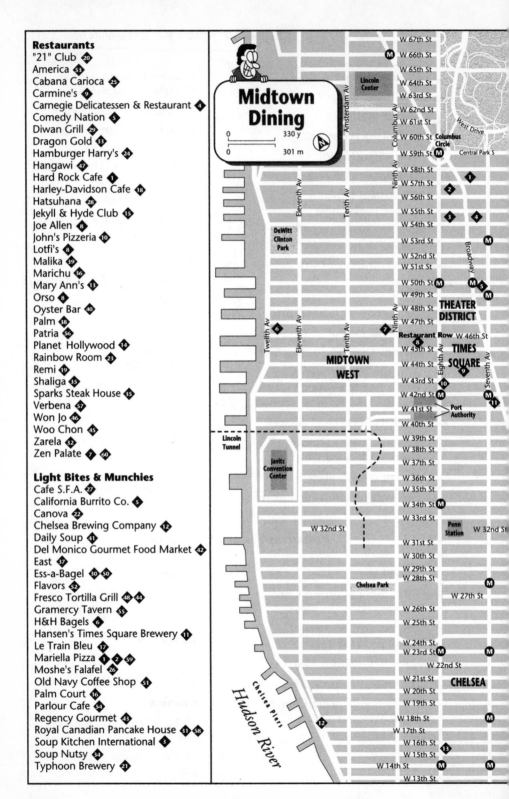

Midtown Dining

118

E 67th St
E 66th St
E 65th St
E 64th St
E 63rd St
E 62nd St
E 61st St
E 60th St
E 59th St
E 58th St
E 57th St
E 56th St
E 55th St
E 54th St
E 53rd St
E 52nd St
E 51st St
E 50th St
E 49th St
E 48th St
E 47th St
E 46th St
E 45th St
E 44th St
E 43rd St
E 42nd St
E 41st St
E 40th St
E 39th St
E 38th St
E 37th St
E 36th St
E 35th St
E 34th St
E 33rd St
E 32nd St
E 31st St
E 30th St
E 29th St
E 28th St
E 27th St
E 26th St
E 25th St
E 24th St
E 23rd St
E 22nd St
E 21st St
E 20th St
E 19th St
E 18th St
E 17th St
E 16th St
E 15th St
E 14th St
E 13th St

Center Drive
East Drive
The Pond
Central Park S

MIDTOWN EAST

Rockefeller Center

Fifth Av
Sixth Av
Madison Av
Park Av
Vanderbilt Av
Depew Pl
Lexington Av
Third Av
Second Av
First Av
York Av
Sutton Pl South
Sutton Pl

From Lower Level
To Upper Level

Roosevelt Island Tram
Queensboro Bridge

Queens

Beekman Place
Mitchell Place

FDR Drive

Grand Central Terminal
Chrysler Building

United Nations

Bryant Park
New York Public Library

MURRAY HILL

Queens–Midtown Tunnel

Tunnel Exit
Tunnel Entrance

Macy's
Empire State Bldg.
Koreatown

Broadway
Park Av. S.

Madison Square Park

East River

Asser Levy Pl

Peter Cooper Village

FLATIRON DISTRICT

Gramercy Park
GRAMERCY PARK

2ND
Perlman Pl

Stuyvesant Town

Union Sq W
Union Sq E
Union Square
Irving Pl
E 16th St

Subway stop Ⓜ

119

Contemporary American

Boat House Café (Upper East Side, $$$$)

Gotham Bar and Grill (West Village/Union Square, $$$$$)

Gramercy Tavern (Union Square/Gramercy Park, $$)

Mark's (Upper East Side, $$$$)

Tavern on the Green (Upper West Side, $$$$)

TriBeCa Grill (Tribeca, $$$$)

Verbena (Union Square/Gramercy, $$$$)

Contemporary Continental

Rainbow Room (Midtown West, $$$$$)

Tavern on the Green (Upper West Side, $$$$)

Deli

Carnegie Delicatessen and Restaurant (Theater District/Midtown West, $)

Second Avenue Deli (East Village, $)

Dim Sum

Golden Unicorn (Chinatown, $$)

Eclectic

Windows on the World (Downtown, $$$$$)

Ethiopian

Abyssinia (SoHo, $$)

French

Florent (West Village, $$)

Jules (East Village, $$$)

L'Ecole (SoHo, $$)

Picholine (Lincoln Center/Upper West Side, $$$$$)

Provence (SoHo, $$$$)

The Odeon (Tribeca, $$$)

Indian

Baluchi's (Upper West Side, Upper East Side, West Village, SoHo, $$)

Bombay Dining (Little India/East Village, $)

Diwan (Midtown East, $$$)

International

NoHo Star (NoHo, $$$)

Italian

Carmine's (Theater District/Midtown West, Upper West Side, $$$)

Il Cortile (Little Italy, $$$)

John's Pizzeria (West Village, Midtown West, Lincoln Center/Upper West Side, Upper East Side, $)

Lombardi's (Little Italy, $$)

Remi (Theater District/Midtown West, $$$$)

Vincent's Clam Bar (Little Italy, $$)

Japanese

Hatsuhana (Midtown East, $$$$)

Iso (East Village, $$$)

Shabu Tatsu (East Village, Upper East Side, Upper West Side, $$)

Korean

Won Jo (Koreatown/Herald Square/Midtown West, $$$)

Mediterranean

Picholine (Lincoln Center/ Upper West Side, $$$$$)

Mexican

Mi Cocina (West Village, $$$)

Zarela (Midtown East, $$$)

Organic Vegetarian

Angelica Kitchen (East Village, $)

Pizza

John's Pizzeria (West Village, Midtown West, Lincoln Center/Upper West Side, Upper East Side, $)

Lombardi's (Little Italy, $$)

Seafood

Oyster Bar (Midtown East, $$)

Vincent's Clam Bar (Little Italy, $$)

Southern

Brothers BBQ (West Village, $$)

Sylvia's (Harlem, $$)

Southwestern

Arizona Café (Upper East Side, $$)

Arizona 206 (Upper East Side, $$$$)

Steak House

Sparks Steak House (Midtown East, $$$$)

Ukrainian Diner

Veselka (East Village, $)

Our Favorite New York Restaurants

20 Mott Street
$$. Chinatown. CHINESE.

This three-level restaurant is one of the moderately elegant choices in Chinatown. The cuisine is true to the best tradition of Hong Kong, and the service attentive and kind—a rarity in this sometimes brusque neighborhood. The menu includes some real Chinese delicacies such as bird's nests and abalone, but we love going there for a banquet: the Chinese-style prix fixe dinner. They'll prepare it for as few as two people, but you get the best choice of dishes and specialties if you arrive with a party of six or more. Our preferred dish is the delicious Peking duck. As at all traditional Chinese restaurants, they welcome families and children and have special seats for the little ones.

20 Mott St. between Pell Street and Chatham Square (two blocks south of Canal Street). ☎ *212/964-0380. Reservations recommended for large parties.* **Subway:** *6/N/R train to Canal stop, and then walk east on Canal to Mott Street and turn right; J/M/Z train to Canal, and then walk west on Canal Street to Mott Street and turn left.* **Main courses:** *$9–$35. AE, DISC, MC, V.* **Open:** *Daily 9am–1pm.*

Restaurants

Arizona 206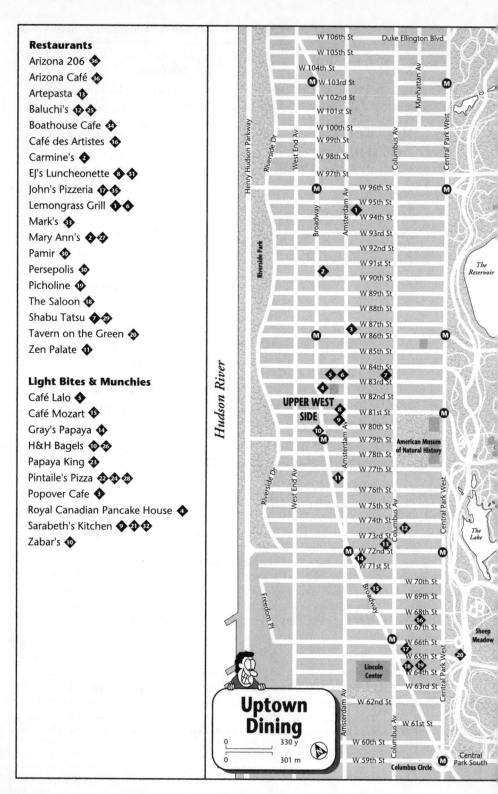
Arizona Café
Artepasta
Baluchi's
Boathouse Cafe
Café des Artistes
Carmine's
EJ's Luncheonette
John's Pizzeria
Lemongrass Grill
Mark's
Mary Ann's
Pamir
Persepolis
Picholine
The Saloon
Shabu Tatsu
Tavern on the Green
Zen Palate

Light Bites & Munchies

Café Lalo
Café Mozart
Gray's Papaya
H&H Bagels
Papaya King
Pintaile's Pizza
Popover Cafe
Royal Canadian Pancake House
Sarabeth's Kitchen
Zabar's

UPPER WEST SIDE

Hudson River

W 106th St
Duke Ellington Blvd
W 105th St
W 104th St
W 103rd St
W 102nd St
W 101st St
W 100th St
W 99th St
W 98th St
W 97th St
W 96th St
W 95th St
W 94th St
W 93rd St
W 92nd St
W 91st St
W 90th St
W 89th St
W 88th St
W 87th St
W 86th St
W 85th St
W 84th St
W 83rd St
W 82nd St
W 81st St
W 80th St
W 79th St
W 78th St
W 77th St
W 76th St
W 75th St
W 74th St
W 73rd St
W 72nd St
W 71st St
W 70th St
W 69th St
W 68th St
W 67th St
W 66th St
W 65th St
W 64th St
W 63rd St
W 62nd St
W 61st St
W 60th St
W 59th St

Manhattan Av
Central Park West
Columbus Av
Amsterdam Av
Broadway
West End Av
Riverside Dr
Henry Hudson Parkway
Riverside Park
Freedom Pl

The Reservoir
The Lake
Sheep Meadow
Central Park South

American Musum of Natural History

Lincoln Center

Columbus Circle

Uptown Dining

0   330 y
0   301 m

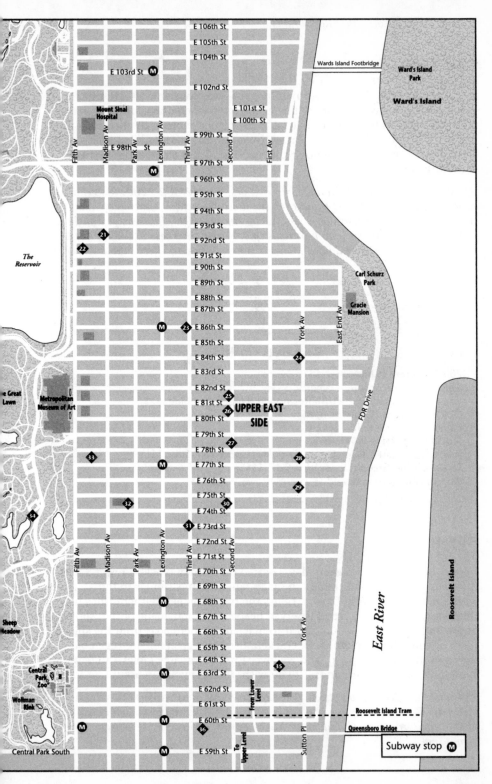

E 106th St
E 105th St
E 104th St
Wards Island Footbridge
Ward's Island Park
E 103rd St Ⓜ
E 102nd St
Ward's Island
E 101st St
Mount Sinai Hospital
E 100th St
E 99th St
E 98th St
E 97th St Ⓜ
E 96th St
E 95th St
E 94th St
E 93rd St
㉑
E 92nd St
㉒
The Reservoir
E 91st St
E 90th St
E 89th St
Carl Schurz Park
E 88th St
E 87th St
Gracie Mansion
Ⓜ
㉓ E 86th St
E 85th St
York Av
E 84th St
E 83rd St
㉔
East End Av
E 82nd St
㉕
The Great Lawn
Metropolitan Museum of Art
㉖ E 81st St
UPPER EAST SIDE
E 80th St
E 79th St
㉗
FDR Drive
E 78th St
㉘
㉝
E 77th St Ⓜ
E 76th St
E 75th St
㉙
㉜
E 74th St
㉚
㉞
㉛ E 73rd St
E 72nd St
Second Av
E 71st St
Fifth Av
Madison Av
Park Av
Lexington Av
Third Av
E 70th St
E 69th St
E 68th St Ⓜ
E 67th St
E 66th St
Roosevelt Island
E 65th St
Sheep Meadow
E 64th St
York Av
East River
㉟
E 63rd St Ⓜ
E 62nd St
From Lower Level
E 61st St
Central Park Zoo
Wollman Rink
E 60th St Ⓜ
Roosevelt Island Tram
㊱
Queensboro Bridge
Ⓜ
Ⓜ
To Upper Level
Sutton Pl
Central Park South
E 59th St Ⓜ
Subway stop Ⓜ

Fifth Av
Madison Av
Park St
Lexington Av
Third Av
Second Av
First Av

123

"21" Club
$$$$$. Midtown West. AMERICAN.

If you want to pay $21 for your hamburger—rated tops, and it better be given what you pay for it—and dine at the table where the Clintons celebrated Chelsea's 17th birthday, or maybe at the regular table of the Kennedys or the Kissingers, then this is the place for you. In this New York landmark, and former speakeasy, you can enjoy really good food and feel like one of the New York powers-that-be.

21 W. 52nd St. between Fifth and Sixth avenues. ☎ *212/582-7200. Reservations required. **Subway:** B/D/F/Q train to 47–50 streets/Rockefeller Center stop, and then walk three blocks north on Sixth Avenue and turn right; however, you might want to take a cab for such an illustrious spot. **Main courses:** $21–$39. AE, DC, DISC, JCB, MC, V. **Open:** Lunch Mon–Fri; dinner Mon–Sat; closed Sun and Aug.*

Best Bets for Kids

20 Mott Street (Chinatown, $$)
America (Union Square/Gramercy, $$$)
Carmine's (Theater District/Midtown West, Upper West Side, $$$)
Golden Unicorn (Chinatown, $$)
Lombardi's (Little Italy, $$)
NoHo Star (NoHo, $$$)
Shabu Tatsu (East Village, Upper East Side, Upper West Side, $$)
Tavern on the Green (Upper West Side, $$$$)
Won Jo (Koreatown/Herald Square/Midtown West, $$$)

Abyssinia
$$. SoHo. ETHIOPIAN.

Here's one you don't see every day. Located on a funky block in lower SoHo, this place dispenses traditional Ethiopian fare, which is similar to Indian but with different spices and flavors. Here's the treat: You get neither dishes nor silverware; instead, your food is served heaped on a tray made of flat, spongy bread, and you tear off chunks of it to make mini-enchiladas from the spicy stews of your choice: lamb, beef, chicken, fish, or vegetable. The vegetable stew and the lamb are great, and we love sitting at the low tables and being allowed to eat with our hands. (If you wish, though, you can ask for a fork.)

35 Grand St. at Thompson Street. ☎ *212/226-5959. Reservations not necessary. **Subway:** C/E train to Spring Street stop, and then walk two blocks south on Sixth Avenue and turn left on Grand Street. **Main courses:** $6–$15. AE. **Open:** Daily 5pm–11pm.*

_{Kids} **America**
$$$. Union Square/Gramercy. AMERICAN.

This is a great place. It feels very much like a hangar for an airplane (make that two airplanes) and the menu is the size of a pre-flight checklist. You can find anything from a peanut butter and jelly sandwich (known here as a "Peoria") to a duck pot pie ("Long Island") to a T-bone steak ("Kansas City") to fried catfish ("Mississippi"). The price is right, too, but don't expect cordon bleu cuisine. Of course, kids are welcome and special chairs are available for them.

9 E. 18th St. between Fifth Avenue and Broadway. ☎ *212/505-2110. Reservations recommended.* **Subway:** *L/N/R/4/5/6 to 14th Street/Union Square stop, and then walk north on Broadway and turn left on 18th Street.* **Main courses:** *$6.95–$18.95. AE, DC, DISC, MC, V.* **Open:** *Daily 11:30am–midnight; Fri–Sat 11:30am–1am.*

Angelica Kitchen
$. East Village. ORGANIC VEGETARIAN.

Ate a little too much yesterday? The wife making remarks about your cholesterol? Take a healthy break in this all-veggie place. The food is good, imaginative, and plentiful, and if you're a real vegetarian, you'll be pleased to know that it's vegan, too. They have a cheese-free onion soup that we'd put up against any French restaurant's, and many good desserts as well. Every day they feature the "daily seasonal creation," which might be one of the best bets on the menu (or at least one of the most interesting).

300 E. 12th St. between First and Second avenues. ☎ *212/228-2909. Reservations accepted for six or more Mon–Thurs.* **Subway:** *L/N/R/4/5/6 train to 14th Street/Union Square stop, and then walk east on 14th Street to Second Avenue and turn right; reach 12th Street and turn left.* **Main courses:** *$5–$12. No credit cards.* **Open:** *Daily 11:30am–10:30pm.*

Arizona 206
$$$$. Upper East Side. SOUTHWESTERN.

This is one of the best restaurants in New York. The food is creative and delicious and the adobe surroundings pleasant and welcoming. You can choose from a smoked venison with garlicky red wine sauce and sweet potato and corn risotto, or a chilled seafood salad of lobster, shrimp, baby octopus, and squid on a bed of grilled cactus hearts. All this goodness comes with a price tag, or course, but those with shallower pockets always have recourse to the Arizona Cafe, with similar flavors and smaller prices (see below).

206 E. 60th St. between Second and Third avenues. ☎ *212/838-0440. Reservations recommended.* **Subway:** *4/5/6 train to 59 Street stop and N/R to Lexington Avenue stop, and then walk one block north on Lexington Avenue, turn right on 60th Street and walk another block east.* **Main courses:** *$21–$29. AE, DC, DISC, MC, V.* **Open:** *Lunch Mon–Fri; dinner daily.*

Arizona Cafe
$$. Upper East Side. SOUTHWESTERN.

The menu at the cafe is simpler than at the Arizona 206 restaurant (see previous) but the food is similarly delicious and imaginative. Imagine a sandwich made of grilled swordfish, guajillo and olive mayonnaise, pancetta, and pickled vegetables accompanied by cumin potato chips; or seared tuna rolls with ginger-wasabi aioli; or maybe lamb quesadilla with red mole and crème fraîche. You get the idea. The setting is more casual than in the restaurant, the prices more friendly, and the atmosphere more lively—maybe too lively in the very crowded evenings, when even the fireplace and the on-tap micro-brewed beer and good margaritas at the bar can't make up for the noise and the chaos. As soon as you sit down, though, everything falls into place.

206 E. 60th St. between Second and Third avenues. ☎ *212/838-0440. Reservations not accepted. **Subway:** 4/5/6 train to 59 Street stop and N/R to Lexington Avenue stop, and then walk one block north on Lexington Avenue, turn right on 60th Street, and walk another block east. **Main courses:** $10–$16. AE, DC, DISC, MC, V. **Open:** Daily noon–midnight; Sun opens at 11:30am for brunch.*

Best Bets for a Romantic Interlude

Gotham Bar and Grill (West Village/Union Square, $$$$$)
Mark's (Upper East Side, $$$$)
Provence (SoHo, $$$$)
Rainbow Room (Midtown West, $$$$$)
Tavern on the Green (Upper West Side, $$$$)
Verbena (Union Square/Gramercy Park, $$$$)
Windows on the World (Downtown, $$$$$)

Baluchi's
$$. Upper West Side, Upper East Side, West Village, and SoHo. INDIAN.

You get a bit classier Indian experience here than in one of the shops on 6th Street—and better food to boot. Preparation is exquisite, with spices delicately proportioned and sauces never achieving the viscous state you often see in cheaper joints. Service is solicitous and unobtrusive. Favorites here include the malai kofta vegetable balls in a creamy tomato sauce and the matar panir (peas and homemade cheese cubes in a cream sauce). There's a decent wine list.

Upper West Side: 283 Columbus Ave. between 73rd and 74th streets. ☎ *212/
579-3900. Subway: 1/2/3/9 to 72nd Street, and then walk one block east and
one block north. Upper East Side: 1565 Second Ave. between 81st and 82nd
streets.* ☎ *212/288-4810. Subway: 6 to 77th Street, and then walk four blocks
north and four blocks east. West Village: 361 Sixth Ave. at Washington Place.*
☎ *212/929-0456. Subway: A/B/C/D/E/F/Q to West 4th Street/Washington
Square, and then walk one block north. SoHo: 193 Spring St. between Sullivan and
Thompson streets.* ☎ *212/226-2828. Subway: C/E to Spring Street, and then
walk one block east. Reservations not necessary. Main courses: $11–$30. AE,
DC, MC, V. Open: Lunch and dinner daily.*

Boathouse Cafe
$$$$. Upper East Side. CONTEMPORARY AMERICAN.
You've seen this place in the movies: If the characters are in New York and
are having lunch on a lake, you can bet it's here. Perched right on the edge
of the water at Central Park's rowing lake, the Boathouse can be quite
romantic, though the food—grilled seafood with creamy risotto or roasted
rack of lamb with polenta and spring vegetables, for example—is not the best
and the tab is expensive. But then again, people come here more for the
ambience than for the food. Lunch, not crowded during the workweek, is a
much better bet than dinner, which is often more crowded and more formal,
though it's lightened by live music Monday through Thursday. By the way,
it's safe and actually very pleasant to walk to the Boathouse after dark from
72nd Street. Of course, don't start wandering behind dark bushes or down
secondary paths far from the main road.

On the Lake in Central Park, East Park Drive and 73rd Street. ☎ *212/517-2233.
Reservations recommended. Subway: 6 train to 68 Street/Hunter College stop, and
then walk three blocks west to Central Park, turn right, enter the park at 72nd
Street, and follow East Park Drive to the Lake. Main courses: $19–$30. AE, CB,
DC, DISC, MC, V. Open: Lunch and dinner daily; closed in winter.*

Bombay Dining
$. Little India/East Village. INDIAN.
Bombay Dining has nothing really from the outside to distinguish it from
the many other Indian restaurants that line both sides of this block. Inside,
though, the place will captivate you. Prices and selection are great and everything is very well prepared. We like getting several of the many appetizers
and types of Indian bread (all very good), but the main dishes are equally
good—it's up to you. *A tip:* the restaurant is BYOB, so stop on First Avenue if
you want beer or wine with your meal. The bodega on the northwest corner
stocks Indian beer—always a good bet.

320 E. 6th St. between First and Second avenues. ☎ *212/260-8229. Reservations
not necessary. Subway: F train to Second Avenue stop, and then walk six blocks
north on Second Avenue and turn right; 6 train to Astor Place stop, and then walk
two blocks east to Second Avenue and turn right, walk to 6th Street and turn left.
Main courses: $4.75–$10.50. AE, MC, V. Open: Lunch and dinner daily.*

Brothers BBQ
$$. West Village. SOUTHERN/CONTEMPORARY AMERICAN.
A very large space, a great bar with lounge, vintage signs covering the walls, and funny melted-looking lamps make this restaurant fashionable but still very laid back and comfortable. The chicken-fried chicken is the best you'll have had in a long time and the mashed potatoes are maybe the best in New York. We love the collard greens too, and the fried okra, and the hush puppies; the new contemporary American dishes they've added to the menu are quite good, as well. You'll never leave hungry, especially not on Monday, which is the night of the "pig out" special.

225 Varick St. at Clarkson Street (Varick is the continuation of Seventh Avenue). ☎ *212/727-2775. Reservations required for groups of 6 or more. **Subway:** 1/9 train to Houston Street stop. **Main courses:** $6.75–$16.75. AE, DC, MC, V. **Open:** Daily 11:30am–11pm; Fri–Sat closes at 2am.*

Cabana Carioca
$$. Theater District/Midtown West. BRAZILIAN.
The portions are big, the prices low, and it's steps from most theaters, making it a good choice for your pre-theater dinner (though it's often a little crowded). The food is good and includes some very nice grilled meat dishes (try the chicken!). The decor is colorful and lively and you'll love the ambience.

*123 W. 45th St. between Sixth and Seventh avenues. ☎ 212/581-8088. Reservations recommended. **Subway:** B/D/F/Q train to 42 Street stop, and then walk three blocks north on Sixth Avenue and turn left. **Main courses:** $5.95–$16.95. AE, DC, DISC, MC, V. **Open:** Daily 11am–11pm.*

Kids Carmine's
$$$. Theater District/Midtown West and Upper West Side. SOUTHERN ITALIAN.
We love the old-fashioned (and once again stylish) dark wood, brass, and mirrors decor of the large dining room. Orders come on an oval platter the size of your grandmother's turkey server, and the heaping portions are about the same as she served, too; each portion is designed for four, so order accordingly. It goes without saying that kids love this place, and it's always hilarious to see the face of the patron who ordered one portion of the (delicious) fried calamari and sees the waiter come back with a twelve-inch mountain of food. Antipasto is delicious and so are many of the entrees and salads. The only bad side is that if you're a party of two you can't taste more than one dish unless you are very hungry, very big people. Desserts are good and come pie-sized, of course. (All this goes for both of Carmine's locations: the original on the Upper West Side and the Midtown location.)

Midtown:** 200 W. 44th St. between Broadway and Eighth Avenue. ☎ 212/ 221-3800. Reservations recommended before 6pm; after 6pm accepted only for parties of six or more. **Subway:** N/R/S/1/2/3/7/9 train to Times Square stop, and then walk two blocks north on Seventh Avenue and turn left on 44th Street. **Upper

West Side: 2450 Broadway between 90th and 91st streets. ☎ *212/362-2200.*
Subway: 1/2/3/9 train to 96th Street stop, and then walk five blocks south on
Broadway. *Main courses* (family style, serves about three): $14.50–$46. AE, DC,
MC, V. *Open:* Tues–Sat 11:30am–midnight; Sun–Mon closes at 11pm.

Carnegie Delicatessen and Restaurant
$. Theater District/Midtown West. DELI.
Are you familiar with traditional deli fare? Pastrami, corned beef, matzo balls,
blintzes, borscht, and so on? If that's your cup of broth, this is the place for
you. Maybe you'd like to sample some of the best pastrami in New York—
and maybe in America? The drawback is that the deli's glamorous location,
its reputation, and the publicity it got since it was made internationally
famous by Woody Allen's movie *Broadway Danny Rose* make it really crowded
all the time, and more expensive than others of the breed (see Second
Avenue Deli, later in this chapter). By the way, don't dream that you can fin-
ish a sandwich all by yourself: There are at
least two pounds of meat in each one.

854 Seventh Ave. at 55th Street. ☎ *212/
757-2245. Reservations not accepted.*
Subway: N/R train to 57 Street stop, and
then walk two blocks south on Seventh
Avenue; B/D/E train to Seventh Avenue stop,
and then walk two blocks north on Seventh
Avenue. *Main courses:* $6.95–$19.95. No
credit cards. *Open:* Daily 7am–3am.

24 Hours of Good Eats

Florent (West Village, $$)
Veselka (East Village, $)
Won Jo (Koreatown/Herald
Square/Midtown West, $$$)

Diwan Grill
$$$. Midtown East. INDIAN.
Subdued elegance, attentive and respectful service, large and comfortable
dining room and, most importantly, delicious food is what you get at this
upscale Indian restaurant. The best deal is the buffet lunch, where you can
stuff yourself on a vast choice of delicacies for $13.95. The ambience is even
more languorous and romantic at dinner time, but there's no buffet.

148 E. 48th St. between Lexington and Third avenues. ☎ *212/593-5425.*
Reservations not necessary. Subway: 6 train to 51st Street, and then walk three
blocks south on Lexington Avenue and turn left on 48th Street. *Main courses:*
$11.95–$16.95. AE, MC, V. *Open:* Lunch and dinner daily.

Florent
$$. West Village. FRENCH BISTRO/DINER.
Missing Paris? You can find it right in the middle of New York's old meat-
packing district, a somewhat desolate though rapidly changing neighborhood where transvestites, truckers, artists, celebrities, and club-going hipsters
mingle and, yes, eat. The best people-watching is late at night, particularly
on Fridays and Saturdays, but Florent is very popular for dinner and brunch
at regular hours as well. The food is very good and fairly priced at any hour.

129

Try the mussels Belgian style—a heaping pile of mussels served in a family-sized salad bowl with french fries on the side. There are also some real French specialties, such as a good boudin noir, a nice steak au poivre, or a good omelet.

*69 Gansevoort St. between Greenwich and Washington streets (Greenwich is the southern continuation of Ninth Avenue). ☎ 212/989-5779. Reservations recommended. **Subway:** A/C/E/L train to 14th Street stop, and then walk one block south on Eighth Avenue, turn right on West 13th Street for one short block and left on Gansevoort Street. **Main courses:** $7.95–$17.95. No credit cards. **Open:** Mon–Thurs daily 9am–5am; Fri–Sun 24 hours.*

Golden Unicorn
$$. Chinatown. CHINESE/DIM SUM.
New Yorkers *love* dim sum and here you can get the whole show. Little carts go around and around, offering a variety of tiny dishes including steamed dumplings (the shrimp ones are very good), braised tripes, and sticky rice (steamed, wrapped in leaves—delicious). You can also order regular dishes from the menu, of course, and the quality is likewise good. They also offer banquets (the Chinese-style prix fixe dinner) in the evening. Eat your fill of dumplings and other little delicacies, but for dessert, wait to go to the bakery downstairs or to the nearby **Chinatown Ice Cream Factory** (see chapter 11). The atmosphere is generally very festive and the lines, especially on Sundays when large Chinese families come in force, might be long.

*18 E. Broadway, three blocks south of Canal Street at Chatham Square. ☎ 212/941-0911. Reservations accepted for large parties. **Subway:** J/M/Z train to Canal stop, and then walk four blocks south on Confucius Plaza (the southern continuation of the Bowery) to Chatam Square and turn left on East Broadway. **Main courses:** $7.95–$35. AE, DC, DISC, JCB, MC, V. **Open:** Daily 9am–10pm, dim sum until 4pm.*

Gotham Bar & Grill
$$$$$. West Village/Union Square. CONTEMPORARY AMERICAN.
Style, elegance, and originality are the three key words that describe this glamorous restaurant and its exquisite food. Chef Alfred Portale is one of the prophets of "new American" cuisine and the originator of many a trend that has spread around the country. (Did you ever wonder who had the idea of piling up food tower-style?) And if the dinner is delicious, desserts are stratospheric, not only delectable but so beautiful to look at that it's almost (only almost) a shame to touch them. Certainly, it's expensive, but go for the prix fixe lunch, where you can net a wonderful experience for $19.98.

*12 E. 12th St. between Fifth Avenue and University Place. ☎ 212/620-4020. Reservations recommended. **Subway:** L/N/R/4/5/6 train to 14th Street/Union Square stop, and then walk two small blocks south on University Place and turn right. **Main courses:** $24–$29. AE, DC, MC, V. **Open:** Lunch Mon–Fri; dinner daily.*

Gramercy Tavern (Tavern Room)
$$. Union Square/Gramercy. CONTEMPORARY AMERICAN.
Top service, top food, and great decor make this one of the top restaurants in New York. It's also one of the most expensive (prix fixe dinner $56) and you have to plan well in advance in order to get a reservation. But all this is for the dining-room. In the tavern room at the front, where the bar is located, you can enjoy simpler yet similarly delicious meals at much more friendly prices. Try the quail with polenta garnished with black olives and greens, or a sandwich of grilled lamb and grilled vegetables. It's a great deal for lunch or for light fare anytime.

42 E. 20th St. between Broadway and Park Avenue South. ☎ ***212/477-0777.*** *Reservations not necessary for Tavern Room.* **Subway:** *R train to 23 Street stop, and then walk three blocks south on Broadway and turn left on 20th Street; 6 train to 23 Street stop, and then walk three blocks south on Park Avenue South and turn right on 20th Street.* **Main courses (tavern menu):** *$6–$17. AE, DC, MC, V.* **Open:** *Lunch Mon–Fri; dinner daily.*

Hatsuhana
$$$$. Midtown East. JAPANESE.
The ambience is elegant but a little heavy on business; the patrons may include a celebrity or two and many Japanese, and the food is sushi at its best (but not only). If you're a purist, you will find many extremely fresh raw fish specialties that are rare in more commonplace Japanese restaurants. Sushi deluxe is a good choice for an assortment of the day's best. The cooked entrees are very good, too; try the tempura, the grilled skewered fish, or the teriyaki salmon. Sit at one of the two sushi bars to admire the master chefs playing knives.

17 E. 48th St. between Fifth and Madison avenues. ☎ ***212/355-3345.*** *Reservations recommended.* **Subway:** *B/D/F/Q train to 47 Street/Rockefeller Center stop, and then walk east on 48th Street.* **Main courses:** *$17–$36. AE, CB, DC, DISC, JCB, MC, V.* **Open:** *Lunch and dinner daily.*

Best Restaurants for the Suit Set

"21" Club (Midtown West, $$$$$)
Sparks Steak House (Midtown East, $$$$)

Il Cortile
$$$. Little Italy. NORTHERN ITALIAN.
Less touristy and more upscale than most, this is probably the best Italian restaurant in Little Italy. True, it's also a little more expensive than its many neighbors, but once you sit at a table you'll understand why. A warm basket of bread, focaccia, and grissini (breadsticks) sustains you while you make your choice between many very good appetizers and entrees. Your options might be the seafood risotto with clams, mussels, octopus, shrimp, and scallops; or pappardelle with a mascarpone sauce; or linguine with fresh shrimp,

lobster, and scallops in a white sauce; or even champagne chicken in a cream sauce with red grapes and escarole.

125 Mulberry St. between Canal and Hester streets. ☎ *212/226-6060.*
Reservations recommended for four and more. **Subway:** *6/N/R train to Canal Street stop, and then walk three blocks east on Canal and turn left on Mulberry Street; J/Z/M train to Canal stop, and then walk three blocks west on Canal and turn right on Mulberry Street.* **Main courses:** *$10.50–$26. AE, CB, DC, DISC, JCB, MC, V.* **Open:** *Daily noon–midnight; Fri and Sat till 1am.*

Indochine
$$$. NoHo/East Village. SOUTHEAST ASIAN.
A very trendy place a few years ago, this nice and pleasant restaurant with an exotic decor is a great choice for an evening of subdued elegance and original food. The atmosphere is still hip but much more relaxed, and the menu offers some delightful southern Asian specialties such as the Cambodian "amok," a sole filet steamed in a banana leaf with lemon grass and coconut milk (our all-time preferred dish) or the tamarind-glazed chicken brochettes. There's also a choice of very tasty appetizers that make a perfect opening.

430 Lafayette St. just south of Astor Place. ☎ *212/505-5111. Reservations suggested.* **Subway:** *6 train to Astor Place stop, and then walk south on Lafayette Street.* **Main courses:** *$13–$18. AE, DC, MC, V.* **Open:** *Dinner Mon–Sat; closed every other Sun (call to check).*

Iso
$$$. East Village. JAPANESE.
This is probably the best deal for sushi in Manhattan. The restaurant is small and simple and the fish is as fresh as it gets, while the prices are moderate. The chefs are inventive and, maybe inspired by the great colorful flower arrangement at the entrance, produce fish and vegetable rolls that spring with color and are as beautiful as they are mouth-watering. Go for the sushi-sashimi for two; it's great, but you have to be hungry! There are also some very nice cooked fish entrees. And leave room for dessert: Unlike other Japanese restaurants, Iso has adopted the western taste for decadent desserts and you can find chocolate Grand Marnier cake besides the classic fresh fruit and ice cream. By the way, the place is not a well-kept secret and you will have to wait in line unless you come early.

175 Second Ave. just north of 11th Street. ☎ *212/777-0361. Reservations not accepted.* **Subway:** *6 train to Astor Place stop, and then walk east to Second Avenue and turn left.* **Main courses:** *$13–$23.50. AE, MC, V.* **Open:** *Dinner Mon–Sat; Sun closed.*

Theme Restaurants

Although we wouldn't put our feet in one of them at prime time (they're so crowded that even if you succeed in getting in, you have to scream to be heard), New York's theme restaurants are a good bet for traditional American fare at decent prices. Also, kids will be happy and you'll be able to find an easy souvenir gift for your buddy back at work. In addition, they're good late at night. The best ones are **Comedy Nation** (1626 Broadway, at 50th Street, ☎ 212/265-5555), **Hard Rock Cafe** (221 W. 57th St. between Broadway and Seventh Avenue, ☎ 212/459-9320), **Harley-Davidson Cafe** (1370 Sixth Ave. at 56th Street, ☎ 212/245-6000), **Jekyll & Hyde Club** (1409 Sixth Ave. between 57th and 58th streets, ☎ 212/541-9505), and **Planet Hollywood** (140 W. 57th St. between Sixth and Seventh avenues, ☎ 212/333-7827).

John's Pizzeria
$. West Village, Midtown West, Lincoln Center/Upper West Side, and Upper East Side. PIZZA.

One of the best pizza places in New York, John's serves up a thin-crusted pie that's well baked and topped with the freshest ingredients, and all at great prices. They have other choices on the menu, but pizza is what everyone comes for. Our big pick is the fresh tomato and mushroom pie, but we always get outvoted by those who prefer Italian sausage and black olives; luckily, you can get half one way and half the other. The downtown location is the original; the decor is more "rough," the lines long, and the pizza at its best. The other locations are a little more elegant, still have very good pizza, and are less crowded.

Downtown: 278 Bleeker St. between Sixth and Seventh avenues. ☎ 212/243-1680. Reservations accepted for six or more. Subway: A/B/C/D/E/F/Q to West 4th Street/Washington Square stop, and then walk one block south on Seventh Avenue and turn right on Bleeker. Upper West Side: 48 W. 65th St. between Columbus Avenue and Central Park West. ☎ 212/721-7001. Subway: 1/9 train to 66 Street-Lincoln Center, and then walk one block south on Columbus Avenue or Broadway and turn left on 65th Street. Upper East Side: 408 E. 64th Street between First and York avenues. ☎ 212/935-2895. Subway: B/Q train to Lexington Avenue stop, and then walk one block north on Lexington Avenue, turn right, and walk three blocks east on 64th Street. Midtown: 260 W. 44th Street at Eight Avenue. ☎ 212/391-7560. Subway: N/R/S/1/2/3/7/9 train to Times Square stop, and then walk two blocks north on Seventh Avenue, turn left on 44th Street, and walk one block west. Main courses: $6–$15.75. No credit cards. Open: Daily 11:30am–12:30am.

Jules
$$$. East Village. FRENCH.

The waiters are French, the atmosphere is French, the food is French, and the check is moderate. Oh, and there's live jazz after 9pm and tables on the sidewalk from which you can observe the East Village crowd with their colorful hair and funky clothing. What more could you want? Of course, the crowd might be rather young and noisy (and plentiful on weekend nights), but once you sit down it feels very European and romantic. And the food is worth it.

Best Restaurant for the Homesick

America (Union Square/ Gramercy, $$$)

65 St. Mark's Place between First and Second avenues. ☎ *212/477-5560. Reservations recommended.* **Subway:** *6 train to Astor Place stop, and then walk two blocks east on 8th Street (8th Street and St. Mark's Place are the same street).* **Main courses:** *$10–$25. AE, MC, V.* **Open:** *Daily 11am–2am.*

Kelley and Ping
$. SoHo. PAN-ASIAN.

The crowd is hip, the food is good, and the atmosphere—like an old colonial building somewhere in the Far East—very nice. It can get insanely crowded though, and then it's a little too noisy and busy for our taste. The Malaysian coconut-seafood soup is delicious, however, and so is the Pad Thai and many of the other dishes, so we keep going back.

127 Greene St. between Houston and Prince streets. ☎ *212/228-1212. Reservations not accepted.* **Subway:** *N/R train to Prince Street stop, and then walk two blocks north on Prince and turn right on Greene.* **Main courses:** *$5.50–$16.50. AE, MC, V.* **Open:** *Daily 11:30am–11:30pm, closed daily 5pm–6pm.*

L'Ecole
$$. SoHo. CONTEMPORARY FRENCH.

A great evening in a top restaurant at moderate prices. Why? Because this is the restaurant of the French Culinary Institute, where potential master chefs are finishing their training. The food is really good and served in style. There's no a la carte, but they offer two possibilities for dinner: from 6–8pm the prix fixe dinner is a four-course menu with several choices of appetizers, entrees, and desserts; from 8–9:30pm there's a five-course tasting menu with no choices but a different combination every evening of the week. We prefer to go for the early prix fixe dinner because then it really feels almost a la carte, given the variety of choices. On the other hand, the later dinner usually includes fancier dishes.

462 Broadway just north of Grand Street. ☎ *212/219-3300. Reservations recommended.* **Subway:** *6 train to Spring Street, and then walk two blocks east on*

Spring Street to Broadway and turn left, walk one and a half blocks south. **Main courses:** *Lunch $7–$14; Dinner only prix fixe $24.95. AE, DC, MC, V.* **Open:** *Lunch Mon–Fri; dinner Mon–Sat; Sun closed.*

Lombardi's

$$. Little Italy. PIZZA.

In serious competition for the "Best Pizza in New York" award, Lombardi's serves a pie that's very thin, very crispy, and made with real Italian toppings. The specialty is the fresh clam pizza, which draws people from all over the five boroughs and beyond. The original Lombardi's was opened in 1905 by Gennaro Lombardi and is supposed to have been the first pizzeria in America. The current owner—a relative of Gennaro—says that many of the pizza chefs now operating in town, including those from John's Pizzeria (see previous), were trained at Lombardi's. Whether true or not, one thing is sure: This is one fine pizza.

32 Spring St. between Mott and Mulberry streets. ☎ **212/941-7994.** *Reservations accepted for six or more.* **Subway:** *6 train to Spring Street, and then walk one block east on Spring Street.* **Main courses:** *$10.50–$20. No credit cards.* **Open:** *Daily 11:30am–11pm; Fri–Sat closes midnight; Sun closes 10pm.*

Mark's

$$$$. Upper East Side. CONTEMPORARY AMERICAN.

Culinary research with delightful results is what characterizes this landmark of classy quality dining, and the elegant decor makes you feel part of a special adventure. The creations of Chef David Paulstich include many dishes where fruit interacts with meat or fish to create surprising and pleasant new flavors. You might be taken aback at the idea of a chocolate sauce on artichokes and squab, or vanilla sauce on celery and turnip puree, but the results are extraordinary. If you want something more traditional, though, you can treat yourself to fresh linguini in a creamy porcini and chicken sauce, or to magnificent fish dishes such as cedar-plank-roasted salmon filet. The great deal here is the three-course pre-theater prix fixe dinner for $29, and the well-priced prix fixe lunch and brunch. Later dinner prix fixe is more expensive at $58.

25 E. 77th Street between Fifth and Madison avenues, in The Mark hotel. ☎ *212/879-1864.* *Reservations recommended.* **Subway:** *6 train to 77th Street stop, and then walk west two and a half blocks on 77th Street to Madison Avenue.* **Main courses:** *$18–$34. AE, CB, DC, JBC, MC, V.* **Open:** *Daily 7am–10:30pm.*

Best Exotic Dining Experiences

Abyssinia (SoHo, $$)
Cabana Carioca (Theater District/Midtown West, $$)
Indochine (NoHo, $$$)
Shabu Tatsu (East Village, Upper East Side and Upper West Side, $$)
Won Jo (Koreatown/Herald Square/Midtown West, $$$)

Mi Cocina
$$$. West Village. MEXICAN.

The service is somewhat uptight and haughty and the place gets really crowded on weekends, but then you decide to go in anyway and you discover that the food is really quite good. This small restaurant offers elegantly presented, spicy, yet light food. The typical Mexican ingredients come together with creative associations of flavors, while delightful sauces accompany more traditional dishes. For example, you can have shrimp in a roasted tomato-chipotle-white wine sauce with spinach and white rice, or an enchilada with fresh tomatillo and poblano chile sauce, and so on. The margaritas are OK but not the best. A good deal is the early bird prix fixe dinner.

57 Jane St. at Hudson Street, one block west of Eighth Avenue. ☎ *212/627-8273. Reservations recommended.* **Subway:** *A/C/E/L train to 14th Street stop, and then walk south one block on Eighth Avenue and turn right on Jane Street.* **Main courses:** *$9.95–$17.95. AE, CB, DC, MC, V.* **Open:** *Dinner daily; lunch Thurs only; Sun brunch.*

Kids NoHo Star
$$. NoHo/East Village. AMERICAN/INTERNATIONAL.

Don't worry about a lack of choices. The menu is eclectic (the Asian menu is available only after 6pm) but the food is well prepared and tasty, with choices like omelets and burgers; roasted chicken; salmon with citrus-beet vinaigrette on a bed of fresh spinach; spicy stir-fried double seafood with garlic sauce; stir-fried sesame scallops; and a really good Caesar salad with the dressing prepared in front of you. Families love to come for brunch and kids are welcome.

330 Lafayette St. at Bleecker Street. ☎ *212/925-0070. Reservations not accepted.* **Subway:** *6 train to Bleecker Street stop, and then look southwest; B/D/F/Q train to Broadway-Lafayette Street stop, and then walk two very small blocks east on Houston Street and make a left on Lafayette Street.* **Main courses:** *$9–$20. AE, CB, DC, DISC, MC, V.* **Open:** *Daily 8am–midnight; Sat–Sun opens 10:30am.*

The Odeon
$$$. Tribeca. FRENCH/AMERICAN.

This trendy art deco diner grew up really wanting to be a French brasserie. The food is reliably good—free-range chicken, seared tuna, and steak frites, but also spinach ravioli and pizza with baby artichokes—and it's a good place to do some celebrity spotting, especially late at night. Brunch is popular and less expensive; try the grilled apple and chicken sausage.

145 W. Broadway at Thomas Street. ☎ *212/233-0507. Reservations recommended.* **Subway:** *1/9 train to Franklin Street stop, and then walk three blocks south on West Broadway.* **Main courses:** *$8.50–$23. AE, DC, MC, V.* **Open:** *Daily noon–2am; Fri–Sat closes at 3am; Sat and Sun opens at 11:30 for brunch.*

Oyster Bar
$$. Midtown East. SEAFOOD.

Tucked away in the lower level of Grand Central Terminal, this historic land-mark has conserved its old New York atmosphere in both the white-tiled din-ing room with arched ceilings and the side room with wood-paneled walls. The menu changes daily so that only the freshest fish is served, but the best reason to go is, of course, oysters: delicious, plentiful, and presented to you by knowledgeable specialists. Another good reason is lunch, particularly for the famous and delicious (and, at $3.95, dirt cheap) clam chowders, but the drawback is that it gets really crowded at lunchtime. (*Note:* A fire ripped through the place not long ago, but it's been restored faithfully, and most of the original elements are still in place. In any case, the quality of the food wasn't affected.)

Grand Central Terminal at the lower level (entrances to Grand Central on 42nd Street between Lexington and Vanderbilt avenues and on Vanderbilt and Lexington avenues between 42nd and 44th streets). ☎ *212/490-6650. Reservations recom-mended. Subway: 4/5/6/7/S train to 42 Street/Grand Central stop, take an exit toward the railroad trains and follow the signs. Main courses: $8.95–$28.95. AE, DC, DISC, JCB, MC, V. Open: Mon–Fri 11:30am–9:30pm.*

Picholine
$$$$$. Lincoln Center/Upper West Side. FRENCH/ MEDITERRANEAN.

Chef Terrance Brennan has deserved much praise for his constantly improv-ing Mediterranean creations. His excellent food, allied with the warm ele-gance of his dining room, produces a perfect dining experience. Have the halibut with eggplant pancakes and tomato confit seasoned with balsamic vinegar and basil oil; or the risotto with wild mushrooms and duck, with asparagus and fava beans seasoned in white truffle oil; or the Moroccan spiced loin of lamb accompanied by vegetable couscous and minted yogurt. Then, go to the cheese tray and enjoy gourmet cheeses matured to perfection in the restaurant's own cheese-aging cellar, under the supervision of a cheese master.

35 W. 64th St. between Broadway and Central Park West. ☎ *212/724-8585. Reservations required. Subway: 1/9 train to 66th Street/Lincoln Center stop, and then walk two blocks south on Broadway to 64th Street and turn left. Main courses: $25.50–$34. AE, DC, MC, V. Open: Lunch Tues–Sat; dinner Mon–Sat; closed Sun.*

Gourmet Bites

Arizona Café (Upper East Side, $$)
Arizona 206 (Upper East Side, $$$$)
Diwan (Midtown East, $$$)
Gotham Bar and Grill (West Village/Union Square, $$$$$)
Gramercy Tavern (Union Square/Gramercy Park, $$)
L'Ecole (SoHo, $$)
Il Cortile (Little Italy, $$$)
Indochine (NoHo, $$$)
Iso (East Village, $$$)
Mark's (Upper East Side, $$$$)
Picholine (Lincoln Center/Upper West Side, $$$$$)
Provence (SoHo, $$$$)
Verbena (Union Square/Gramercy Park, $$$$)
Won Jo (Koreatown/Herald Square/Midtown West, $$$)
Zarela (Midtown East, $$$)

Provence
$$$$. SoHo. PROVENCAL FRENCH.
You'll love the atmosphere of this little piece of southern France planted in SoHo. The delightful garden, the warm interior, and the great food all contribute to make it one of the area's favorites. Start with the fish soup and continue with braised rabbit with olives and fava beans accompanied by chickpea cakes, or maybe poached fish with aioli broth, or monkfish with artichokes and crayfish. There are many more choices in this fashionable restaurant, which offers good values for lunch.

38 MacDougal St. between Prince and Houston streets. ☎ *212/475-7500. Reservations recommended.* **Subway:** *C/E train to Spring Street stop, and then walk one block north on Sixth Avenue, bear right at the beginning of MacDougal and walk another block north.* **Main courses:** *$14–$21. AE.* **Open:** *Lunch and dinner daily.*

Rainbow Room
$$$$$. Midtown West. CONTEMPORARY CONTINENTAL.
The thing to do is to dress up in your most elegant dancing clothes and go for a magic evening of dinner and dancing, taking a spin or two on the revolving floor while the orchestra plays, in between oysters Rockefeller and duck a l'orange that's flambee'd at your table. You can languidly admire the lights of New York spread out at your feet while waiting for a luscious dessert. Of course, you can also opt for a somewhat simpler evening (call in

advance for a schedule of live entertainment, which involves a $20 charge) or simply take advantage of the view from the lounge next door.

30 Rockefeller Plaza, 65th floor, between 49th and 50th streets and Fifth and Sixth avenues. ☎ *212/632-5000. Reservations required. Jacket/tie required.* **Subway:** *B/D/F/Q train to 47–50 streets/Rockefeller Center stop, and then walk one half block east.* **Main courses:** *$27–$32. AE, DC, DISC, MC, V.* **Open:** *Dinner Tues–Sun; Sun brunch; closed Mon.*

Lunch Deals in Midtown East

A great area for finding very good food at very decent prices is the area between Grand Central and the United Nations. The armies of office workers in this area have supported the development of an incredible number of lunch deals. There are very good salad bars—try **Del Monico,** on Lexington Ave. between 42nd and 41st streets (☎ **212/661-0510**), or the **Regency Deli,** 801 Second Ave. between 42nd and 43rd streets (☎ **212/661-3322**)—and great restaurants such as the Spanish Basque **Marichu,** at 342 E. 46th St. between First and Second avenues (☎ **212/370-1866,** reservations recommended); the famous **Palm** steak house, at 837 Second Ave. between 44th and 45th streets (☎ **212/687-2953**); or the Thai **Shaliga,** at 834 Second Ave. (☎ **212/573-5526**). The best deals though, are the lunch specials. At the Japanese chain **East** (210 E. 44th St. between Second and Third avenues, ☎ **212/687-5075**) you can have a huge lunch box for $8.50, and they make some of the best tempura in town; at **Malika** (210 E. 43rd St. between Second and Third avenues ☎ **212/681-6775**), you can have a great Indian buffet lunch for $10.95; and at the many Chinese places around (try **Dragon Gold,** 913 Second Ave., between 48th and 49th streets, ☎ **212/223-0888**) you can have a lunch special for as little as $4.50.

Remi

$$$$. Theater District/Midtown West. NORTHERN ITALIAN.
Elegance, fine decor, and terrific food are what attracts patrons to this Venetian restaurant, which is among the best Italian places in New York. It's in a great location for pre-theater dinner, but you have to be careful not to be distracted by your taste buds and miss the show. Try duck-filled pasta and seared tuna, or goose prosciutto with truffle oil, baby greens, and shaved Parmesan followed by a loin of lamb with black olive sauce, or maybe fried baby artichokes in parsley-and-garlic sauce ricotta and spinach pasta.

145 W. 53rd St. between Sixth and Seventh avenues. ☎ *212/581-4242. Reservations required.* **Subway:** *B/D/E train to Seventh Avenue stop, and then walk east on 53rd Street.* **Main courses:** *$16–$29. AE, CB, DC, JBC, MC, V.* **Open:** *Lunch Mon–Fri; dinner daily.*

The Saloon
$$. Lincoln Center/Upper West Side. AMERICAN.
Located just in front of Lincoln Center and with a large dining room that nevertheless fills up some nights, this restaurant is also one of the best buys in the area. The ambience is pleasant and the moderately priced food is okay—not a cordon bleu spot, but some of the typical American dishes are quite good. We like their nachos (a meal on their own) and the pan-roasted organic chicken breast with fricassee of wild mushrooms, roasted potatoes, pearl onions, and smoked bacon (wow!). The quesadillas are not bad at all, and their salads are really nice (try the avocado salad—s'yummy).

*1920 Broadway at 64th St. ☎ 212/874-1500. Reservations recommended. **Subway:** 1/9 train to 66 Street/Lincoln Center, and then walk two blocks south on Broadway. **Main courses:** $8.50–$16.95. AE, CB, DC, DISC, MC, V. **Open:** Daily 11:30am–midnight; Fri–Sat closes at 1am; Sat–Sun opens at 11am for brunch.*

Second Avenue Deli
$. East Village. DELI.
If pastrami is the specialty of the Carnegie Deli (see previous), corned beef is the trademark here. The crisp and tasty pickles on the table make a perfect side for the long list of delicious kosher specialties on the menu. The chopped liver and the matzo ball soup are tops, but any of the sandwiches are great, too.

*156 Second Ave. at 10th Street. ☎ 212/677-0606. Reservations recommended for large parties. **Subway:** 6 train to Astor Place stop, and then walk two blocks east to Second Avenue and turn left. **Main courses:** $6.75–$20.95. AE. **Open:** Daily 7am–midnight; Fri–Sat closes at 2am.*

⭐Kids Shabu Tatsu
$$. East Village, Upper East Side, and Upper West Side. JAPANESE.
Have you ever made "shabu"? This is cooking for yourself on the wok-like grill built into the table in front of you. Lots of fun, really, and very tasty, with all the little pickles and sauces that come with the raw slices of meat, veggies, and seafood. Kids (maybe not toddlers) absolutely love it. If you don't feel in the mood for do-it-yourself dinner, just order one of the very good entrees on the menu. It might get quite crowded, so go early if you want to avoid standing in line.

*Downtown: 216 E. 10th St. between First and Second avenues. ☎ 212/477-2972. **Subway:** 6 train to Astor Place stop, and then walk east to Second Avenue, turn left and walk north to 10th Street. **Upper West Side:** 483 Columbus Ave. between 83rd and 84th streets. ☎ 212/874-5633. **Subway:** B/C to 81 Street/Museum of Natural History stop. **Upper East Side:** 1414 York Ave. at 75th Street. ☎ 212/472-3322. **Subway:** 4/5/6 train to 77th Street stop. Reservations accepted for four or more. **Main courses:** $8–$18. AE, DC, MC, V. **Open:** Sun–Thurs 5pm–11:45pm; Fri–Sat 3pm–2am.*

Sparks Steak House

$$$$. Midtown East. STEAK HOUSE.

One of the best steak houses in Manhattan, it's also one of the most expensive, but at least you get what you pay for. The steaks are excellent, the lobsters are monsters, and the wine list is one of the best in the city. Beware of the lengthy wait at rush hours, though.

210 E. 46th St. between Second and Third avenues. ☎ *212/687-4855. Reservations required. Jacket requested.* **Subway:** *4/5/6/7/S train to 42 Street/Grand Central stop, and then walk four blocks north on Lexington Avenue, turn right on 46th Street, and walk one block east.* **Main courses:** *$19.95–$29.95. AE, CB, DC, MC, V.* **Open:** *Lunch Mon–Fri; dinner Mon–Sat; closed Sun.*

Sylvia's

$$. Harlem. SOUL FOOD.

If you decide to visit Harlem, or to go for one of the great gospel masses in the area, Sylvia's is the place to eat. What we like best—and think is a great excursion in itself—is to go just for the Sunday gospel brunch. It's a great deal, the food is really good and cheap, and the singing is superb. They could use a better sound system, but the atmosphere is so nice and the singers so good that it doesn't really matter. We love the pancakes and fried chicken for brunch, or the unique ribs if you want something more substantial. If you go for dinner Sunday night, there's open-mike gospel after hours.

328 Lenox Ave. (one block west of Fifth Avenue) between 126th and 127th streets. ☎ *212/996-0660. Reservations accepted for 10 or more.* **Subway:** *2/3 train to 125th Street stop, and then walk one block north on Lenox Avenue.* **Main courses:** *$8–$16. AE, DISC, MC, V.* **Open:** *Mon–Sat 7:30am–10:30pm; Sun brunch 12:30pm–7pm.*

Kids Tavern on the Green

$$$$. Upper West Side. CONTEMPORARY AMERICAN/CONTINENTAL.

A magical setting perfect for a celebration is the best description of this New York landmark. Ask to be seated in the Crystal room with Tiffany glass and crystal chandeliers, or in the garden in summer for the best setting. The food is good and a children's menu is available. Go for a delicious grilled pork porterhouse or for the great choice of pastas. There are also many mouth-watering starters. The service is known to be friendly and unpretentious but it might be slow at times.

In Central Park at 67th Street. ☎ *212/873-3200. Reservations recommended.* **Subway:** *1/9 train to 66 Street/Lincoln Center stop, and then walk west to the Park entrance and follow the path.* **Main courses:** *$12.50–$29.75. AE, DC, MC, V.* **Open:** *Lunch Mon–Fri; dinner daily; Sat–Sun brunch; Sat open until 1am.*

TriBeCa Grill

$$$$. Tribeca. CONTEMPORARY AMERICAN.

As you'd expect from a restaurant owned by actor Robert De Niro, the ambience here is active and chic, and you're all but certain to spot celebrities, but guess what? It's also a very good restaurant. Start with the Asian-scented appetizers—crisp fried oysters with garlic-anchovy aioli or seared tuna with sesame noodles—and continue with barbecued breast of duck or a braised lamb shank with sweet-potato agnolotti and braised Swiss chard. Desserts are outstanding. De Niro also owns the nearby **Nobu,** an expensive Japanese restaurant that's so popular you need reservations weeks in advance.

375 Greenwich St. at Franklin Street, one block east from the Hudson River. ☎ *212/941-3900. Reservations recommended.* **Subway:** *1/9 to Franklin St. stop, and then walk two blocks west on Franklin Street.* **Main courses:** *$19–$27. AE, DC, MC, V.* **Open:** *Lunch Mon–Fri; dinner daily; Sun brunch.*

Verbena

$$$$. Union Square/Gramercy. CONTEMPORARY AMERICAN.

This romantic and quietly elegant restaurant is in perfect harmony with the spirit of the surrounding Gramercy Park, which is probably the most romantic neighborhood in Manhattan. A mild country touch enhances the innovative cooking and pampers your taste buds. The menu is seasonal, but if you're there in the fall or early winter be sure not to miss the butternut squash ravioli with cheese and cinnamon. Deserts are delightful. The verbena crème brûlée, the house trademark, is light, surprising, and served in far too small a quantity for our taste. In spring and summer, the garden terrace is very pleasant as well.

54 Irving Place between 17th and 18th streets. ☎ *212/260-5454. Reservations recommended.* **Subway:** *L/N/R/4/5/6 train to 14th Street/Union Square stop, and then walk one block east to Irving Place, turn left and walk one block north.* **Main courses:** *$18–$27. AE, DC, MC, V.* **Open:** *Lunch Mon–Sat; dinner daily; Sun brunch.*

Veselka

$. East Village. UKRAINIAN DINER.

This institution of the East Village has gained its popularity for consistently good food around the clock at great prices. We love their pancakes for breakfast, their ice cream sodas on a summer afternoon, or a bowl of their excellent borscht in the evening. Their entrees are great, too: Try the stuffed cabbage (regular or vegetarian) or the meatloaf. Recently renovated, it lost some of the old-fashioned character but kept the great food.

144 Second Ave. at 9th Street. ☎ *212/228-9682. Reservations not accepted.* **Subway:** *6 train to Astor Place stop, and then walk two blocks east.* **Main courses:** *$1.95–$11.50. AE, MC, V.* **Open:** *Daily 24 hours.*

Vincent's Clam Bar

$$. Little Italy. ITALIAN/SEAFOOD.

One of the oldest restaurants in Little Italy, this old-fashioned family-style place offers large servings of pasta and seafood at great prices. The specialty is the hot sauce, which has many fans but is suggested only for those who really like it hot. We prefer the clams, oysters, calamari, and mussels, which are all quite good.

119 Mott St. at Hester Street. ☎ *212/226-8133. Reservations suggested.* **Subway:** *B/D/Q train to Grand Street stop, and then walk three blocks west on Grand Street, turn left on Mott Street, and walk south; 6/J/M/N/R/Z train to Canal stop, and then walk on Canal to Mott Street and walk north.* **Main courses:** *$7.75–$15. AE, DC, MC, V.* **Open:** *Daily 11:30am–1:30am; Fri–Sat closes at 3am.*

Windows on the World

$$$$$. Downtown. ECLECTIC.

Perched at the top of the World Trade Center, this renovated 107th-floor restaurant is simply breathtaking and features tables set in such a way that you're guaranteed to have an unobstructed view from everywhere. It's an unforgettable experience. The food, which had been of disappointing quality for a long time, has now quite improved under the direction of new chefs. The eclectic menu—the theme is "best dishes of the world"—includes some good choices, and you are in for a quite pleasant meal; still, if food is your only motivation, there are definitely better choices for the price. *Be warned:* Lunch isn't a great money-saver here. The restaurant charges a $15 per-person service charge on top of your lunch bill.

One World Trade Center, 107th Floor, on West Street between Liberty and Vesey streets. ☎ *212/524-7000. Reservations recommended well in advance.* **Subway:** *1/9/N/R train to Cortland Street stop, and then up the internal passage to the World Trade Center; C/E trains to World Trade Center stop.* **Main courses:** *$25–$35. AE, CB, DC, DISC, MC, V.* **Open:** *Lunch Mon–Fri; dinner daily; Sun buffet lunch.*

Kids Won Jo

$$$. Koreatown/Herald Square. KOREAN.

The special fare here is an authentic Korean barbecue that you cook yourself at the grill built into the table. It's quite different from the wok-like plate for Japanese shabu (see Shabu Tatsu, previous), and, to our taste, more satisfactory. The barbecue is a full meal, including meat, noodles, and vegetables. There are also many other Korean specialties and a choice of delicately broiled fish. Children love this place, and really young ones are provided with high chairs.

23 W. 32nd St. between Fifth and Sixth avenues. ☎ *212/695-5815. Reservations recommended.* **Subway:** *B/D/F/N/Q/R train to 34 Street, and then walk two blocks south on Sixth Avenue and turn left on 32nd Street.* **Main courses:** *$9.95–$19.95. AE, MC, V.* **Open:** *Daily 24 hours.*

Zarela
$$$. Midtown East. MEXICAN.

If you want a burrito, go elsewhere, 'cause what we have here is the temple
of real upscale gourmet Mexican cuisine. Creative dishes accompany tradi-
tional ones revisited with innovative spirit and style. Try the fantastic duck
with a sauce of apricots, prunes, pineapples, red chiles, and tomatoes; or the
shrimp braised with poblano, onions, and queso blanco. The one very tradi-
tional entree is the fajitas, and you never had 'em so good. Save room for
dessert, though, because they're extraordinary—among the best in the city;
the burst of flavor is only matched by the festivity of the restaurant decor.
The Margaritas are first class, as are the homemade tortilla chips and salsa,
and the service is very friendly and attentive.

953 Second Ave. between 50th and 51st streets. ☎ *212/644-6740. Reservations
required.* **Subway:** *6 train to 51 Street stop, and then walk two blocks east on 51st
Street and turn right on Second Avenue.* **Main courses:** *$12.95–$16.95. AE, DC.*
Open: *Lunch Mon–Fri; dinner daily.*

Chapter 11

Light Bites & Munchies

In This Chapter

➤ Where to find a fast snack

➤ What about street food?

➤ Where to find a sweet treat

➤ Where to take a break

OK, chapters 9 and 10 told you where to have a nice dinner and a great lunch, but we all know that the three basic meals are only the base from which we work—particularly when we're on vacation. As a matter of fact, vacation almost *demands* that we stuff ourselves with whatever uncommon treats we find.

With that in mind, this chapter runs through your main New York City snack options.

Afternoon Tea

The one great English institution, as everybody knows, is high tea (parliamentary democracy is OK, too), and New Yorkers have been appreciating this treat more and more. You can get afternoon tea at any pastry shop and at department store coffee shops, but a few restaurants actually specialize in real High Tea, such as **Anglers and Writers** (see the "Brunch" section, following); **Palm Court,** inside the Plaza Hotel (768 Fifth Ave. between 58th and 59th streets, ☎ 212/546-5350), where you pay $22 and mingle with the cream of New York ladies; and **Danal** (see the "Brunch" section, following).

Brunch

If you don't like afternoon tea, you can always try the same places for breakfast or brunch. The best are **Anglers and Writers** (420 Hudson St. at St. Luke's Place, in the West Village, ☎ 212/675-0810); **Danal** (90 East 10th St. between Third and Fourth avenues, ☎ 212/982-6930); **Popover Cafe** (551 Amsterdam Ave. between 86th and 87th streets, ☎ 212/595-8555); the **Royal Canadian Pancake House,** which is a great place for kids and has servings big enough for a hungry lumberjack or two (three locations: 1004 Second Ave. at 53rd Street, ☎ 212/980-4131; 180 Third Ave. at 17th Street ☎ 212/777-9288; and 2286 Broadway between 82nd and 83rd streets, ☎ 212/873-6052); and, last but not least, **Sarabeth's Kitchen** (three locations as well: 423 Amsterdam Ave. between 80th and 81st streets, ☎ 212/496-6280; 1295 Madison Ave. between 92nd and 93rd streets, ☎ 212/410-7355; and 945 Madison Ave. between 74th and 75th streets, inside the Whitney Museum, ☎ 212/570-3670).

Snacking While Shopping

What's more exhausting than shopping? You may need a little lift, and the best place to get it could be right there in the store. At Saks Fifth Avenue, **Cafe S.F.A.** is a really pleasant spot for a break—or for a more substantial fare (611 Fifth Ave., 8th floor, ☎ 212/940-4080); at Bloomingdale's you should stop at **Le Train Bleu** (1000 Third Ave., 6th floor, ☎ 212/705-2100); at ABC Carpet & Home, the **Parlour Cafe** is a great place for desserts (38 East 19th St., ☎ 212/677-2233). There's even a **Coffee Shop** with a high-toned sandwich menu in the Old Navy Clothing Company (610 Sixth Ave., ☎ 212/645-0663).

Coffee Break

The java craze that's swept the city during the past couple of years has produced a mind-boggling number of coffee parlors. There's a **Starbucks** on just about every corner, so we won't bother giving addresses—just walk out your hotel door and you're almost bound to see one. **Barnes & Noble** has opened nice cafes in several of its locations (among them 54th Street and Third Avenue, 66th Street and Broadway, and Astor Place), though—guess what!—they serve Starbuck's coffee, too. **Dean & Delucca** is a little more than a coffee shop and a little more New Yorky than the Seattle-based Starbucks, and has several stores around town (see the section "Delis and Salad Bars" later in this chapter). You'll also find **New World Coffee, Timothy's Coffees of the World,** and **Dalton's Coffee** shops scattered wherever you look. We still think the best coffee in town is at **Ferrara** (see the section "Pastries & Sweet Breaks" later in this chapter).

If you're looking to stock up on beans (and grab a quick cup, too), take a trip to **Porto Rico Importing Company** (201 Bleecker St., between Sixth Avenue and MacDougal Street, ☎ 212/477-5421; 107 Thompson St. between Prince and Spring, ☎ 212/966-5758; or 40½ St. Marks Place, between First and Second avenues, ☎ 212/533-1982). You'll find a mind-boggling assortment of beans, teas, and coffee accessories and ephemera, and get to watch the staff—buzzed out of their minds from the coffee smell—rush around like hummingbirds on speed. (*Note:* The main branch on Bleecker Street is the best stocked and the most fun.)

The Doughnuts That Ate Manhattan

What's the surest sign that the economy really has gone global? Maybe the fact that Southern doughnut kings **Krispy Kreme** have opened four wildly successful branches right in the heart of New York City. Sure, we've always had doughnuts—there was always Dunkin, and the ever-reliable Twin Donuts—but they always, *always* took second fiddle to the traditional breakfast bagels and bialys. New Yorkers fell hard and fast for Krispy's doughnuts, though, and early reports are that bagel sales are starting to suffer. What's the world coming to? Krispy made its first New York beachhead in **Chelsea,** at 265 W. 23rd St. (☎ 212/620-0111), then marched uptown, opening branches on **125th Street** and at 141 W. 72nd St. on the **Upper West Side,** between Broadway and Columbus Ave. (☎ 212/724-1100). Another was opened at **Penn Station,** the better to lure in unsuspecting commuters, and by the time you read this they will have started corrupting our youth by opening a branch on 8th Street, near the NYU campus in the **West Village.** Krispy central command says that together, the NYU and 72nd Street branches will have the capacity to produce *over 5,000 doughnuts an hour.* We are surely doomed.

Best Bagels in New York

Although the competition has been going on for some time, the winner has not yet been crowned. We leave the decision to you; here are the two top competitors: **H&H Bagels** (three locations: 2239 Broadway at 80th Street, ☎ 212/595-8003, open daily 24 hours; 1551 Second Ave. at 80th Street, ☎ 212/734-7441; and 639 W. 46th St. between Eleventh Avenue and the West Side Highway, ☎ 212/595-8000); and **Ess-A-Bagel** (two locations: 831 Third Ave. at 51st Street, ☎ 212/980-1010; and 359 First Ave. at 21st Street, ☎ 212/260-2252). Down in the West Village, **Bagels on the Square** (7 Carmine St., near the intersection of Bleecker and Sixth Avenue in the West Village, ☎ 212/691-3041) is less traditional with their product, which means the bagel cognoscenti pretty much shun them. Still, one of their warm multi-grain bagels with butter is mighty fine. In general, our suggestion wherever you go is to look for the **hot bagel** sign, which indicates that bagels are baked fresh on the premises.

If da Place Is Doity, Don't Eat 'Dere

A word of warning for the food scene in New York: In the last couple of years there's been an increasing number of hepatitis cases reported, largely brought about by the poor hygienic conditions during food preparation. Although the city has reacted with stricter rules and controls, it's a good idea to keep an eye on what and where you eat. Don't eat in places that look dirty, and look around for customers; if it's a very popular place, it's also likely to be safe. These basic rules are particularly important for street carts—one of the major sources of problems— and for sandwiches and salad bars in delis.

A Slice of Heaven

Pizza in New York is as ubiquitous as yellow cabs. Here are some of the tastier slices in town: **California Pizza Oven** (122 University Place at 12th Street, ☎ 212/989-4225); **Mariella Pizza** (225 W. 57th St. at Broadway, next to the Hard Rock Cafe, ☎ 212/757-3016, with two other locations at 960 Eighth Ave. and 180 Third Ave. at the corner of 16th Street); **Pintaile's Pizza** (29 E. 91st St. between Madison and Fifth avenues, ☎ 212/722-1967, with two other locations on York Avenue at 84th Street and 77th Street), whose small 91st Street storefront is ideally located for a little break from Museum Mile (and the dough is organic, too); **St. Marks Pizza** (23 Third Ave. at St. Mark's, ☎ 212/420-9531); **Two Boots to Go-Go** (74 Bleecker St. between Broadway and Lafayette, ☎ 212/777-1033; and 75 Greenwich Ave. at Seventh Avenue, ☎ 212/633-9096). If you're visiting the Cathedral of St. John the Divine, drop into **Koronet Pizzeria,** on Broadway between 110th and 111th streets (☎ 212/222-1566). Just one of their aptly named "jumbo slices" will get you through the rest of the day.

Delis & Salad Bars

Delis and salad bars are a great place to have a good and inexpensive lunch. Most of the best ones are clustered in central Midtown, where lots of offices are to be found. The famous and popular ones have an incredible selection of American and Asian dishes, from roasted turkey with gravy and mashed potatoes to crispy sesame chicken and broccoli, plus large selections of fresh and cooked vegetables, fruit, and fish (whole carp and salmon, not just little fish fragments). On the west side, go to **Flavors** (8 W. 18th St. between Fifth and Sixth avenues, ☎ 212/647-1234), or **Canova** (140 W. 51st St. between Sixth and Seventh avenues, ☎ 212/969-9200), which also has a Mongolian barbecue where you select your choice of extremely fresh thinly sliced veggies, meat, and fish, and then the cooks sauté it with the sauce of your choice. On the east side, the best choices are **Del Monico Gourmet Food**

Market (Lexington Avenue between 42nd and 41st streets, ☎ **212/661-0510;** 320 Park Ave., ☎ **212/317-8777;** and 55 East 59th St., ☎ **212/751-5559**), and **Regency Gourmet** (801 Second Ave. between 42nd and 43rd streets, ☎ **212/661-3322**), which has a great selection of fresh baked and grilled fish. Downtown, our preferred choice is **Grassroots** (520 Broadway, just south of Spring Street, ☎ **212/344-2444**), where you have a choice of gourmet organic dishes, mostly vegetarian though you also find great and wonderfully prepared chicken and cheese. Another good place is **Dean & De Luca** (the mother ship—with a large grocery—is at 560 Broadway between Prince and Spring streets, ☎ **212/226-6800,** but there are branches all over town: 75 University Place at 13th Street, ☎ **212/473-1908;** 1 Wall Street Court, ☎ **212/514-5368,** and 121 Prince St., between Mercer and Greene streets, ☎ **212/254-8776,** are only some addresses).

"But Who on Earth Is Ray?!?"

You'll be asking yourself that question while strolling the streets of Manhattan, where it seems like most of the pizza joints are called Ray's something or other. Well, Ray actually did exist. One of the first successful pizza places was Famous Ray's Pizza of Greenwich Village (465 Sixth Ave. at 11th Street). As a result, today his name is used as a synonym for "best pizza in New York" by all those pizza parlors that claim Ray's heritage. Ray's pizza became famous for the large amount of cheese on top. So, if you like your slice overloaded, that's the place to go. (The newest trend is for thin and crusty pizza with a not-too-greasy topping, but sometimes that grease is so *good*.)

Fast & Cheap

It's best to stay away from the national fast food chains—why eat generic when you can have a New York taste sensation?—but if you're in a rush and don't want pizza or a bagel, then try one of the more interesting chain options.

Various places around town offer Mexican food, such as **California Burrito Co.** (several locations all around the city, including 750 Seventh Ave. at 49th Street, ☎ **212/265-4433;** and 4 World Financial Center, 250 Vesey St., ☎ **212/233-6800**) or **Fresco Tortilla Grill** (also several locations, among them 36 Lexington Ave. between 23rd and 24th streets, ☎ **212/475-7380;** and 546 Third Ave. between 35th and 36th streets, ☎ **212/685-3886**), which has really good food and fast deliveries.

For sandwiches, **Blimpy's,** which got its start across the river in Hoboken, New Jersey, is a reliable and easy-to-find choice: They're *everywhere.*

If you really have to go to a McDonald's, then go to the Wall Street branch (160 Broadway at Cortlandt Street, ☎ **212/385-2063**), where the door is opened for you by a doorman wearing a tuxedo, you wait to be seated, there's live piano accompaniment for lunch, and the latest Dow Jones quotes flash by on an electronic screen.

A Dog with Everything

In New York, hot dogs take the place of apple pie in that old "Mom and apple pie" thing (and they almost take the place of mom). If you're in a rush, on the fly, or just in a New York state of mind, they're a great choice, especially in cold weather. Great and cheap places for hot dogs in Manhattan are **Papaya King** (179 E. 86th St. at Third Avenue, ☎ **212/369-0648**), which also offers fruit shakes, and **Gray's Papaya** (2090 Broadway at 72nd Street, ☎ **212/799-0243**; and 402 Sixth Ave. at 8th Street, ☎ **212/260-3532**), which also offers tropical drinks and is open 24 hours.

The other place to get hot dogs in the city is at one of the innumerable…

Street Carts

You'll find street carts selling just about everything. Most of them cater to office crowds and starving workers with little time, so you're more likely to see them in busy areas like Midtown, around hospitals, and near government buildings. These are also the ones that offer the best quality food, in general. In the morning, until 11am, there are breakfast carts that offer decent coffee and a selection of doughnuts, generally mediocre bagels, and muffins; at lunch time, you can have hot dogs, skewers, or falafel—a pita pocket filled with fried chick pea balls, lettuce, tomatoes, and sesame sauce. The best is **Moshe's Falafel** (at the southeast corner of 46th Street and Sixth Avenue— see the write-up in chapter 9), but there are equivalents on the east side around 42nd Street. Potato knishes are another popular item, as are the legendary and almost totemic soft pretzels. *Hint:* Hot dogs, pretzels, and knishes should never cost you more than about a buck a pop. If someone tries to charge you more than, say, $1.50, you're being ripped off. Go elsewhere.

You Want Some Fries with That?

New Yorkers like to think that everything good in the world started here, and while for the most part that's true, there are exceptions, a recent one being the invasion of **Belgian-style French fries.** If you've ever been to Europe, you know about this one: shops that sell nothing but fries, but with a mind-boggling list of toppings, many of them based on mayonnaise—yes, mayonnaise, just in case the fries don't have *enough* cholesterol by themselves. The fries are made fresh as you order them, and are just the right combination of hot, crispy on the outside, and fluffy on the inside. As for the toppings, you have the option of going traditional with catsup or choosing from such odd-ball but delicious choices as Parmesan peppercorn, Mediterranean pepper mayonnaise, blue cheese, Hawaiian pineapple mustard, Dijon mustard, hot or mild curry sauce, or any one of a dozen others.

150

As of this writing, two Belgian fry places have opened downtown, but if their popularity is any yardstick, there may be dozens by the time you get here. In the East Village, check out **Pommes Frites,** 123 Second Ave., between 7th and 8th streets (☎ **212/674-1234**); and in the West Village, try **Le Frite Kot,** 148 W. 4th St., between Sixth Ave. and Washington Square Park (☎ **212/979-2616**). Orders generally run from $2.50 to $4, depending on size, and fancy toppings are an extra 50¢.

A Nice Bowl of Chicken Soup—and More

Another recent craze in New York is to have soup for lunch. Probably thinking that it is a more healthy and "dietetic" choice—and certainly heart-warming in winter—office crowds line up at the many soup joints that have opened in the city. The most famous is **Soup Kitchen International** (259A W. 55th St. at Eighth Avenue, ☎ **212/757-7730**, but don't phone unless you want a very rude answer), celebrated in the New York-based TV serial *Seinfeld;* the soup is as good as they say. Other good places are **Daily Soup,** with locations all around town (21 E. 41st St. at Madison Avenue, ☎ **212/953-7687**; 325 Park Ave. South, ☎ **212/531-7687**) and **Soup Nutsy** (148 E. 46th St. at Lexington Avenue, ☎ **212/927-8800**).

I Scream, You Scream...

The number of places to have ice cream or frozen yogurt has multiplied in recent years, especially with the craze for reduced-fat treats. Basically every deli in New York sells freshly made frozen yogurt and ready-made ice cream. Chains such as **Haagen Dazs** and **Baskin Robbins** have stores in the city, but the best of all is **Ben & Jerry's** ice cream. Not only is their ice cream delicious—the Vermont-based firm uses natural and fresh ingredients—but they redistribute part of their profits to various good causes, including the protection of the environment and support to impoverished children.

In addition to chains, some New York-based firms make terrific homemade ice cream. The best is **Moondog Ice Cream** (three locations in Manhattan: 378 Bleecker St. between Perry and Charles streets, ☎ **212/675-4540**; 166 Bleecker St. between Sullivan and Thompson streets, ☎ **212/260-9740**; and One Hundred Forty Seventh Ave. A between 9th and 10th streets, ☎ **212/328-0167**), which offers innovative and traditional flavors, all like homemade and all good. Try chocolate-orange, coconut, or peanut butter, or go wild with cardamom or black chocolate stout. Be prepared to line up for after-dinner treats in summer; it's worth it!

If you feel in the mood for something different, the **Chinatown Ice Cream Factory** (65 Bayard St. between Mott and Elizabeth streets, ☎ **212/608-4170**) has wonderful exotic flavors such as ginger, lichee, and papaya. Their ice cream is delightful and well worth the detour, and perfect after a meal in Chinatown.

Folk Music & Falafel

Back in the 1960s, the area around **MacDougal Street** in Greenwich Village was a hotbed of folk music, coffee houses, and Bohemian living. Nowadays, the folk music is mostly gone and the coffee houses survive in a somewhat less revolutionary form, but that staple of MacDougal Street Bohemian cuisine—the falafel—keeps going strong. Never had a falafel? You're in for a treat. What it is is a pocket of pita bread stuffed with mashed and fried chick peas, lettuce, tomatoes, white sauce, and maybe onions and/or hot sauce, depending on where you go. They're filling, delicious, and each one will only cost you a couple bucks. While MacDougal is lined with falafel shops (all of which are good) the most legendary—and the smallest—is **Mamoun's Falafel,** near the corner of W. 3rd St. Look closely, 'cause the storefront isn't much more than a doorway wide. They're open till all hours, and are almost always crowded, so don't count on getting a seat at one of the few tables. If the weather is good, take your food a block north to Washington Square Park and have a picnic. (For Midtown falafel, see the box on **Moshe's** in chapter 9.)

Pastries & Sweet Breaks

You feel like something sweet? **Ellen's Cafe and Bake Shop** (270 Broadway at Chambers Street, ☎ 212/962-1257) is a spot where you can have good muffins and maybe meet New York's mayor and other big wheels when they take their coffee break from the neighboring city hall. If you're on the east side, you can find delicious challah bread, rugelach, and cookies at **Moishe's Kosher Bake Shop** (115 Second Ave. at 8th Street, ☎ 212/378-2890). At **Ferrara** (195 Grand St. between Mulberry and Mott streets, ☎ 212/226-6150) you can find the best coffee in town and a great selection of Italian ice cream and pastries, to stay or to go. Another Italian place worth a visit is **Veniero's** (342 E. 11th St. at First Avenue, ☎ 212/674-7070); choose your pastry and sit down for a hot drink (go for the creamy stuff); we love it and we're not the only ones: It's often crowded.

If you're on the west side, there are several great places to have coffee and dessert in style: **Café Mozart** (154 W. 70th St. between Broadway and Columbus Avenue, ☎ 212/595-9797) for a Viennese atmosphere, and **Café Lalo** (201 W. 83rd St. between Amsterdam Avenue and Broadway, ☎ 212/496-6031). And if you're visiting the Cathedral of St. John the Divine, stop at the **Hungarian Pastry Shop** (1030 Amsterdam Ave. between 110th and 111th streets, ☎ 212/866-4230), which has great cookies and good desserts.

Greenwich Village has a number of pastry shops on Bleecker Street, but none is better than **The Magnolia Bakery** (401 Bleecker Street at W. 11th

St., ☎ **212/462-2572**), where scrumptious homemade cakes, pastries, and pies are baked following tried-and-true recipes.

Brew Me a Cold One—NYC Microbreweries

If you feel like a beer, you have the choice to go to one of the regular bars (see chapter 20) or check out one of the microbreweries that sprung up like mushrooms over the last 3 or 4 years (though natural selection has begun to weed out the weaker ones). Some make really good beer and often offer more than pub food. If you want the latest news on the beer scene, check out **The New York City Beer Guide** website at **www.nycbeer.org/toc.html**, which lists addresses, reviews, special events, and more.

The **Chelsea Brewing Company** (Pier 59 at 18th St., ☎ **212/336-6440**) is New York's largest microbrewery and our preferred one. Not only is the beer great, but you have a really great view over the Hudson River. The best time to show up is at sunset on the large terrace.

Another great one is **Heartland Brewery** (35 Union Square West, ☎ **212/ 645-3400**), which has a good and large selection. Others are the **Typhoon Brewery** (22 E. 54th St., ☎ **212/754-9006**) and **Hansen's Times Square Brewery** (160 W. 42nd St., ☎ **212/398-1234**), which is actually a good place to bring kids.

If you're over in Brooklyn Heights to catch the view from the Promenade, stop in to the Brooklyn Heights branch of the **Park Slope Brewing Company,** located at 62 Henry St. (☎ **718/522-4801**), only a few blocks from the entrance to the Brooklyn Bridge walkway. A full range of their home-brewed beer is always on tap, from a light Belgian blonde ale to a heady porter and a truly amazing Irish dry stout.

Part 5

Ready, Set, Go! Exploring New York

Now that you have a place to hang your hat and food in your stomach, you're ready to do what you went to all this trouble for in the first place: See the city. The following chapters will help you decide what you want to see and help you figure out how you're going to see it.

There are so many things to see in New York that you'll have to prioritize the "top sights," always tailoring your list to your specific interests. Beyond the major institutions, hosts of lesser-known attractions are available in each area.

Then of course there's shopping to consider. New York is, after all, capitalism central; there are famous major department stores like Macy's and Bloomingdale's, glamorous Fifth Avenue boutiques, funky downtown clothing shops, and clusters of interesting small shops where you can find just about anything made by the hand of man—and some other stuff, too. You'll have to plan well in order to sandwich your shopping in between hitting the attractions.

In this section we recommend several itineraries that take in the major sights, giving you some constructive help in shaping your itinerary but allowing plenty of leeway so that your trip doesn't become too regimented. Last, but hardly least, is nightlife. You may already have booked tickets for a show (see chapter 4), but you probably have some other evenings to play with, and we'll provide you with the background to make spontaneous choices as the spirit moves you.

Chapter 12

Should I Just Take a Guided Tour?

In This Chapter

➤ Orientation tours

➤ River cruises

➤ Architectural and historical tours

➤ Special-interest tours

There are several reasons to take a tour, some of them good, some of them (if you'll forgive the pun) misguided. As we mentioned in chapter 1, one option is to arrange a package or an escorted tour that will take you sightseeing around the city. Of course, if you're not very mobile, a guided tour is a way to safely cover more ground than you might be able to by yourself. And if you're a very nervous traveler who wants a lot of structure, a guided tour will mean at least a few hours in which you don't have to do anything but look and listen.

If you think, however, that a tour is going to teach you the city rather than just show it, guess again. We really are talking about sight*seeing*. Tour guides (that's the person up front, screaming into the mike to be heard above the roar of traffic) aren't always well-informed, and when they are, aren't always comprehensible. Keep this in mind when making your decision.

Time-Savers

The rule for sightseeing tours is do your homework: A little studying-up on New York's history and architecture will go a long way toward preparing you to understand what you'll see. Fortunately, there are dozens of great books on the city, some written from a general perspective and some on a very specific topic. If you're particularly interested in architecture, Gerard R. Wolfe's *New York: A Guide to the Metropolis* (McGraw-Hill, 1988) is an invaluable reference. Read it before you go and you may know more than your tour guide.

Here's the Church & Here's the Steeple— Orientation Tours

Several companies offer general city tours. None of the them are renowned for erudition, accuracy, or comprehensibility.

New York Apple Tours offers a multitude of tours using double-decker London buses. In good weather, you can sit up top in the open. The largest dose is the full-city, 46-stop, two-day, hop-on, hop-off tour ($25 adults, $16 children under 12). The smaller tours ($16 adults, $10 children) include a downtown tour that runs day and night; an uptown tour that basically circles Central Park, passing through Harlem; and a Hudson River waterfront tour that covers some of the same sights as the downtown tour. New York Apple also runs a State of Liberty Express that includes the full-city tour plus the lady ($39 adults, $23 kids). Operates daily, opens at 9am Eighth Avenue at 50th Street; Seventh Avenue at 41st Street, ☎ **800/876-9868** or 212/944-9200. Subway: C/E to 50th Street stop; N/R/S/1/2/3/7/9 to Times Square stop.

Dollars & Sense

Sometimes you can save money on tours by booking in advance—for example, **New York Apple Tours** will give you a 10% discount if you reserve ahead.

Gray Line New York Tours offers pretty much the same options as New York Apple, plus a lot of other permutations, including helicopter and harbor tours. Prices are generally lower and you see the same stuff. Gray Line also uses double-deckers, and they have trolleys (one nice trolley tour goes through Central Park). They have a 2-day Grand Tour ($27 adults, $13.50 children under 12), a Grand Tour plus Statue of Liberty ($33/$19), and uptown or downtown tours ($17/$8.50). Operates daily, opens at 9am Port

Authority Bus Terminal, Eighth Avenue at 42nd Street, ☎ **212/397-2600.**
Subway: A/C/E to Port Authority, or N/R/S/1/2/3/7/9 to Times Square and
walk.

New York Double-Decker Tours is another variation on the theme. This
one is probably the cheapest, but you get what you pay for. The 2-day hop-
along tour costs $17 for adults, $10 for children under 12. 350 Fifth Ave. (at
34th Street), Suite 6104, ☎ **212/967-6008.**

Dollars & Sense

Say you're a reader. Say you read five books about New York history before
you came. Why not take a bus tour for $1.50, courtesy of the Transit Authority,
and narrate it yourself? You could take the no. 1 all the way down Fifth
Avenue from Museum Mile to 42nd Street, and then change to the 104 and
go across to Times Square, up Broadway through the Theater District, past
Lincoln Center, and on to the Upper West Side. Or stay on the no. 1 all the
way to City Hall and Battery Park. A little ingenuity (and $1.50) goes a long
way.

Rollin' on the River—Cruises Around Manhattan
Seeing Manhattan from the water has to be one of the most romantic ways
to experience the city. It's also the way millions of people in an earlier era
first saw it, when they arrived by ship and were processed at Ellis Island.
Although the Circle Line is the most famous (see below), there are quite a
few other interesting options. The water-borne cruises generally get better
marks than do the buses for the quality and depth of the guides' narration.

New York Stories

Want to see the Hudson Canyon? Rent a submarine. Before the melting of the
glaciers at the end of the last Ice Age, when the ocean's level was much lower,
the Hudson River extended another 100 miles. This trench now lies offshore
below the Atlantic Ocean.

The main **Circle Line Sightseeing Cruise** is the 3-hour, 35-mile circum-
navigation of Manhattan ($20 adults, $10 children). That means you see

Lower Manhattan from both sides, pass through Spuyten Duyvil—sounds like a monster, doesn't it? It's actually a spot at the top of the island, where the Harlem River meets the Hudson—go under the George Washington Bridge, and then pass down through Hell Gate, the often turbid spot where the East River and the Harlem River meet. Above Midtown, the view is kind of boring. There's a snack bar aboard; this cruise runs March to December.

Recognizing that not everyone wants so much time on the water, Circle Line also has an "express cruise" for fidgeters that lasts only 2 hours, is a bit cheaper ($17 adults, $9 children), and runs April to November. Other options include a 2-hour family cruise (weekends, May–July; $15/$5); a Harbor Lights Cruise (daily, May–Oct; $20/$10); and a DJ cruise that runs from 10pm–midnight, Friday and Saturday (May–Oct; $20). A jazz cruise operates sporadically in the summer. Pier 83, at West 42nd Street and Twelfth Avenue, ☎ **212/563-3200.** Subway: A/C/E to Port Authority, or N/R/S/1/2/3/7/9 to Times Square and walk.

New York Stories

The Circle Line's boats are former World War II landing craft used by the U.S. Navy. Some are combat veterans.

Seaport Liberty Cruises leave from South Street Seaport and offer a touch of Old New York. At 1 hour, the cruise is shorter than the Circle Line and nearly half as expensive ($12 adults, $6 children under 12), but it covers the best sights: southern Manhattan, the Statue of Liberty, and Ellis Island. The restored vessels are more picturesque. Nighttime music cruises—with the option of jazz, blues, or rock—are offered in the warmer months (May–Sept; call for details and prices). The basic cruise runs April to November (weekends only in Dec and Mar). Pier 16, at South Street Seaport, ☎ **212/ 630-8888.** Subway: 2/3/4/5 to Fulton Street.

New York Waterways is another company that offers a harbor cruise, this one lasting 1½ hours and costing $16 for adults and $8 for children. What sets Waterways apart, though, is two interesting, all-day cruises upriver into the Hudson Valley. The Sleepy Hollow cruise ($35) docks at Tarrytown; from there, you take a bus to Philipsburg Manor, a working Dutch Colonial farm, and Sunnyside, the whimsical, gem-like home of Washington Irving, author of *The Legend of Sleepy Hollow*. The Kykuit Cruise ($60) takes in Philipsburg as well as one of the Rockefeller estates (Kykuit), which has a

Dollars & Sense

When you call to reserve a cruise, don't forget that most of the companies offer a **senior discount,** sometimes of 50% off the full adult fare.

collection of art, antique cars, and a beautiful view. The cruise is very popular and reservations are necessary. The harbor cruise runs daily (Mar–Nov), and the others run Thursday to Sunday (Memorial Day–Oct). Pier 78 at West 38th Street and Twelfth Avenue, ☎ **800/533-3779.** Subway: A/C/E to Port Authority, or N/R/S/1/2/3/7/9 to Times Square and walk.

If you're the "star to steer by" type, two sailing ships offer cruises of the harbor. The ***Petrel*** is a 1938-vintage 70-foot Sparkman & Stephens wooden yacht that offers 2-hour sailings for around $20 for adults and $13 for children, depending on when you go. The boat sails daily from May to September. Call for times and definitely for reservations, since the *Petrel's* capacity is only 35 passengers. No narration. Battery Park, near the Staten Island Ferry Terminal, ☎ **212/825-1976.** Subway: 1/9 to South Ferry.

The schooner ***Pioneer,*** built in 1885, had her rig cut down and did time as a barge before being restored to her original condition. Once used to carry lumber (the square doors in the bow are where the logs were slid in), the boat is 110 feet long. In contrast to the *Petrel,* where you're just a passenger, here you're allowed to help sail the ship. Cruises, lasting two hours ($16 adults, $6 children) are not narrated; reservations are strongly recommended. The boat sails daily, May to September, from South Street Seaport just behind the huge four-master *Peking.* ☎ **212/748-8786.** Subway: 2/3/4/5 to Fulton Street.

Extra! Extra!

Spirit Cruises (☎ 212/727-2789) and **World Yacht (☎ 212/630-8100)** run romantic, formal dinner cruises with entertainment included on big, swanky boats, but you're likely to pay up to $80 per adult for the cruise and meal.

Billed as "America's only gay sailing tea dance," the **Sea Tea** excursion departs from Pier 40 (2 blocks below Christopher Street), and the $15 charge includes a buffet dinner. The boat boards at 6pm, departs at 7:30pm, and returns at 10pm. Sundays only. Tickets can be purchased in advance (even through Ticketmaster, ☎ **212/307-7171**) or at 5pm on Pier 40. Information: ☎ **212/675-HELP.** Tickets: ☎ **800/988-1181** or 212/242-3222. Subway: 1/9 to Christopher Street, walk west to river, then south to Pier 40.

George Washington Slept Here—Architectural & Historical Tours

Most of the walking tours listed in this section will take you to various neighborhoods in Manhattan and tell you more than you're likely ever to find out by yourself outside of a college history classroom. Many operators will give you a good price on a private tour, or you can be hooked up with a group. Ask about group size when you call to reserve.

Big Onion Walking Tours has highly educated, enthusiastic guides who take you through the neighborhoods of Lower Manhattan. They also visit Ellis Island and Governors Island. Price: $9–$15. ☎ **212/439-1090.**

Joyce Gold History Tours of New York have been around for 20 years. The tours are on foot, on weekends, and in neighborhoods from Harlem to Wall Street. Weekends, Mar–Nov; $12. ☎ 212/242-5762.

Citywalks cover Midtown and downtown, but are particularly good for the neighborhoods at the southern end of the island. $12. ☎ 212/989-2456.

Adventure on a Shoestring is exactly that: For a low price they take you on a weekend tour of New York neighborhoods. The organization operates something like a club, so that, in addition to the public tours (which cost $5), they offer special tours that you get access to by paying a $40 membership fee. ☎ 212/265-2663.

The Museum of the City of New York runs tours on weekends, sometimes theme-oriented, sometimes focused on neighborhoods. You couldn't ask for more solid institutional backing. ☎ 212/534-1672, ext. 206.

Special-Interest Tours
Special tours that focus on one feature of the city can be great fun. Try one of these:

➤ **Big Onion** (see above) runs a multi-ethnic eating tour that runs (or walks) the gamut of cuisine, from Italian to Chinese.

➤ **Urban Explorations,** in addition to neighborhood tours, does such specials as garden tours and a gay and lesbian tour. $12. ☎ 718/721-5254.

➤ The **New York City Transit Museum** offers a variety of tours dealing with the city's subways and their history, including occasional "Nostalgia Train" rides aboard a 1928-model subway. Call at least a week ahead for information and to make reservations. $9–$15. ☎ 718/243-8601.

➤ **Radical Walking Tours** uncovers the subversive history of New York, from anarchism to the Civil Rights movement. $6. ☎ 718/492-0069.

➤ **Wild Food Tours** offers a walk on the wild side—go to Central Park, find edible plants, and eat them, guided by a naturalist and ecologist. Suggested contribution, $10. ☎ 718/291-6825.

➤ **Harlem Spirituals** offers gospel and jazz tours that combine a tour of Harlem with performances and southern food. $33–$75, depending on events. ☎ 212/757-0425.

Free Walking Tours
To prove that you can get something for nothing, the following free walking tours are offered by various groups in the Midtown area.

➤ The **Grand Central Partnership** (☎ 212/818-1777) tours 42nd Street, including the Chrysler Building and Grand Central, on Fridays at 12:30pm, departing from the Whitney Museum at Philip Morris, 42nd St. and Park Avenue.

➤ The **34th Street Partnership** conducts a tour with an architectural historian and an architect, Thursdays at 12:30pm Call ☎ 212/868-0521 for information.

➤ One of the things that's looking up in Times Square is the tour given through the **Times Square Business Improvement District**. The guides are actors and take you through the Theater District on Fridays at noon. Meet at the Embassy Theater, Broadway and 46th Street.

Don't Forget

Refer back to Chapter 1 for information about the **Big Apple Greeter** personalized neighborhood tours (☎ **212/669-2896,** fax 212/669-3685), which you'll have to book before you travel. Also don't forget the "Guide to Lesbian & Gay New York Historical Landmarks" published by and available from the Organization of Lesbian and Gay Architects and Designers (☎ **212/475-7652**).

Chapter 13

New York's Top Sights from A to Z

In This Chapter

➤ Attractions indexed by location and type

➤ Full write-ups of all the top attractions in town

➤ Your personal Greatest Hits list and a worksheet for making your choices

---

In this chapter, we start off with indexes that list all the top sights by location and by type (museums, parks, historic buildings, and so on), so that, for instance, when you come out of the Metropolitan Museum of Art and say "What else is there to do around here?" you can turn to the Midtown East listing and find the nearest museum. After that, we review all the big sights, giving you the info you need to get there, get in, and see what you came to see.

Even working just from this list, though, there's much more than you could possibly see unless you're planning a really long trip, so here's what you do: Defy everything your parents and teachers ever told you about defacing books and scrawl your relative level of interest right in the margins next to the reviews. Rank them using a scale of 1 to 5, with #1s being number ones—your numero uno, big-pick, must-see attractions—and #5s being the sights you could live without seeing. At the end of the chapter we've provided a chart where you can list these all out together, and in chapter 16 we give some pointers on linking these sights logically, so you don't have to go ping-ponging all over the island to get from one sight to another. Chapter 17 provides some help in narrowing your focus if you find yourself with too much to do and too little time to do it.

Note where we've indicated sights especially suited to travelers with children, so that you can keep everybody happy.

Quick Picks—New York's Top Attractions at a Glance
Index by Location

Upper West Side

American Museum of Natural History

Cathedral of St. John the Divine

Central Park

Upper East Side

Central Park

Guggenheim Museum

Metropolitan Museum of Art

Midtown West

Empire State Building

Intrepid Sea-Air-Space Museum

Museum of Modern Art

New York Public Library and Bryant Park

Rockefeller Center

Times Square

Midtown East

Chrysler Building

Fifth Avenue

Grand Central Terminal

St. Patrick's Cathedral

United Nations

23rd Street to Canal Street

Flatiron Building and District

Gramercy Park

Greenwich Village

Little Italy

SoHo

Washington Square

Downtown

Battery Park City and Hudson River Park

Brooklyn Bridge

Chinatown

Ellis Island

New York Stock Exchange

St. Paul's Chapel

South Street Seaport and Museum

Staten Island Ferry

Statue of Liberty

Wall Street

World Trade Center

Index by Type of Attraction
Museums

American Museum of Natural History

Ellis Island

Guggenheim Museum

Intrepid Sea-Air-Space Museum

Metropolitan Museum of Art

Museum of Modern Art

South Street Seaport and Museum

Parks

Battery Park City and Hudson River Park

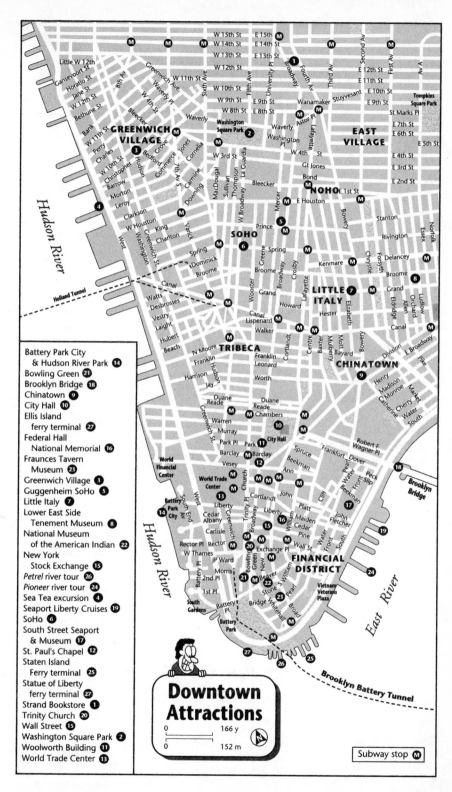

Downtown Attractions

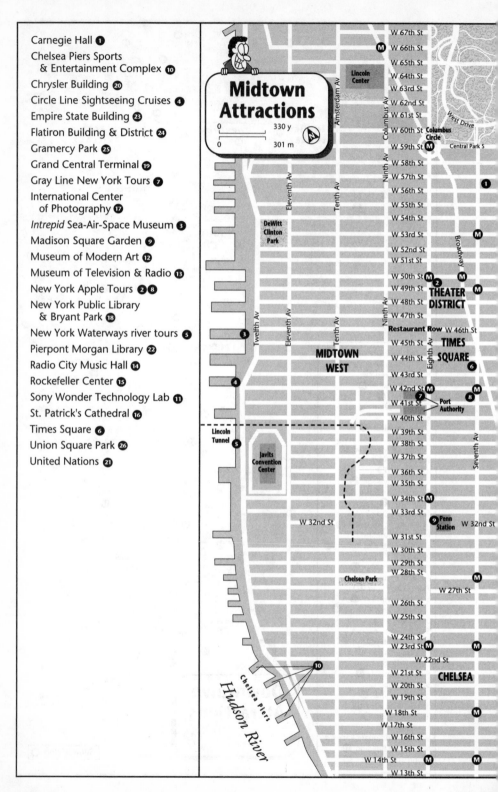

Carnegie Hall ❶

Chelsea Piers Sports
& Entertainment Complex ❿

Chrysler Building ⓴

Circle Line Sightseeing Cruises ❹

Empire State Building ㉓

Flatiron Building & District ㉔

Gramercy Park ㉕

Grand Central Terminal ⓳

Gray Line New York Tours ❼

International Center
of Photography ⓱

Intrepid Sea-Air-Space Museum ❸

Madison Square Garden ❾

Museum of Modern Art ⓬

Museum of Television & Radio ⓭

New York Apple Tours ❷❽

New York Public Library
& Bryant Park ⓲

New York Waterways river tours ❺

Pierpont Morgan Library ㉒

Radio City Music Hall ⓮

Rockefeller Center ⓯

Sony Wonder Technology Lab ⓫

St. Patrick's Cathedral ⓰

Times Square ❻

Union Square Park ㉖

United Nations ㉑

**Midtown
Attractions**

0   330 y

0   301 m

Lincoln
Center

West Drive

Columbus
Circle

Central Park S

Amsterdam Av

Columbus Av

Ninth Av

Eleventh Av

Tenth Av

Broadway

W 67th St

W 66th St

W 65th St

W 64th St

W 63rd St

W 62nd St

W 61st St

W 60th St

W 59th St

W 58th St

W 57th St

W 56th St

W 55th St

W 54th St

W 53rd St

W 52nd St

W 51st St

W 50th St

W 49th St

W 48th St

W 47th St

Restaurant Row   W 46th St

W 45th St

W 44th St

W 43rd St

W 42nd St

W 41st St

W 40th St

W 39th St

W 38th St

W 37th St

W 36th St

W 35th St

W 34th St

W 33rd St

W 32nd St

W 31st St

W 30th St

W 29th St

W 28th St

W 27th St

W 26th St

W 25th St

W 24th St

W 23rd St

W 22nd St

W 21st St

W 20th St

W 19th St

W 18th St

W 17th St

W 16th St

W 15th St

W 14th St

W 13th St

THEATER
DISTRICT

TIMES
SQUARE

Eighth Av

Seventh Av

MIDTOWN
WEST

Twelfth Av

Eleventh Av

Tenth Av

DeWitt
Clinton
Park

Lincoln
Tunnel

Javits
Convention
Center

Port
Authority

Penn
Station   W 32nd St

Chelsea Park

CHELSEA

Chelsea Piers

Hudson River

166

Abigail Adams Smith Museum ⑰

American Museum
of Natural History ②

Central Park Zoo/
Wildlife Conservation Center ⑮

The Children's Museum
of Manhattan ①

Dakota Apartments/
Strawberry Fields ③

El Museo del Barrio ⑥

Frick Collection ⑭

Gracie Mansion ⑪

Guggenheim Museum ⑩

International Center
of Photography ⑧

Jewish Museum ⑨

Lincoln Center ④

Metropolitan Museum of Art ⑫

Museum of the City
of New York ⑦

Rock-climbing wall
at Harmony Atrium ⑤

Roosevelt Island Tram ⑱

Whitney Museum ⑬

Wollman Rink ⑯

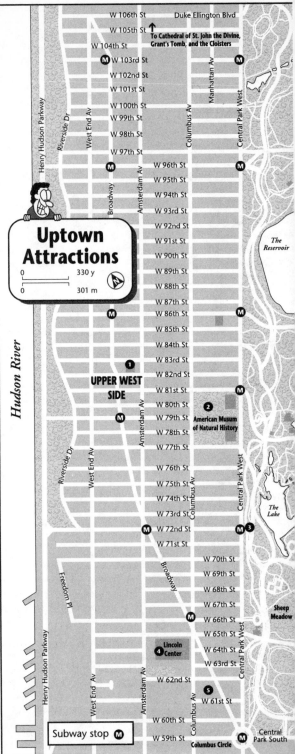

Uptown Attractions

0 ——— 330 y
0 ——— 301 m

W 106th St
W 105th St
W 104th St
W 103rd St
W 102nd St
W 101st St
W 100th St
W 99th St
W 98th St
W 97th St
W 96th St
W 95th St
W 94th St
W 93rd St
W 92nd St
W 91st St
W 90th St
W 89th St
W 88th St
W 87th St
W 86th St
W 85th St
W 84th St
W 83rd St
W 82nd St
W 81st St
W 80th St
W 79th St
W 78th St
W 77th St
W 76th St
W 75th St
W 74th St
W 73rd St
W 72nd St
W 71st St
W 70th St
W 69th St
W 68th St
W 67th St
W 66th St
W 65th St
W 64th St
W 63rd St
W 62nd St
W 61st St
W 60th St
W 59th St

Duke Ellington Blvd

To Cathedral of St. John the Divine,
Grant's Tomb, and the Cloisters

UPPER WEST
SIDE

American Museum
of Natural History

Lincoln
Center

The
Reservoir

The
Lake

Sheep
Meadow

Central
Park South

Columbus Circle

Hudson River

Henry Hudson Parkway
Riverside Dr
West End Av
Broadway
Amsterdam Av
Columbus Av
Manhattan Av
Central Park West
Freedom Pl

St. John's/ Grant's Tomb Area

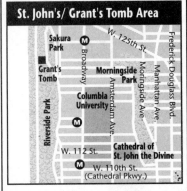

Sakura
Park

Grant's
Tomb

Morningside
Park

Columbia
University

W. 125th St.

W. 112 St.

Cathedral of
St. John the Divine

W. 110th St.
(Cathedral Pkwy.)

Broadway
Amsterdam Ave.
Morningside Ave.
Manhattan Ave.
Frederick Douglass Blvd.
Riverside Park

Take the 1/9 to 110th St. for
St. John's; to 116th or 125th st.
for Grant's Tomb.
For the Cloisters, take the A train
to 190th St. and continue north
into Ft. Tryon Park.

Subway stop Ⓜ

E 106th St
E 105th St
E 104th St
Wards Island Footbridge
Ward's Island Park
E 103rd St Ⓜ
Ward's Island
E 102nd St
E 101st St
E 100th St
Mount Sinai Hospital
E 99th St
E 98th St
E 97th St
Ⓜ
E 96th St
E 95th St
E 94th St
E 93rd St
E 92nd St
E 91st St
E 90th St
E 89th St
Carl Schurz Park
E 88th St
E 87th St
Ⓜ
Gracie Mansion
E 86th St
E 85th St
E 84th St
E 83rd St
E 82nd St
E 81st St
UPPER EAST SIDE
E 80th St
E 79th St
E 78th St
E 77th St
Ⓜ
E 76th St
E 75th St
E 74th St
E 73rd St
E 72nd St
E 71st St
E 70th St
E 69th St
E 68th St
Ⓜ
E 67th St
E 66th St
E 65th St
E 64th St
E 63rd St
Ⓜ
E 62nd St
From Lower Level
E 61st St
Roosevelt Island Tram
E 60th St
Ⓜ
Ⓜ
To Upper Level
E 59th St
Ⓜ
Queensboro Bridge

The Reservoir

MUSEUM MILE

Madison Av
Park Av
St
Lexington Av
Third Av
Second Av
First Av
York Av
East End Av
FDR Drive

The Great Lawn

Metropolitan Museum of Art

Fifth Av
Madison Av
Park Av
Lexington Av
Third Av
Second Av
York Av
Sutton Pl

Sheep Meadow

Central Park Zoo

Wollman Rink

Central Park South

East River

Roosevelt Island

6
7
8
9
10
11
12
13
14
15
16
17
18

Parks *continued*

Central Park

New York Public Library and
Bryant Park

United Nations

Washington Square Park

**Historic Buildings &
Architecture**

Brooklyn Bridge

Chrysler Building

Empire State Building

Flatiron Building and District

Grand Central Terminal

Guggenheim Museum

New York Public Library and
Bryant Park

New York Stock Exchange

Rockefeller Center

Statue of Liberty

United Nations

World Trade Center

Neighborhoods

Chinatown

Flatiron Building and District

Gramercy Park

Greenwich Village

Little Italy

SoHo

South Street Seaport and
Museum

Times Square

Wall Street

Churches

Cathedral of St. John the
Divine

St. Patrick's Cathedral

St. Paul's Chapel

The Top Sights

Kids American Museum of Natural History

Lions and tigers and bears (some of them shot by Teddy Roosevelt),
as well as renowned dinosaur displays, are among the attractions at
this enormous museum, which covers four city blocks. There are also displays of gems, meteorites, and minerals, as well as areas devoted to Native
American culture. Recent renovations have brought the museum up to date,
and there are interactive exhibits for kids. The IMAX theater has a screen
four stories tall (it'll cost you an extra couple dollars to get in to see it,
though). Allow at least a couple of hours to visit. Note that the Hayden
Planetarium is being demolished and a new facility will not be opened until
2000.

Central Park West between 77th and 81st streets (it occupies four blocks). ☎ *212/
769-5100.* **Subway:** *B/C train to 81 Street stop (at the north-east corner of the
museum), and then walk south along the front to the entrance.* **Bus:** *The M10
(north/south bus running on Central Park West, Eighth Avenue Uptown, and
Seventh Avenue Downtown) and the M79 (cross-town bus running on 79th Street)
are very convenient and stop right at the museum.* **Open:** *Sun–Thur 10am–
5:45pm; Fri–Sat 10am–8:45pm.* **Suggested Admission:** *$8 adults, $4.50
children between 2 and 12 (free under 2), $6 seniors.*

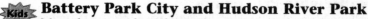

Battery Park City and Hudson River Park

More than a residential complex, Battery Park City is a great place to spend some time outside on the grass or look at the spectacular views of the Statue of Liberty, Ellis Island, and the harbor. Clustered around North Cove, a high-toned yacht basin, are shops and outdoor cafes. Check out the indoor Winter Garden and, outdoors, the funny bronze sculptures all over the place, showing strange figures and animals coming out of the ground. Kids love it.

On the Hudson River between Battery Park and Harrison Street, in addition, there's a pedestrian (plus bikes and roller blades) promenade that stretches all the way from Hudson River Park to Chelsea Piers up at 22nd Street, where you'll even find miniature golf. **Subway:** *1/9 train to Cortland Street or C/E train to World Trade Center, and then walk west toward the river.* **Bus:** *M10 (north/south bus running on Seventh Avenue/Varick Street Downtown and Eighth Avenue/Hudson Street Uptown) and M9 (cross-town bus running on East Broadway, Park Row, and West Street).* **Open:** *From dawn to dusk.*

> **Kid-Friendly Attractions**
>
> ➤ American Museum of Natural History
>
> ➤ Battery Park City and Hudson River Park
>
> ➤ Central Park
>
> ➤ Ellis Island
>
> ➤ Intrepid Sea–Air–Space Museum
>
> ➤ Metropolitan Museum of Art
>
> ➤ South Street Seaport and Museum
>
> ➤ Statue of Liberty
>
> ➤ United Nations
>
> ➤ World Trade Center

Brooklyn Bridge

"O harp and altar, of the fury fused" Hart Crane wrote of this bridge's graceful web of cables and impressive towers of stone. Whether you stroll halfway out to get a view of lower Manhattan or cross over to Brooklyn Heights, John Roebling's stone-and-steel marvel is a necessary visit. Begun in 1867, the construction was plagued with disasters and was not finished until 1883. (Crane also said "only in darkness is thy shadow clear," but you should be advised to go in daylight.)

Sidewalk entrance to the bridge is on Park Row, just across from City Hall south of Chambers Street. **Subway:** *4/5/6 train to Brooklyn Bridge/City Hall; you'll be just across the street from the entrance.* **Bus:** *M1 (north/south bus running down Broadway and up Center Street/Lafayette/Park and Madison avenues), though traffic congestion makes the subway a better choice.*

Brooklyn Heights Promenade

If you're walking across the Brooklyn Bridge, have a little extra time, and want a great view of Manhattan, take this tiny walking tour: When you reach the Brooklyn end of the bridge, go down the stairs, make a right when you hit the bottom, walk through the park to Henry Street, take Henry to Montague Street, make a right and walk till the street runs out. There you'll see the entrance to the promenade, which stretches for approximately one-half mile, lined by beautiful homes and overlooking the East River and a gorgeous stretch of skyline. Make sure you have film in your camera. After you've strolled and had your fill of the view, retrace your steps to Montague Street and explore for a while; this is one of the most charming neighborhoods in the city. When you're done, either backtrack and walk back across the bridge or catch the subway (2/3/4/5/M/N/R) at the intersection of Montague and Court streets.

Cathedral of St. John the Divine

Though it's still far from finished—even though it's been under construction for more than a century—St. John's is already the largest gothic cathedral in the world. It's an impressive and inspiring sight—not least for the fact that it's brought together all the diverse cultures of the city of New York. Begun in 1892, it is only two-thirds finished, but that's because no cheating is allowed: The cathedral is being built using traditional Gothic engineering and stone-cutting techniques, which European masters are teaching to young American apprentices. Different chapels commemorate various ethnic groups and traditions. It's a great idea to take a tour ($3), offered at 11am Tues–Sat and at 1pm on Sun. There are three services per day during the week (7:15am; 12:15pm; and 5:30pm) and four on Sun (8am, 9am, 11am, 7pm).

1047 Amsterdam Ave. between 110 and 113 streets. ☎ *212/316-7540.*
Subway: *1/9 train to Cathedral Parkway (110th Street) stop, and then walk one block east to Amsterdam Avenue and you'll see the Cathedral towering overhead.* ***Bus:*** *M11 (running up Tenth/Amsterdam Avenue and down Columbus/Ninth Avenue).* ***Suggested Admission:*** *$1 adults, 50¢ children under 18 and seniors.* ***Open:*** *Mon–Sat 7am–6pm; Sun 7am–7:30pm.*

Strawberry Fields Forever

The **Dakota Apartments,** where John Lennon lived and where he was murdered in 1980, are located on Central Park West between 72nd and 73rd streets. If you're a fan, it's worth a visit to see the place (the outside, at least—only residents are allowed into the building and courtyard) and to take a walk through **Strawberry Fields,** a public garden located immediately across from the building, in Central Park.

Even if you're not a fan, though, it's worth stopping to stare at the Dakota, which is one of the most magnificent buildings in the city. While you're standing there, keep this fact in mind: When the building was constructed in 1881, this neighborhood was so far away from the bustling hub of the city that it was considered the countryside, and in fact it *was* surrounded by farmland for a number of years. Detractors told the building's developer that he might as well be building in the Dakotas—and the name stuck.

Central Park

Who hasn't heard of Central Park? Without it, living in New York would be unbearable. It has 58 miles of paths winding through 843 acres. This is where Shakespeare in the Park and SummerStage take place (see chapter 19), and where you will find The Boathouse Restaurant and Tavern on the Green (see chapter 10). You can also rent a rowboat at the Loeb Boathouse (☎ 212/517-2233) for a paddle around the lake; take your child for a ride on the carousel to the sound of calliope music; skate at Wollman Rink (see chapter 14); or walk, rollerblade, picnic, run, fly a kite, play catch, or anything else you can think of. The farther north you go in the park, the fewer people, though even some areas at midpoint can be pretty secluded (for instance, the wooded Ramble at about 74th Street: beautiful, crisscrossed by paths, but spooky as darkness approaches). The largest open spaces are the Sheep Meadow and the recently restored Great Lawn, while the focal point of the park is the Mall and the Belvedere Fountain.

From 59th to 110th streets, between Fifth Avenue and Central Park West (the continuation north of Eighth Avenue). Information Center ☎ *212/794-6564.* ***Subway:*** *A/B/C/D/1/9 train to Columbus Circle stop for the southwest main entrance; N/R train to Fifth Avenue stop for the southeast main entrance.* ***Bus:*** *Buses run along both sides of Central Park and make several stops; the M10 runs up and down Central Park West, whereas the M1, M2, M3, and M4 run south down Fifth Avenue on the East side of the Park (they go north on Madison Avenue).* ***Open:*** *24 hours.*

Chinatown

Ever restless and expanding, Chinatown is one of New York's largest and most famous ethnic neighborhoods. From the brash, bustling market of Canal Street, the activity radiates in all directions. Baxter Street, East Broadway, and the smaller cross streets are lined with Chinese shops, groceries, herbalists, and restaurants. Whether you want dim sum or acupuncture, Chinatown is the place. (See map of Chinatown and Little Italy later in this chapter.)

South of Canal Street between Broadway and East Broadway. ***Subway:*** *J/M/N/R/Z/6 train to Canal stop and you'll be right in the center of action.* ***Bus:*** *Forget it; it gets too crowded. If you insist on taking the bus get on the M1 (running down Fifth/Park Avenue/Broadway and up Center Street/Park/Madison Avenue).*

Dollars & Sense

A great spot for one-stop shopping in Chinatown is the **Pearl River Chinese Department Store** (☎ 212/431-4770), located upstairs on the northeast corner of Canal Street and Broadway. You can get everything from Chinese groceries, soaps, and toiletries to clothing, kitchenware, and traditional musical instruments.

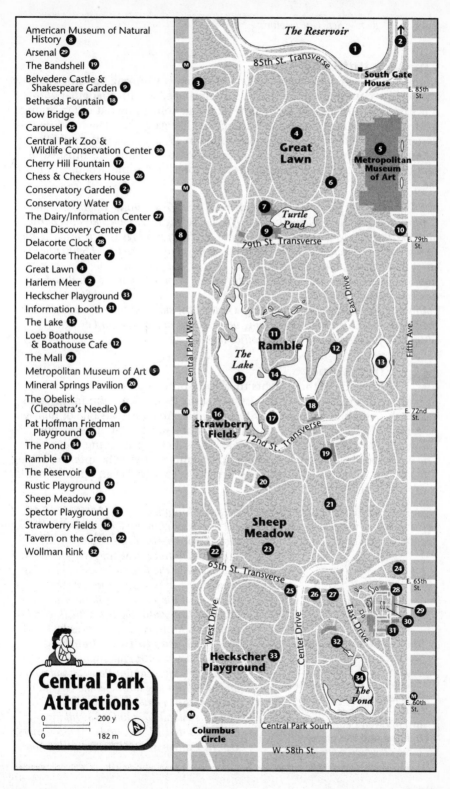

Chrysler Building

Number 405 Lexington Avenue is one of the most stunning buildings in New York or any city. Surmounted by a shiny steel needle, with triangular windows that are illuminated at night, it looks like something out of Oz. Strange steel sculptures are poised on its battlements like gargoyles. The building was designed by William Van Alen and finished in 1930, and was the world's tallest building until 1931, when the Empire State Building was finished. Be sure to visit the lobby—an art deco tour de force in chrome, wood, and marble.

*405 Lexington Ave. at 42nd Street. **Subway:** 4/5/6/7/S train to 42 Street/Grand Central stop, and then follow the exit signs for Lexington Avenue, pass the barrier, and take the passage in front of you toward the right; it brings you right inside the Chrysler at the lower level. If you miss this exit, get up to street level, cross the street walking east, and there it is. **Bus:** The bus is a good idea only well away from rush hours. Take the M104 from the Upper West Side (runs down Broadway and crosses town at 42nd Street) and the M42 across town on 42nd Street; they both stop right in front of the building. On the East side and from Downtown, take the M101, M102, and M103 (running up Third Avenue and down Lexington Avenue). **Open:** 8am–6pm, during office hours.*

Ellis Island

This is one of those sights that is not only impressive, but moving. Between its opening in 1892 and its closing in 1954, 12 million immigrants passed through here on their way to a new life. An enormous pile of luggage pays mute testimony to their sufferings and hopes, while another exhibit shows the demography of the Unites States as it changed during the period. The enormous Registry Hall is where immigrants waited to be interrogated by officials; a good many of them were sent back. There's also an optional audio tour and a documentary film.

*New York Harbor. ☎ **212/363-7620** for general information, 212/269-5755 for ticket and ferry information. **Transport:** Ferry from Battery Park. **Subway to ticket booth:** 4/5 train to Bowling Green stop and 1/9 train to South Ferry stop. (Note: ride in the first five cars, as the platform at arrival is shorter than the train.) Once out of the station, walk through the Park heading south; the ticket booth is a little fortress at the edge of the trees by the promenade. **Bus to ticket booth:** M1 (running down Fifth/Park Avenue/ Broadway), M6 (running down Broadway) and M15 (running down Second Avenue). **Admission:** Ferry plus Statue of Liberty and Ellis Island $7 adults, $3 children between 3 and 17 (free under 3), $5 seniors. **Open:** Daily 9:30am–5pm (extended hours in summer).*

New York Stories

The Empire State Building was once hit by an airplane—a B-25 Air Force bomber, to be exact—which rammed into the 79th floor of the building in heavy fog in 1945. Ten people in the building and the plane's three crewmen were killed.

Empire State Building
Finished in 1931, the Empire State building took only a little more than 400 days to build. Its height (including the TV antenna added in the 1950s) is 1,472 feet. The magnificent art deco tower surmounting the building was originally supposed to be a dock for airships, but only two dirigibles ever tried it. (Would you? Yikes!) On a clear day you can see up to 10 miles from the observation deck, and on any day you can pretend you're Cary Grant and Deborah Kerr in *An Affair to Remember*.

Fifth Ave. at 34th Street. ☎ *212/736-3100.* **Subway:** *B/D/F/N/Q/R train to 34th Street, and then walk east on 34th Street and turn right on Fifth Avenue to the entrance.* **Bus:** *The M2/M3/M4/M5 run down Fifth Avenue and stop right in front of the entrance.* **Admission to observation deck:** *$6 adults, $3 children under 12 and seniors (children under 5 free).* **Open:** *Daily 9:30am–11:30pm (You can stay up until midnight.)*

Tourist Traps

Here is a trap you set yourself: When you go to the Empire State Building, you'll notice that they post the visibility. When they say the visibility is zero, they mean zero. The staff will gladly refund your money and let you try another day, but only before you go up. We've seen plenty of people go up disbelieving and come down with glum faces. Save your money and come another day.

Flatiron Building and District
Although it wasn't the first skyscraper (the Tower Building was; see sidebar), the Flatiron is one of the foremost architectural icons of the city, and, though only 20-stories tall, was the tallest building in the world for a short time. Opened in 1902, the building's triangular site at the intersection of Broadway, Fifth Avenue, and 23rd Street accounts for its distinctive shape. Its real name was the Fuller Building, but New Yorkers thought it looked like a flatiron.

The area surrounding the building, the Flatiron District, sports some beautiful architecture and runs roughly from 14th to 23rd streets and between Park Avenue South to Sixth Avenue. Once grungy, the district has now been spruced up with the addition of boutiques, restaurants, and nightlife.

New York Stories

The first skyscraper, the 11-story Tower Building, went up at 50 Broadway in 1889. It used "curtain wall" construction, with an iron skeleton on which slabs of stone were hung.

175 Fifth Ave. where Fifth Avenue and Broadway cross at 23rd Street. **Subway:** *N/R train to 23 Street stop and you're right there.* **Bus:** *M6 and M7 down Broadway or M2/M3/M5 down Fifth Avenue for a magnificent view of it; they stop right there, too.*

Gramercy Park

This delightful little enclosed park is surrounded by 19th-century buildings and gives a real sense of a bygone era. It's not large (and not open, either: only the residents have a key), but the atmosphere is unique and magic, especially in the morning and at dusk. Do wander in the streets around Gramercy Park, south on Irving Place and east around Stuyvesant Square from 17th to 15th streets between Second and Third avenues; this neighborhood is the eastern pendant to the Flatiron District (see above) and is dotted by beautiful former mansions and houses.

The park is at Lexington Avenue between 21st and 20th streets. **Subway:** *L/N/R/4/5/6 train to 14 Street/Union Square stop, and then walk north on Park and turn right to start at Gramercy Park.* **Bus:** *M1 on Park Avenue and M101/M102/M103 down Third Avenue.*

Grand Central Terminal

Finished in 1913, this Beaux Arts masterpiece has been under intensive restoration for a while now, but by the time you read this it should be looking like its old self, only new. Now, if they could just get rid of the elevated road around it...

From outside, note the ornamented clock; inside, look up 12 stories to the vibrant blue ceiling, on which the stars of the zodiac are traced in 24-karat gold. The renovation calls for new shops and even an art gallery. After years of neglecting its landmarks (or worse, tearing them down, like they did to the much-lamented old Penn Station), maybe this restoration represents a turning point for New York.

New York Stories

Despite what you may have heard, there ain't no such place as Grand Central Station. Its official name is Grand Central *Terminal*.

The main entrance is on 42nd Street at Park Avenue. **Subway:** *S/4/5/6/7 train to 42 Street/Grand Central.* **Bus:** *M1/M2/M3/M4 running up Madison Avenue and M101/M102/M103 running down Lexington Avenue will stop you right there—but avoid it, as it's jammed all the time.*

Greenwich Village

The village is the prime wandering area of the city, with crooked streets, trees, and a spectrum of architecture running from wood frame houses to 1850s brownstones to low-rises of the 1920s and 1930s. The largest open space in the Village is Washington Square Park (see following), and one of its architectural gems is the Jefferson Market Courthouse, now a branch of the public library; a melange of Gothic, Victorian, and Venetian styles, it occupies a triangular site where Sixth Avenue, Greenwich Avenue, and West 10th Street meet. The balcony, 100 feet up, was used by firewatchers who kept a lookout over the Village. Long a tolerant and artistic community, the Village was home at one time or another to Edgar Allan Poe, Mark Twain, Edith Wharton, John Reed, and Jackson Pollock. Now it houses coffee shops, jazz clubs, restaurants, and small theaters.

From Houston Street to 14th Street and from the Hudson River to Broadway. **Subway:** *A/B/C/D/E/F/Q train to West 4 Street/Washington Square to be at the center of it all.* **Bus:** *M2/M3/M5 run Downtown on Fifth Avenue and bring you only steps from Washington Square.*

8th Street ❾	McSorley's Old Ale House ❼
Astor Place & "The Cube" ❽	Porto Rico Importing Company ⓯
Bagels on the Square ⓮	The Public Theater ❽
The Blue Man Group: Tubes ❽	Sea Tea excursion ⓱
The Blue Note jazz club ⓭	Second Avenue Deli ❹
Canal Jean Co. ⓴	St. Mark's Place ❻
The Fantasticks ⓰	Strand Bookstore ❷
Grace Church ❸	Tower Records ⓲
Guggenheim SoHo ⓳	Union Square & the Greenmarket ❶
Jefferson Market Courthouse ❿	The Village Vanguard jazz club ⓫
Little India ❺	Washington Square Park ⓬

Solomon R. Guggenheim Museum

You can go either to see the art inside or simply to look at the building outside. The exhibition has to be pretty good to live up to Frank Lloyd Wright's controversial design (it is Wright's only building in New York), which suggests both a shell and a beehive. Inside, it's a unique exhibition space, with a long curving ramp that glides past the exhibits (you either love it or feel like you're in a parking garage, and you either take the easy path walking down or get a workout walking up). The museum's addition, the Tower Galleries, holds the permanent collection of 20th century art.

107 Fifth Avenue at 88th Street. ☎ *212/423-3500. **Subway:** 4/5/6 train to 86th Street stop, and then walk three blocks west to Fifth Avenue, turn right, and walk two blocks north to the entrance. **Bus:** The bus is a good idea because it brings you closer: Take the M1/M2/M3/M4 up Madison and walk one block west (it does south on Fifth), or the M86 cross-town on 86th Street. **Admission:** $8 adults, $5 seniors, children under 12 free; Fri 6–8pm pay what you wish. **Open:** Sun–Wed 10am–6pm; Fri–Sat 10am–8pm.*

Intrepid Sea-Air-Space Museum

The *Intrepid*, a battle-scarred aircraft carrier from World War II, is the center of what is considered the largest naval museum in the world. Forty aircraft of various periods crowd the flight deck of the carrier, and other vessels on display include the submarine *Growler* and the lightship *Nantucket*. Memorabilia and naval displays are housed below decks.

New York Stories

So, how do you think the "Houston" in Houston Street is pronounced? You'll immediately be pegged as a tourist if you answer "*Hew-ston*"; in fact, it's pronounced "*How-ston.*"

Hudson River at 46th Street, Pier 86, west of Twelfth Avenue. ☎ *212/245-0072. **Subway:** A/C/E train to 42nd Street stop, and then continue west on 42nd Street for four blocks, or change to the bus. **Bus:** M42 cross-town bus running on 42nd Street or, even better, the M50 cross-town bus running west on 49th Street and east on 50th Street. **Admission:** $10 adults, $5 children under 11 (one child under 6 free, additional children under 6 $1 each), $7.50 seniors. **Open:** Daily 10am–5pm, summer Sun open until 6pm, winter closed Mon–Tues. Note: Last admission one hour before closing time.*

Little Italy

Not what it once was, Little Italy is still a great place for a stroll. Most of the Italians are gone, but the tenements that housed them are still there, and you'll still see some old-timers who remember the way it was. Mulberry Street between Houston and Canal Streets is the core of the neighborhood, and you'll find plenty of Italian restaurants, groceries, and shops there.

*Subway: 6 train to Spring Street stop, and then walk east to Mulberry. **Bus:** M1 down Broadway and up Lafayette Street and M103 up and down Third Avenue and Bowery.*

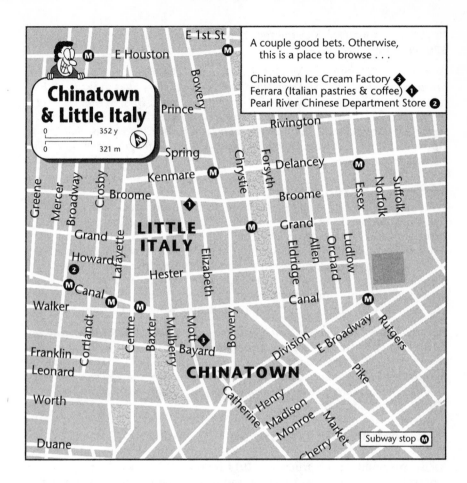

A couple good bets. Otherwise, this is a place to browse . . .

Chinatown Ice Cream Factory ❸
Ferrara (Italian pastries & coffee) ❶
Pearl River Chinese Department Store ❷

Subway stop Ⓜ

Metropolitan Museum of Art

Kids The Met is simply awesome, and follows an approach so comprehensive that they even number 200,000 baseball cards among the treasures in their collection. Among the highlights are the Egyptian collection and the Temple of Dendur, which stands in its own glass-walled space overlooking Central Park. Paintings by Breughel, Rembrandt, Vermeer, Manet, and every other major (and minor) artist could keep you wandering and contemplating for days. Then there's American wing, with its airy sculpture garden and fine collection of paintings, furniture, silver, and objects, as well as room from a Frank Lloyd Wright house. The Chinese galleries have recently been expanded; the recreation of a Ming Dynasty scholar's courtyard is a serene and meditative spot. Samurai swords, Greek and Roman statuary, Colt revolvers with gold chasing, Sheraton sofas—there are objects to fascinate anyone, young or old. That's why the Met is the city's top tourist destination, with 5 million visitors a year. Tours of various parts of the collection are conducted several times an hour, and you can also take a self-guided audio tour or the

181

"highlights" tour. Check at the tour bureau in the Great Hall, or call ☎ **212/ 570-3930** for schedules.

On the edge of Central Park, at Fifth Avenue and 82nd Street. ☎ **212/535-7710. Subway:** *4/5/6 train to 86 Street stop, and then walk three blocks west to Fifth Avenue, turn left, and walk along the Park to the entrance.* **Bus:** *M1/M2/M3/M4 up Madison and down Fifth Avenue.* **Suggested admission:** *$8 adult, $4 seniors, children under 12 free; includes admission to the Cloisters (see chapter 14).* **Open:** *Tues–Sun 9:30am–5:15pm; late nights Fri–Sat until 9pm. Note: No strollers allowed on Sun. Closed Mon.*

Museum of Modern Art

With a collection that includes such late–19th century art as *Starry Night* by Van Gogh and works of Fauvism, Cubism, Futurism, Surrealism, German Expressionism, Abstract Expressionism, and every other *ism* that's come down the pike, MOMA is said to hold the greatest collection of modern art in the world. A good place to start or end your visit is in the sculpture garden, designed by Philip Johnson, and if you're there in the afternoon, be aware that the museum shows films in its on-site theater and that the showings are free with admission. Check the schedule when you arrive.

West 53rd Street, between Fifth and Sixth avenues. ☎ *212/708-9480.* **Subway:** *E/F train to Fifth Avenue stop, and then walk west on 53rd Street for half a block.* **Bus:** *M1/M2/M3/M4/M5 down Fifth Avenue and M5/M6/M7 up Sixth Avenue.* **Admission:** *$8.50 adults, $5.50 seniors, children under 16 free; Thurs and Fri 5:30–8:30pm, pay what you wish.* **Open:** *Sun–Tues 11am–6pm, Thurs–Fri Noon–8:30pm; closed Wed.*

New York Public Library and Bryant Park

The main research library of the New York Public Library is housed in a Beaux Arts building constructed in 1911 on the site of the old Croton Reservoir. With its impressive facade and its two famous guarding lions, it looks just like what it is: a temple of learning. The library regularly mounts exhibitions of prints, manuscripts, and documents, and tours of the building are conducted at 11am and 3pm and include—when it's not closed for renovation, which it is now—the Main Reading Room, which is the largest unsupported hall in the city.

Bryant Park is the library's back yard, and is also the largest illuminated park in the world. With its gravel paths and green iron chairs, it has a Parisian feel and is a favorite picnic lunch spot for New Yorkers who work in Midtown. Recently renovated, it's cleaner and more beautiful than ever, and two restaurants have been added at the back of the museum. There are free films and performances during the summer.

Fifth Avenue between 42nd and 41st streets. ☎ *212/869-8089.* **Subway:** *B/D/F/Q train to 42 Street stop, and then walk east along Bryant Park to Fifth Avenue and turn right to the main entrance.* **Bus:** *M1/M2/M3/M4/M5 down Fifth Avenue and M5/M6/M7 up Sixth Avenue.* **Open:** *Main Reading Room Mon, Thurs, and Sat 10am–6pm; Tues–Wed 11am–6pm; closed Sun.*

It's a Bird, It's a Plane...

It's the **Roosevelt Island Aerial Tramway,** which connects Manhattan with tiny Roosevelt Island, 2 miles long, about 800 feet wide, and nestled in the East River between Manhattan and Queens. The trip across on the tramway is *extremely* romantic and provides a great view (especially at night, when everything's lit up). On the island itself there's not much to see—some apartment buildings, the ruins of two old hospitals, a couple of historic buildings, and a few gardens and fields—but it's a revelation to stand there in the relative quiet and watch Manhattan *happen* only about 100 yards away.

The tramway is located at Second Avenue and 60th Street, near the ramp to the Queensboro Bridge, and runs every 15 minutes on the quarter hour from 6am until after 2am daily (though there's been talk of ending service earlier; check before you get aboard). Tickets in each direction cost $1.50 for adults, 75¢ for seniors; children under 5 ride free. Call ☎ **212/832-4543** for schedules and information.

New York Stock Exchange

The stock exchange building, which dates from 1903, is a classical temple for dollar worship, and from the observation gallery you can watch the world's largest stock frenzy in action. Be there early if you want to avoid a long wait in line; admission is free, but the tickets are given out starting at 9am.

20 Broad Street at Wall Street. ☎ *212/656-5165.* **Subway:** *4/5 train to Wall Street stop to be right there, N/R train to Rector Street stop, and then walk east to Wall Street.* **Bus:** *M1/M6 down Broadway and up Trinity Place, but you're better off with the subway.* **Admission:** *Free.* **Open:** *Mon–Fri 9am–4:30pm.*

Rockefeller Center

Rockefeller Center is a massive complex consisting of 18 buildings, at the center of which is the GE building, a 70-story art deco tower. The entertainment ranges from the outdoor skating rink to Radio City Music Hall, where the Rockettes perform (call ☎ **212/632-4041** for backstage tours, and see chapter 19 for more info), to the NBC Studios, which you can also tour (call ☎ **212/664-4000**). There's a huge underground concourse beneath the Center, full of stores and restaurants. For a self-directed tour of the complex, pick up the map at 30 Rockefeller Center.

Between Fifth and Sixth avenues and from 48th to 51st streets; Promenade main entrance between 49th and 50th streets on Fifth Avenue. ☎ *212/632-3975.* **Subway:** *B/D/F/Q train to 47–streets/ Rockefeller Center to be right in the middle of it.* **Bus:** *M1/M2/M3/M4/M5 down Fifth Avenue and M5/M6/M7 up Sixth Avenue.*

New York Stories

The Promenade at Rockefeller Center—the main entrance between 49th and 50th streets on Fifth Avenue, from which the complex extends—is also known as the Channel Gardens, since it divides La Maison Francaise on its south side from the British Building on its north side.

St. Patrick's Cathedral

Construction began in 1858 and wasn't completed until 1906, but today St. Patrick's is the largest Catholic cathedral in the United States. Its Gothic spires and white marble facade are one of the city's most familiar sights. Mass is held eight times a day from Monday through Friday (7, 7:30, 8, and 8:30am; noon; 12:30, 1, and 5:30pm) and on Sunday (7, 8, 9, and 10:15am; noon; 1, 4, and 5:30pm), and five times a day on Saturday (8 and 8:30am; noon; 12:30 and 5:30pm).

New York Stories

James Renwick Jr., who designed St. Patrick's Cathedral, was only 25 years old when he received the commission to design Grace Church, the cathedral's pre-cursor, located on Broadway at 11th Street.

Fifth Avenue between 50th and 51st streets. ☎ *212/753-2261. Subway: B/D/F/Q train to 47–50 streets/Rockefeller Center, and then walk west to Fifth Avenue. Bus: M1/M2/M3/M4/M5 down Fifth Avenue and M1/M2/M3/M4 up Madison Avenue. Open: Daily 7am–8:30pm, Sat opens at 8am.*

St. Paul's Chapel

Manhattan's oldest church, St. Paul's is 10 years older than the country itself, having been completed in 1766. George Washington worshiped here (his pew is in the north aisle), and a service was held here following his inauguration; New York was the capital at the time. Only one service is still celebrated: 8am on Sunday. (Incidentally, the church was constructed of stone quarried right here in town. Imagine that.)

Broadway between Fulton and Vesey streets. ☎ *212/602-0872. Subway: 2/3/4/5/J/M/Z train to Fulton Street stop and A/C train to Broadway/Nassau Street stop, and then walk west on Fulton Street and turn right on Broadway. Bus: M1/M6 down Broadway and up Trinity Place. Open: Daily 9am–3pm, Sun opens at 7am Closed Sat.*

SoHo

This neighborhood is named after its location (*So*uth of *Ho*uston Street) and is famed for the cast iron architecture of its old industrial buildings, for the artists who moved into the area a couple of decades ago, and for the shops and restaurants that came more recently. (See the shopping and dining chapters for more information.) Unlike other parts of the city, such as Midtown, SoHo still has the feeling of 19th-century New York, with long stretches of historic buildings not dwarfed by high-rise monstrosities. (See map of Greenwich Village and SoHo earlier in this chapter.)

From Canal Street to Houston Street and between Lafayette and Sixth Avenue. **Subway:** *A/C/E/N/R trains to Prince or Canal Street stops, 1/9 trains to Spring or Canal Street stops, 6 train to Bleecker Street stop, or B/D/F/Q trains to Broadway/Lafayette Street stop.* **Bus:** *M6/M1 down Broadway and M6 up Sixth Avenue will leave you at the west and east borders of this neighborhood; M21 crosstown bus on Houston Street will leave you at the northern edge.*

Kids South Street Seaport and Museum

Although as a museum it can't hold a candle to Mystic Seaport in Connecticut, South Street Seaport is a major tourist attraction. With its cobbled streets, the warehouses of Schermerhorn Row (ca. 1811–1812), and the restored buildings of Cannon's Walk, the Seaport recalls commerce in the great days of sail. The museum's ships include the *Peking,* an enormous four-master built of steel; the lightship *Ambrose*; and the restored fishing schooner *Lettie G. Howard.* You can actually sail on another schooner, the *Pioneer* (see "River Cruises" in chapter 12). There are two large indoor shopping complexes: one in the Fulton Fish Market building and the other in Pier 17. The deck on the third floor of Pier 17 has one of the best views in the city, upriver through the cables of the Brooklyn Bridge and downriver to lower Manhattan.

On the East River, east of Water and Pearl streets, between John Street and Peck Slip. ☎ *212/669-9400. Museum: 12 Fulton Street between Water and South streets.* ☎ *212/748-8600.* **Subway:** *2/3/4/5/J/M/Z train to Fulton Street stop, and then walk east on Fulton and you'll be right in the middle of it all.* **Bus:** *The M15 (down Second Avenue and up First) leaves you right there, at Fulton and Water streets.* **Museum admission:** *$6 adults, $3 children, $5 seniors.* **Open:** *Daily 10am–5pm; Apr–Sept closes at 6pm and has a late night till 8pm on Thurs.*

Staten Island Ferry

These big old hulks are one of the symbols of New York City (remember *Funny Girl?*), and used to cost only 50¢. We know what you're thinking: "Yeah, they *used* to cost 50¢, but what are they up to now?" Well, that's the funny thing: Now they're free. Some new and doubtlessly more efficient boats have been added, but there's no deck space where you feel the breeze in your hair, so wait for one of the older models, and then take an evocative trip out to see the skyline and the Statue of Liberty. The runs are very frequent, especially at peak time: every 20–30 mins. during the day, more infrequently (every hour) late at night.

Staten Island Ferry Terminal on Peter Minuit Plaza at the end of South Street and State Street (the southern continuation of Broadway). ☎ **212/806-6940.** **Subway:** *1/9 train to South Ferry and N/R train to Whitehall Street/South Ferry and you'll see the terminal on the waterside, towering over you.* **Bus:** *M1/M6 down Broadway and M15 down Water Street have their terminus in front of the Terminal.* **Fare:** *Free.* **Open:** *24 hours.*

Statue of Liberty

Kids

The Statue of Liberty, a gift to the United States from France, is an international symbol of freedom and, at 450,000 pounds, an incredible technological feat. Its interior iron skeleton was designed by Gustave Eiffel three years before his famous tower was completed, and the finished statue was unveiled in October 1886. At night, when the torch is illuminated, the statue makes for a deeply impressive sight (especially from the water—from the Staten Island Ferry, for example), but if you want to visit it up close and personal, you're in for a long wait unless you get up really early. If you do make it, you can take an elevator to the top of the statue's base, which is 89 feet high, or climb all 354 steps to Liberty's crown. (Visitors can no longer climb up to the torch.)

When Liberty Ain't Worth It

The Statue of Liberty is a great sight, but in the summer you may want to see it from the water or outside on the grounds. On a hot summer day, visiting inside the lady will be like being inside a U-boat: hot, fetid, cramped, and tiring. The lines may be up to three hours long, unless you arrive early in the morning.

On Liberty Island in New York Harbor. ☎ **212/363-7620** *for general information, 212/269-5755 for ticket and ferry information.* **Transport:** *By ferry from Battery Park.* **Subway to ticket booth:** *4/5 train to Bowling Green stop and 1/9 train to South Ferry stop; Note: Ride in the first five cars, since the platform at arrival is shorter than the train. Once out of the station, walk through the Park heading south; the ticket booth is a little fortress at the edge of the trees by the promenade.* **Bus to ticket booth:** *M1 (running down Fifth/Park Avenue/Broadway), M6 (running down Broadway), and M15 (running down Second Avenue).* **Admission:** *Ferry plus Statue of Liberty and Ellis Island $7 adults, $3 children between 3 and 17 (free under 3), $5 seniors.* **Open:** *Daily 9:30am–5pm (extended hours in summer).*

Times Square

The corner of Seventh Avenue and 42nd Street is one of the most heavily trafficked spots in the city, and there is no mystery as to why: Times Square has undergone a renaissance. Sleaze is down, healthy attractions are up, and Disney is in. It's like an amusement park without rides. The neon signs are bigger and more astounding than ever, from the steaming tea cup to the Claes Oldenburg–like giant light switch of Con Ed. Even the police department has a glowing sign with letters that flash on and off. Times Square is also the gateway to the Theater District (see chapter 18).

At the intersection of Broadway and Seventh Avenue, between 42nd and 44th streets. **Subway:** *1/2/3/7/9/N/R/S train to 42 Street/Times Square stop.* **Bus:** *M6/M7 down Seventh Avenue and M104/M10 down Broadway offer a perfect view of the Square.*

🌟 Kids **United Nations**

Often misunderstood yet increasingly called upon to clean up and police the world, the United Nations has its headquarters on a beautiful 18-acre site overlooking the East River. A guided one-hour tour will explain the history and purpose of the U.N.—from its founding at the close of World War II to the completion of its New York complex in 1952 through to its present budget crisis—and will show you the General Assembly Hall and the Security Council Chamber. Although you're not allowed to picnic on the grounds, be sure not to miss them. There's a lovely rose garden just near the promenade that overlooks the river, Roosevelt Island, and Brooklyn. The many sculptures that have been given to the U.N. by member states range from St. George slaying a dragon made out of ICBMs to the huge, bronze, geode-looking thing at the entrance, which was recently donated by Italy.

United Nations Plaza, on First Avenue between 42nd and 48th streets, Visitor entrance at 46th Street. ☎ **212/963-7713.** **Subway:** *4/5/6/7/S train to 42 Street/Grand Central stop, and then walk east on 42nd Street to First Avenue, turn left, and walk to the visitor entrance at 46th Street.* **Bus:** *Much more convenient than the subway, take the M15 down Second Avenue and up First Avenue, the M104 down Broadway and 42nd Street, and the M42 cross-town on 42nd Street.* **Admission:** *Free to the park and lobby; guided tours $7.50 adults, $3.50 children, and $5.50 seniors. Note: children under 5 are not allowed on the guided tours.* **Open:** *9:15am–4:45pm; tours every 30 mins. from 9:15am–4:15pm; no tours weekends Jan–Feb.*

New York Stories

Washington Square was once used as a graveyard (thousands of victims of Yellow Fever lie under the ground) and also as a site of public executions.

Wall Street

Wall Street has come to be synonymous with the whole section of lower Manhattan that's dominated by finance. There are 65 Fortune 500 companies headquartered in New York, and more international firms have offices here than in any other American city. However, these are things you can't see;

what you can see are the skyscrapers in which the fortunes are won and lost, and which make the landscape of Wall Street impressive. On weekdays, the area teems with corporate types, and you can stand back and listen to the hum of activity (if you can find room to stand, that is); at night and on weekends, though, the area's pretty dead. While you're here, visit the Stock Exchange (see previous).

Between Broadway and South Street. **Subway:** *4/5 train to Wall Street stop, N/R to Rector Street.* **Bus:** *M1/M6 down Broadway and up Trinity Place.*

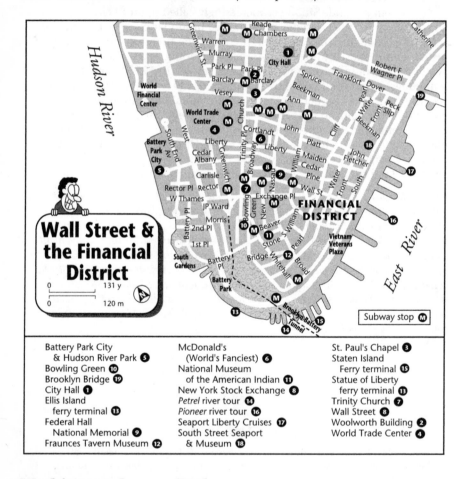

Battery Park City & Hudson River Park ❺	McDonald's (World's Fanciest) ❻	St. Paul's Chapel ❸
Bowling Green ❿	National Museum of the American Indian ⓫	Staten Island Ferry terminal ⓯
Brooklyn Bridge ⓳	New York Stock Exchange ❽	Statue of Liberty ferry terminal ⓭
City Hall ❶	*Petrel* river tour ⓮	Trinity Church ❼
Ellis Island ferry terminal ⓭	*Pioneer* river tour ⓰	Wall Street ❽
Federal Hall National Memorial ❾	Seaport Liberty Cruises ⓱	Woolworth Building ❷
Fraunces Tavern Museum ⓬	South Street Seaport & Museum ⓲	World Trade Center ❹

Washington Square Park

At the base of Fifth Avenue, Washington Square Park until recently had the highest concentration of drug dealers in the Downtown area, but during his re-election campaign Mayor Rudolph Giuliani made its cleanup a centerpiece of his own personal war on drugs. Dealers or none, it's always been a raucous, carnivalesque scene, with street musicians, chess players, NYU students (the college campus surrounds the park), skateboarders, people walking their dogs, joggers and strollers, and even families with kids taking in and adding to the atmosphere. The park is dominated by the Washington Arch, designed by Stanford White. A bit of trivia: White's murderer was tried at the nearby Jefferson Market Courthouse (see previous, under Greenwich Village).

At the southern end of Fifth Avenue, below 8th Street. **Subway:** *A/B/C/D/E/F/Q train to West 4 Street/Washington Square stop, and then walk one block east.* **Bus:** *M2/M3/M5 down Fifth Avenue; M8 cross-town on 8th Street (eastbound) and 9th Street (westbound).*

⭐Kids **World Trade Center**
The World Trade Center twin towers lack the aesthetic appeal of other buildings (they look like the boxes that the Chrysler Building and the Empire State Building came wrapped in), but the view from 1,350 feet above the street is impressive, especially if you go outside to the rooftop promenade. There's much more to the complex than just the towers: stores, restaurants (including Windows on the World—see chapter 10), a hotel, and a plaza used for performances in the summer.

Between Church and West streets and from Liberty to Vesey streets. ☎ *212/* **435-4170; Top of the World,** *2 World Trade Center,* ☎ **212/323-2340.** **Subway:** *C/E train to World Trade Center stop and 1/9/N/R to Cortland Street stop.* **Bus:** *M6 up Church Street and M10 down Varick Street.* **Admission to the Top of the World:** *$10 adults, $5 children, $8 seniors.* **Top of the World Open:** *Daily 9:30am–9:30pm; in summer open until 11:30pm.*

Worksheet: Your Must-See Attractions

Enter the attractions you most would like to visit to see how they'll fit into your schedule. Then use the date book below to plan your itinerary.

Attraction and location	Amount of time you expect to spend there	Best day and time to go

DAY 1

Morning:

Lunch:

Afternoon:

Dinner:

Evening:

DAY 2

Morning:

Lunch:

Afternoon:

Dinner:

Evening:

DAY 3

Morning:

Lunch:

Afternoon:

Dinner:

Evening:

DAY 4

Morning:

Lunch:

Afternoon:

Dinner:

Evening:

DAY 5

Morning:

Lunch:

Afternoon:

Dinner:

Evening:

Chapter 14

More Fun
Stuff to Do

> **In This Chapter**
>
> ➤ More sights and activities for art lovers, animal lovers, history buffs, book-worms, and others
>
> ➤ Places to ice skate and rock climb, right in town
>
> ➤ Spots for Sports—Yankee Stadium and more

If you have a particular interest—and almost everyone does—then the Top Sights listed in the last chapter only scratch the surface. Here's some stuff that's buried a little lower.

New York for the Art Lover

At the north end of the island in Fort Tryon Park are **The Cloisters** (☎ **212/923-3700**), constructed from portions of medieval and early Renaissance European cloisters that were shipped across the Atlantic. The Cloisters belong to the Metropolitan Museum of Art, house a collection of medieval art (including an impressive series of unicorn tapestries), and have a commanding view of the Hudson and the New Jersey Palisades. Admission (which includes admission to the Met downtown) is $8 adults (half price for seniors) and free for children under 12. Hours are Tuesday–Sunday 9:30am–4:45pm from November–February; open a half hour later March–October. You reach the Cloisters via the A train or the M4 bus on Madison Avenue. The bus takes you right to the museum but will be a *very* long ride. The subway brings you to the entrance to Ft. Tryon park: Get off at the 190th Street stop and take the elevator up to street level (don't walk up the long ramp—it takes you out of your way). Once you get outside you'll see the park entrance. It's a very lovely walk, and you'll see signs pointing you toward the Cloisters.

The **Whitney Museum** (☎ 212/570-3676), at 945 Madison Ave. (at 75th Street), has a spectacular collection of modern American art—Hopper, Bellows, O'Keefe, and others—and a new exhibition gallery is being added for the permanent collection. The Whitney Biennial, the show that artists (and most everyone else) love to hate, showcases the good, the bad, and the ugly in contemporary art (next Biennial: spring 1999). The museum is open Wednesday–Sunday, 11am–6pm and stays open an extra couple of hours on Thursday nights, when admission is free. (Otherwise, admission is $8 adults, $6 seniors, and free for kids under 12.) Take the 6 train to the 77th Street stop.

The **Frick Collection** (☎ 212/288-0700) is housed in one of the grand mansions of Old New York, built by Henry Clay Frick at 1 E. 70th St. (at Fifth Avenue). The rooms feel like the rooms of a home—an extremely elegant one—rather than a museum, and the collection includes works by Titian, Rembrandt, Vermeer, and Whistler. Admission is $5 adults, $3 seniors. (Children under 10 not admitted). Hours are 10am–6pm Tuesday–Saturday, 1pm–6pm Sunday. Take the 6 train to the Hunter College/68th Street stop, walk west to Fifth Ave., and then walk two blocks north.

Where the Wild Things Are—New York Zoos

Kids The **Bronx Zoo/Wildlife Conservation Park** (☎ 718/ 367-1010) is one of the great zoos of the world, and the largest metropolitan zoo in the country. There are 4,000 animals living on 265 acres; a Children's Zoo; the Bengali Express Monorail, which passes over elephants, Siberian tigers, and other exotic beasts; and 17 rare snow leopards. In spring, the butterfly tent may be set up, allowing you to share space with 1,000 of the critters. The zoo is open daily 10am–4:30pm from November–March ($3 adults, $1.50 seniors and kids under 12, under 2 free); 10am–5pm Monday–Friday and 10am–5:30pm Saturday–Sunday from April–October ($6.75 adults, $3 seniors and kids under 12, under 2 free). To get there, take the 2 train to Pelham Parkway stop, and then walk 2 blocks west; if you're not so adventuresome, take the Liberty Line B11 bus, which stops on Madison Avenue and runs express to the Zoo; this route costs $4. (Bring exact change: bill, or coin.) Liberty schedule: ☎ 718/652-8400.

Kids If you don't have time to get to the Bronx, the **Central Park Zoo/Wildlife Conservation Center** (☎ 212/861-6030) has some great exhibits (animals), though it can't match the size of its northerly cousin. Among the animals you'll see are the red pandas, which look like a cross between a raccoon, a fox, and a giant panda; the polar bears, whom you can watch doing laps from an observatory below the level of their pond; and the rain forest house, full of screaming birds and squirming things. At Fifth Avenue and 64th Street, the zoo is convenient, and at $2.50 adults, $1.25 seniors, and 50¢ for kids 3–12, the zoo is cheap. Open Monday–Friday

10am–5pm, weekends 10:30am–5:30pm. The closest subway is the N/R train to the Fifth Avenue stop at 59th Street, or follow the directions to the Frick Collection but walk south instead of north.

New York for the History Buff

Kids The Heritage Trails are self-guided walking tours that bring you to the discovery of historic Downtown Manhattan. The four trails, all marked by dots of different colors on the pavement and at intersections, start at the **Federal Hall National Memorial,** 26 Wall St. at Broad Street (☎ 212/767-0637). A guided tour of the trails is also available on weekdays. You can get an accompanying booklet for $5 at the Federal Hall on weekdays or at local bookstores; otherwise, a marker at each site gives you historical information. The red trail goes north to City Hall, the Blue one east to South Street Seaport, the orange one west to Battery Park City, and the Green one south on a circuit that ends at Bowling Green, passing by many historical landmarks. All the trails are great. To get there, take the 4/5 train to the Wall Street stop or the N/R train to Rector Street stop, or hop the M6 Broadway bus or the M1 down Fifth Avenue/Park Avenue/Broadway.

Fraunces Tavern is the place where General George Washington bid farewell to his troops in 1783. This building is a 1917 reconstruction of the early New York landmark, and though it's not historical, at least it's old. There are a couple of period rooms, a restaurant that on any other site would probably not survive, and a small museum. Located at 54 Pearl St. (at Broad St.); ☎ 212/425-1778. Admission is $2.50 adults, $1 seniors, children under 7 free. Hours are Monday–Friday, 10am–4:45pm; weekends noon–4pm. To get there, take the 1/9 train to South Ferry stop, or the 4/5 train to Bowling Green stop.

Who's buried in **Grant's Tomb?** Ulysses S., who saved the Union but is also remembered for a corrupt presidency. The tomb itself is a copy of a mausoleum that was one of the Seven Wonders of the ancient world, and it recently underwent an almost $2 million renovation (we spiffed it up just for you). Admission is free, and there are sometimes free jazz concerts around the tomb in the summer. Located at 122nd Street and Riverside Drive, it's open daily from 9am–5pm (for info, call ☎ 212/666-1640). By subway, take the 1/9 to the 125th Street stop; walk west and then south along Riverside Park.

The **Museum of the City of New York** (☎ 212/534-1672), at the top of Museum Mile (1220 Fifth Ave. at 103rd Street), has decorative arts, artifacts, and objects related to the history of the city from its Dutch beginnings onward. There are elegant displays of furniture, a re-creation of John D. Rockefeller's bedroom, theater history material, and lots of information. Admission is $5 adults, $4 seniors and children, or $10 for families, and it's open Wednesday–Saturday 10am–5pm and Sunday 1pm–5pm. Take the 6 train to 103rd Street, and then walk west toward Central Park.

New York for the Bookish

One of the great buildings of the city, the often overlooked **Pierpont Morgan Library** (☎ 212/685-0610), is housed in a 1906 mansion designed by McKim, Mead, and White (designers of the late, lamented Penn Station, among other great buildings), in the style of an Italian palazzo. J. P. Morgan's collection of medieval and Renaissance manuscripts, rare books, and drawings is second to none; the exhibits are fascinating; and the library room is worth the visit alone. There's also an indoor atrium/cafe that's a great place to sit with a book. The library is located at 29 E. 36th Street at Madison Avenue. Suggested admission is $5 adults, $3 seniors, children under 12 free. The Library is open Tuesday–Friday 10:30am–5pm, Saturday 10:30am–6pm, and Sunday noon–6pm. Take the 6 train to the 33rd Street stop, and then walk two blocks east and four blocks south.

Whatever your discipline (or lack thereof), you should be able to find a box full of books at the **Strand Bookstore** (☎ 212/473-1452). The largest used bookstore in the world, the store advertises "eight miles of books," most of which are half price. The original store is at Broadway and 12th Street (take the 4/5/6/N/R/L train to the 14 Street/Union Square stop and walk south), and there's a newer, monstrously huge Strand (☎ 212/732-6070) at 95 Fulton St., near the South Street Seaport (2/3/4/5 train to the Fulton Street stop, and then walk east).

Extra! Extra!

Have a hankering for fruits and vegetables fresh from the soil? You're not near-ly as out of luck as you might think: The **Union Square Greenmarket** is open for business each Monday, Wednesday, Friday, and Saturday. Farmers and vendors from all around the tri-state area truck their wares into town to bring a touch of the country to us city-folk. You can pick up homemade cheeses, cider, fresh fruit, home-baked pies and cookies, and other rural treasures, all without having to drive to Vermont. (Union Square is located where Park Avenue meets Broadway, at 16th Street.)

Ice Skating, Rock Climbing, & Other Ways to Work off Dessert

Kids The new **Chelsea Piers Sports and Entertainment Complex** (☎ 212/336-6666) has everything for the physically fit and/or obsessed, including a four-story golf range (fun to do, funnier to watch) honeycombed with cubicles where you can hook and slice away in privacy; two indoor skating rinks; an indoor pool; a 90,000 square–foot field house; and a 40-lane bowling alley. There are also facilities for weight training, indoor rock climbing, boxing, basketball, volleyball, gymnastics...pretty much everything other than telemark skiing. Afterward, enjoy a rub at the spa (☎ 212/336-6780), or a beer at the Chelsea Brewing Company (☎ 212/336-6440). The complex is located on four Hudson River piers between 17th and 23rd street. Take the C/E train to the 23 Street stop and walk west; or take the A/C/E train to the 14th Street stop or the L train to the Eighth Avenue stop, walk to the river, and then follow the walking/riding/running path north.

If you're staying in (or even passing through) the Lincoln Center area, you can make a quick ascent of the New York Sports Club's **rock-climbing wall** at the Harmony Atrium on the west side of Broadway between 61st and 62nd streets. For $9, you get use of the necessary equipment and 2 attempts.

Kids At **Wollman Rink** (☎ 212/396-1010) you get your chance to pretend you're in an old movie and go ice skating in Central Park. Located near the southeast corner of the park, Wollman is romantic, large, oddly shaped, and extremely crowded on weekends. Admission is $6 adults, $3 children, and $3.50 for the skates. (Pack a small padlock if you plan to do this, for your locker.) The closest stop is Fifth Avenue on the N/R train; walk west along Central Park South, take the path into the Park midway along it, and walk until you see the entrance to the rink. The rink at *kids* **Rockefeller Plaza** (☎ 212/332-7654), is even more famous, and, especially when the Christmas tree is lit, very, *very* romantic. It's also tiny, so go during off hours. Admission is $7–$8.50 adults and $6–$6.75 children; skate rental is $4. Take the B/D/F/Q to the Rockefeller Center stop.

New York's Corridors of Power

What is there to see at **City Hall?** First, there's the building itself, a French Renaissance/Georgian structure that dates from 1802–1811 and features an illuminated public clock from 1832. The interior houses interesting paintings, historical objects such as George Washington's desk, and the elegant city council room. Take the 4/5/6 train to the Brooklyn Bridge/City Hall stop; the building is surrounded by City Hall Park, right across the street from the Brooklyn Bridge.

The mayor of New York actually lives uptown at **Gracie Mansion,** an elegant Federal-period building that began its existence in 1799 as the home of the merchant Archibald Gracie. The city's most famous mayor, Fiorello La Guardia, was the first to occupy it (in 1942). The first floor is open to the public ($4 adults, $3 seniors), and the surrounding Karl Schurz Park and view of the East River and Hell Gate are lovely. Guided tours are given from March–November on Wednesdays at 10am, 11am, 1pm, and 2pm; reservations are required (☎ 212/570-4751). The mansion is at 89th Street and East End Avenue. Take the 4/5/6 train to the 86th Street stop and walk east; then go three blocks north.

More Gorgeous Buildings to Stare at

While you're downtown, you might check out the **Woolworth Building** at 233 Broadway. The Woolworth chain has fallen on hard times these days, but when Cass Gilbert's Gothic tower was finished (1913), Mr. Woolworth was still flush, and paid $15.5 million cash for the structure. Besides the stunning exterior, it has gorgeous mosaic ceilings, a marble staircase, and statues of people involved in the building. For a time, it was the tallest building in the world, and was known as "The Cathedral of Commerce." Take the 4/5/6 train to Brooklyn Bridge/City Hall stop; the Woolworth Building is at Broadway and Park Place.

Another of Gilbert's buildings is the Beaux Arts–style **U.S. Customs House,** which is home to the National Museum of the American Indian (see the section "Museums of Many Cultures" later in this chapter). Close by is the 1846 **Trinity Church** (☎ 212/602-0800), which is yet another building that laid claim to the title "tallest building in New York" for many years. The building is gothic in inspiration, and has a 281-foot steeple. Hard to believe now, dwarfed as it is by everything around it, but back in the old days you could see that spire for miles. Buried in the churchyard are Robert Fulton, Alexander Hamilton, and many other famous Americans. Free guided tours are given daily at 2pm, and after 11:15am on Sunday. Services are held Monday–Friday at 8am, 12:05pm, and 5:15pm; Saturday at 9am; and Sunday at 9am and 11:15pm. The church is open 7am–6pm, Monday–Friday; 8am–4pm Saturday; 7am–4pm Sunday. Take the 4/5 train to the Wall Street stop and walk west, or take the 1/9/N/R to the Rector Street stop and walk east.

If you're walking up Broadway at around 11th Street, stop and take a look at **Grace Church,** a lovely 1849 Gothic Revival structure set in an island of manicured lawns, trees, and shrubbery so perfect you'd swear it was beamed here direct from some English country village. If the lines of the church look a little bit familiar, that's because it was designed by architect James Renwick Jr., who thirty years later would design St. Patrick's Cathedral.

Take Me out to the Ball Game

Kids You're some decades late for visiting the legendary Ebbets Field or the Polo Grounds, but you can still catch a Yankees game in The House That Ruth Built—unless Steinbrenner moves the team away, as he keeps threatening to do. **Yankee Stadium** (☎ 718/293-6000) is at 161st Street and River Avenue in the Bronx; take the C/D/4 train to the 161st Street/Yankee Stadium stop. The New York Mets play at **Shea Stadium** (☎ 718/507-8499), which is located at 16th Street and Roosevelt Avenue in Flushing, Queens. Take the 7 train to the Willets Point/Shea Stadium stop. The New York Knicks, who have struggled to become the Boston Red Sox of hoop by winning and then breaking the city's heart, play at **Madison Square Garden** (Seventh Avenue between 31st and 33rd streets). Tickets are tough to get, but call ☎ 212/465-JUMP to give it a shot. Take the 1/2/3/9/A/C/E train to the 34th Street/Penn Station stop.

Museums of Many Cultures

New York is renowned for its dozens (hundreds, thousands) of cultures, and there isn't room to list all the institutions devoted to them. Here are three that fall into the "biggest, best, or only" category.

The **National Museum of the American Indian, George Gustav Heye Center** (☎ 212/668-6624) is located at 1 Bowling Green in the U.S. Customs House (1907), designed by Cass Gilbert a few years before the Woolworth Building (see "More Gorgeous Buildings to Stare at" earlier in this chapter). The largest such collection in the world, it displays only a selection of the *million* objects collected by George Gustav Heye. The site was opened in 1994 and is curatorially up to date. Admission is free; hours are 10am–5pm daily, with late hours on Thursdays (to 8pm). Take the 4/5 train to Bowling Green stop or the 1/9 train to South Ferry stop; then walk north.

El Museo del Barrio (1230 Fifth Ave. at 103rd Street, ☎ 212/831-7272) is the only museum in the country devoted to Puerto Rican and Latin American art and objects. At the top of Museum Mile, it has pre-Columbian art, Christian religious artifacts, photographs, sculpture, paintings, and decorative arts. Admission is $4 adults, $2 seniors, and free for children under 12. Hours are Wednesday–Sunday 11am–5pm. Take the 6 train to the 103rd Street stop and walk west.

The **Jewish Museum** (☎ 212/423-3230) has an impressive collection of Judaica that stretches back several thousand years and is the largest of its kind in the country. It's housed in a recently renovated mansion on Museum Mile at 1109 Fifth Ave. (at 92nd Street). Admission is $7 adults, $5 seniors, children under 12 free; open Sunday–Thursday 11am–5:45pm and extra hours (until 8pm) on Tuesday, when you pay what you wish. Take the 6 train to the 96th Street stop, walk west to Fifth Avenue, and then go four blocks south.

Pictures That Move & Pictures That Don't

The **International Center of Photography** (☎ 212/860-1777) holds one of the world's best photo collections. Admission is $4 adults, $2.50 seniors, $1 children up to age 12. It's open Tuesday–Sunday 11am–6pm; it's also open late hours Tuesday night (6pm–8pm), when you pay what you wish. Located at 1130 Fifth Avenue at 94th Street; take the no. 6 train to 96th Street and Lexington Avenue, then walk 3 blocks west (toward Central Park). Their **midtown branch** concentrates on rotating exhibits and is located close to Times Square, at 1133 Sixth Avenue at 43rd Street (☎ 212/768-4680).

For moving pictures, visit the **Museum of Television and Radio** (☎ 212/621-6800), not surprisingly one of the most high-tech museums around. Its library of 75,000 TV and radio programs—even commercials—goes back as far as 1920. You can search via computer for the moment you want to relive and then watch it on an individual monitor, whether it's the "I hate Quantas" ad or Edward R. Murrow's courageous unmasking of Senator Joe McCarthy. Admission is $6 adults, $4 seniors, $3 children up to age 12. Hours are Tuesday–Sunday noon–6pm, with late hours on Thursday (to 8pm). Located at 25 W. 52nd St. (between Fifth and Sixth avenues); take the B/D/F/Q train to 47–50 streets/Rockefeller Center stop, or the N/R to the 49th Street stop and walk north on Sixth Avenue to 52nd Street, and then turn right.

Who Lived Where?

There are many historic houses in New York, but two of the most fascinating are the **Abigail Adams Smith Museum** (☎ 212/838-6878) and the **Lower East Side Tenement Museum** (☎ 212/431-0233). The former house was actually the carriage house belonging to the daughter of President John Adams. It was restored by the Colonial Dames of America, and has nine period rooms with furnishings dating from 1800–1830. Located at 421 E. 61st St. between First and York avenues (M31 cross-town bus on 57th Street and up York Avenue or M15 north on First Avenue and south on Second); admission is $3 adults, $2 seniors, and free for children under 12. Hours are Tuesday–Sunday 11am–4pm, with late hours on Tuesday (to 9pm), but only in July. The museum is closed in August.

At the other end of the social scale is the Tenement Museum, a fascinating, accurate, and sobering reconstruction of a New York tenement (the kind of place where most of those people who went through Ellis Island wound up). The museum is at 97 Orchard St. at Broome Street; group tours only, but the guides are very informative. Reservations are strongly recommended. Admission is $8 adults, $6 seniors; tours are at 1pm, 2pm, and 3pm Tuesday–Friday, and every 45 minutes Saturday–Sunday from 11am to 4:15pm. Take the F train to the Delancey Street stop, and then walk two blocks east to Orchard and turn left one block.

Good Bets if You've Got the Kids in Tow

Kids One good bet for kids is the **Museum of Television and Radio** (see the section "Pictures That Move and Pictures That Don't" earlier in this chapter), and for even more technodazzle, try the **Sony Wonder Technology Lab** (☎ 212/833-8100), which has a display on the history of technology and three floors of video, robots, and all the latest equipment to experiment with. Even small children can get something out of this place, and older kids and adults will be totally absorbed. Admission is free, and the staff limits the number of people who can use the facility at one time. Open Tuesday–Sunday 10am–6pm. The Lab is located at 550 Madison Ave. Take the E/F train to the 53rd Street stop, walk one block east to Madison, turn north, walk up to 56th Street, and turn left. (The entrance is on 56th Street.)

Skateboard Jungle

If you're traveling with a teen—particularly one of those baggy-pants-wearing, grunge-music-listening, Generation X–type teens—consider veering east off Broadway at 8th Street and walking around **Astor Place** and **St. Mark's Place.** Odd traffic patterns mean that Astor Place is usually free of cars, and this means it's a haven for downtown skate punks, who zip around and hang out on the sidewalk. Check out **the cube** right in the center of the area: It's a great big piece of modern art that sits perched on one of its corners and will spin if you give a mighty push.

Right at the eastern end of Astor is St. Mark's Place, a veritable time machine of a street where underage 70s-style punks (some with multicolored mohawk haircuts and multiple body piercings—how quaint!) wallow in teen angst. Your kids'll love it.

Of course, the natural choice is **The Children's Museum of Manhattan** (☎ 212/721-1234), which has such absorbing activities as three-dimensional recreations of the Dr. Seuss books, a special playroom for kids under age 4, and special daily activities. Children who are almost in double digits may get bored, however. Admission is $5 for adults and children (free for those under 2) and $2 for seniors. During the school year, the hours are Monday, Wednesday, and Thursday 1:30pm–5:50pm, Friday–Sunday 10am–5pm; in the summer, Wednesday–Monday 10am–5pm. The museum is at 212 W. 83rd St. between Broadway and Amsterdam avenues. Take the 1/9 train to the 79th Street stop, walk north on Broadway to 83rd, and turn right.

Chapter 15

Charge It! A Shopper's Guide to New York

In This Chapter

➤ Where to go to daydream

➤ Where to go when you know what you want

➤ Where to go when you don't know what you want

➤ Where to find it cheap

➤ When to go

New York is synonymous with shopping. There are shops everywhere, selling everything you need, many things you don't need, and things you didn't even know existed. Where else can you find a store that sells animal skeletons?

Prices, of course, achieve the same variety, but the good news is that you can find top-quality goods at bargain prices if you're at the right spot at the right time.

In this jungle of possibilities, here are a few simple and straightforward guidelines:

➤ A few shops—department stores and others—are so famous that you visit them as you would an attraction (see the next section, "The Big Names," for an alphabetical listing). They are, though, really good places to do your shopping and are not necessarily overpriced.

➤ There are some areas of the city where you find the tops in fashion, jewelry, housewares, and so on (see the section "Prime Hunting

Grounds" later in this chapter). These are prime neighborhoods for window shopping, but also for some special buys.

➤ Finally, there are some shops where you go for particular objects, such as an electric appliance or antiques (see the section "Where to Find That Thingie You Wanted—Specialty Shopping" later in this chapter), and where you are sure to pay a fair price, often lower than what you would pay anywhere else in the country.

At this point, you're ready to make your selection and shop, shop, shop 'til you drop, pick up a few choice items, or just get overwhelmed with it all.

Shopping Hours

No such thing. Remember, this is the city that doesn't sleep, and what's the sense in staying up if you can't go out and buy dishes at 10pm?

Honestly, business hours vary widely according to the type of shop and neighborhood. Call around. Some places (especially in high business areas like Wall Street) open at 8am while others (especially in funkier neighborhoods) don't open until 11am. You can count on most shops to stay open until at least 7pm or 8pm, though a few close earlier and a good number stay open much later.

Note that some fancy fashion and jewelry stores—such as Tiffany & Co. and some European designer stores—close on Saturdays during the summer.

Paying Your Taxes

Sales tax in New York is 8.25% for most goods, although some luxury goods—such as cigars—get a higher tax. There has been a move towards abolishing the sales tax for clothes and shoes, but no luck yet, except during well-publicized tax-free weeks.

The Big Names

London has its Harrod's and New York has its own world-famous stores. Many are department stores; others are the flagships of some top chain stores. They're all worth a visit, especially if you love shopping.

Here they are in alphabetical order:

ABC Carpet & Home. 888 Broadway at 18th Street (☎ 212/473-3000); 4/5/6/L/N/R train to 14th Street/Union Square stop. This store is more an attraction than a real shop. You go there more for the Kiplingesque atmosphere than for the generally pricey goods (though once in a while you'll find a bargain). Even if you don't buy anything, a visit will be like a stroll in Ali Baba's cavern. (*Note:* Some beautiful Oriental rugs and kilims are to be found on the second floor of ABC's rug store, right across the street on the west side of Broadway.)

Barneys. 660 Madison Avenue at 61st Street (☎ **212/826-8900**), N/R train to Fifth Avenue stop. Open until 9pm every night. Not just for men, and not just clothes.

Bergdorf Goodman and **Bergdorf Goodman Man.** 754 Fifth Ave. at 57th Street and 745 Fifth Ave. at 58th Street (☎ **212/753-7300**). N/R train to Fifth Avenue stop. The most exclusive department store, and priced to stay that way.

Bloomingdale's. 1000 Third Ave. at 59th Street (☎ **212/355-5900**). 4/5/6 train to 59 Street stop or N/R train to Lexington Avenue stop. Probably the best department store in New York.

Brooks Brothers. 346 Madison Ave. at 44th Street (☎ **212/682-8800**) and 1 Liberty Plaza at Church and Liberty streets (☎ **212/267-2400**). Home of the most traditional men's clothes, and with a selection for women and children, too. If your grandfather was a banker he probably bought his shirts here.

Kids **The Disney Store.** The original store is at 711 Fifth Ave. at 55th Street (☎ **212/702-0702**). E/F train to Fifth Avenue stop. It recently opened branches at 210 W. 42nd St. (☎ **212/221-0430**); 39 W. 34th St. (☎ **212/279-9890**); and 141 Columbus Ave. (☎ **212/362-2386**).

Lord and Taylor. 424 Fifth Ave. at 39th Street (☎ **212/391-3344**). B/D/F/Q train to 42nd Street stop and 7 train to Fifth Avenue stop. Go there not only for the moderate prices, but also for the animated Christmas windows if you're in town at the right time.

Kids **FAO Schwarz.** 767 Fifth Ave. at 58th Street (☎ **212/644-94000**). N/R train to Fifth Avenue stop. Toy heaven for kids. Life-size stuffed animals and long lines at holiday time.

Macy's. Herald Square at West 34th Street, Sixth Avenue, and Broadway (☎ **212/695-4400**). B/D/F/N/Q/R train to 34th Street stop. Large, comprehensive, less elegant than Bloomingdale's.

Saks Fifth Avenue. 611 Fifth Ave. at 50th Street (☎ **212/753-4000**). E/F train to Fifth Avenue stop. Lavish and stylish; shopping here will make you feel like Zsa Zsa Gabor.

Tiffany & Co. 727 Fifth Ave. at 57th Street (☎ **212/755-8000**). N/R train to Fifth Avenue stop. Maintaining the tradition of the great artist Louis Confort Tiffany. Even if you don't go in, stare in the window and pretend you're Audrey Hepburn.

Kids **Warner Brothers Studio Store.** 1 E. 57th St. at Fifth Avenue (☎ **212/754-0300**). N/R train to Fifth Avenue stop. If you need Bugs or Daffy plastered on a shirt, bag, or sundry item, this is your place.

New York Stories

You want it, you want it, you want it, but you just can't afford it? But maybe you can. A few shops specialize in **quality copies of famous designers' accessories**, such as handbags and jewelry (and we're not talking about illegal knock-offs here). The quality is top, so why not? The best are **Saurez** (450 Park Ave., ☎ 212/753-3758) for designer handbags and **René Collections** (1007 Madison Ave., ☎ 212/327-3912) particularly for evening bags and jewels.

Prime Hunting Grounds

New York has three prime shopping areas: the Upper East Side/Madison Avenue for the classic, elegant stuff; the Downtown/SoHo area for the trendy chic shopping; and Midtown/Fifth Avenue for many famous stores and boutiques. These are the centers of New York's fashion statement, but not exclusively; plenty of other elegant and trendy shops can be found, and in these neighborhoods you can acquire things for the house, the body, and, sometimes, the soul.

Madison Avenue

The stretch of Madison Avenue between 57th and 78th streets is where you'll find most of the big names of fashion design as well as a slew of other elegant stores. It's a pleasure to window shop here, but if you can afford it, you're also in for one of the most pleasant shopping sprees of your life—you'll feel as if you've died and gone to Paris. Below 57th Street, Madison becomes more commercial in a down-to-earth way.

The best way to shop this neighborhood is to start at one of the two ends and walk your leisurely way through. Take the 6 train to the 77th Street stop and walk south; or take the 4/5/6 train to the 59th Street stop or N/R train to Lexington Avenue stop and walk north.

You'll find top European fashion designers' shops, such as the sleek **Giorgio Armani** (760 Madison Ave. at 65th Street, ☎ 212/988-9191) and his younger line at **Emporio Armani** (601 Madison Ave., at 60th Street, ☎ 212/317-0800); the sometimes outrageous **Moschino** (803 Madison Ave. at 68th Street, ☎ 212/639-9600); the very special **Dolce & Gabbana** (825 Madison Ave. at 69th Street, ☎ 212/249-4100); and the famous **Valentino** (747 Madison Ave. at 65th Street, ☎ 212/772-6969).

American fashion is there, too, and you'll find **Calvin Klein** (654 Madison Ave. at 60th Street, ☎ 212/292-9000), **Eileen Fisher** (521 Madison Ave. at 53rd Street, ☎ 212/759-9888), and **Polo/Ralph Lauren and Polo Sport** (867 Madison Ave. at 72nd Street, ☎ 212/606-2100).

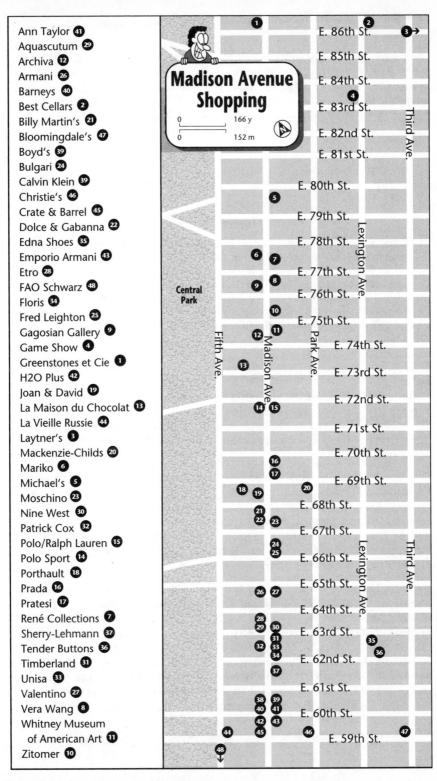

Ann Taylor **41**
Aquascutum **29**
Archiva **12**
Armani **26**
Barneys **40**
Best Cellars **2**
Billy Martin's **21**
Bloomingdale's **47**
Boyd's **39**
Bulgari **24**
Calvin Klein **39**
Christie's **46**
Crate & Barrel **45**
Dolce & Gabanna **22**
Edna Shoes **35**
Emporio Armani **43**
Etro **28**
FAO Schwarz **48**
Floris **34**
Fred Leighton **25**
Gagosian Gallery **9**
Game Show **4**
Greenstones et Cie **1**
H2O Plus **42**
Joan & David **19**
La Maison du Chocolat **13**
La Vieille Russie **44**
Laytner's **3**
Mackenzie-Childs **20**
Mariko **6**
Michael's **5**
Moschino **23**
Nine West **30**
Patrick Cox **32**
Polo/Ralph Lauren **15**
Polo Sport **14**
Porthault **18**
Prada **16**
Pratesi **17**
René Collections **7**
Sherry-Lehmann **37**
Tender Buttons **36**
Timberland **31**
Unisa **33**
Valentino **27**
Vera Wang **8**
Whitney Museum
    of American Art **11**
Zitomer **10**

Madison Avenue Shopping

0 — 166 y
0 — 152 m

Central Park

E. 86th St.
E. 85th St.
E. 84th St.
E. 83rd St.
E. 82nd St.
E. 81st St.
E. 80th St.
E. 79th St.
E. 78th St.
E. 77th St.
E. 76th St.
E. 75th St.
E. 74th St.
E. 73rd St.
E. 72nd St.
E. 71st St.
E. 70th St.
E. 69th St.
E. 68th St.
E. 67th St.
E. 66th St.
E. 65th St.
E. 64th St.
E. 63rd St.
E. 62nd St.
E. 61st St.
E. 60th St.
E. 59th St.

Third Ave.
Lexington Ave.
Park Ave.
Madison Ave.
Fifth Ave.

For the top of elegance in Italian shoes and leather, there is **Prada** (28 E. 70th St., ☎ **212/327-4200**). For domestic elegance, there is **Coach** (595 Madison Ave. at 57th Street, ☎ **212/754-0041**). If your yen is for elegant linen, you might like to visit **Pratesi** (829 Madison Ave. at 69th Street, ☎ **212/ 288-2315**), the Italian boutique that serves the European royal houses.

Tourist Traps

"Rolex, anybody?" Thousands of street vendors in tourist areas offer watches at cheap prices. They're fake, of course, and cheat the manufacturers of the original out of profit, but as long as you're aware of these facts, you won't get ripped off. You can find fake Rolexes and other big-name watches for as little as $25 if you bargain, or even less for smaller models or if you buy more than one. But why bother? They're cheap watches, so the glass or the finish will probably come off quite easily and it won't be worth repairing.

SoHo

It started with art galleries, emerging designers, and cutting-edge boutiques; now it's a prime shopping area with a huge variety of stores covering the whole price scale from top to bottom, plus plenty of places to have a break (see chapters 11 and 13). Note that in this arty neighborhood most shops do not open before 11am.

This area is like a big rectangle enclosed by Grand Street to the south, West Broadway to the west, Broadway to the east, and Houston to the north. The best way to shop it is to get in at one of the four corners and walk up and down or left and right (pretend you're hoeing a field). Take the A/C/E train to the Canal Street stop, the C/E to the Spring Street stop, the N/R train to the Canal or Prince Street stop, the 6 train to the Bleecker Street stop, or the B/D/F/Q train to the Broadway/Lafayette Street stop.

You'll find many young American fashion designers such as **Anna Sui** (113 Greene St., ☎ **212/941-8406**) and **Todd Oldham** (123 Wooster St., ☎ **212/226-4668**), but as well as foreign designers such as the French **Tehen** (122 Greene St., ☎ **212/431-5045**), the Australian **Country Road** (411 West Broadway, ☎ **212/343-9544**), and the Italian **Dolce and Gabbana** (434 W. Broadway between Prince and Spring Streets, ☎ **212/ 965-8000**). You'll also find **MiuMiu** (100 Prince St., ☎ **212/334-5156**), the young line of the Italian designer shoe store **Prada** (see the section "Madison Avenue" earlier in this chapter).

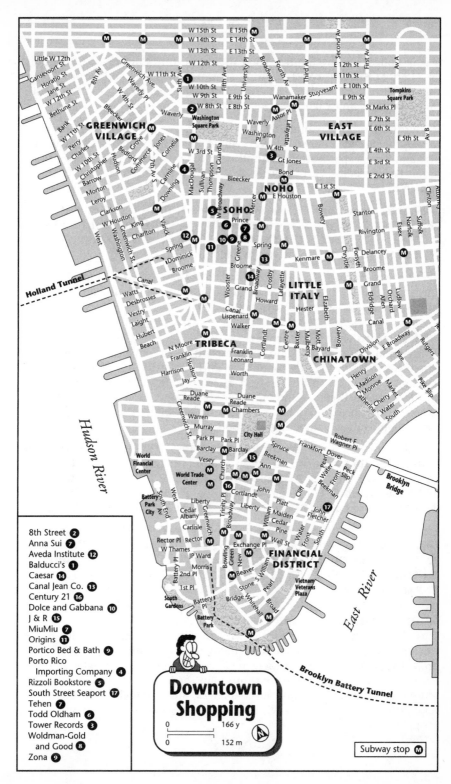

Downtown Shopping

8th Street	②	
Anna Sui	⑦	
Aveda Institute	⑫	
Balducci's	①	
Caesar	⑭	
Canal Jean Co.	⑬	
Century 21	⑯	
Dolce and Gabbana	⑩	
J & R	⑮	
MiuMiu	⑦	
Origins	⑪	
Portico Bed & Bath	⑨	
Porto Rico Importing Company	④	
Rizzoli Bookstore	⑤	
South Street Seaport	⑰	
Tehen	⑦	
Todd Oldham	⑥	
Tower Records	③	
Woldman-Gold and Good	⑧	
Zona	⑨	

0 — 166 y
0 — 152 m

Subway stop Ⓜ

If your budget is more limited, you can always go to **Caesar** (487 Broadway, ☎ 212/941-6672) for SoHo fashion at affordable prices, and **Canal Jean Co.** (504 Broadway, between Spring and Broome streets, ☎ 212/226-1130), for good prices on casual wear.

If your thing is body pampering, take advantage of the **Aveda Institute** (233 Spring St., ☎ 212/807-1492), where you can buy natural beauty products and have a spa treatment. Another store for cosmetics and body products is **Origins** (402 W. Broadway, ☎ 212/219-9764), the natural cosmetics branch of Estée Lauder.

Other interesting stores include **Portico Bed & Bath** (139 Spring St., ☎ 212/941-7722) for trendy linens and soaps, **Wolfman-Gold and Good** (117 Mercer St., ☎ 212/431-1888) for tabletop wares, and **Zona** (97 Greene St., ☎ 212/925-6750) for trendy home furnishings.

There also is **Rizzoli** (454 W. Broadway, ☎ 212/674-1616), a large, pleasant, and elegant bookstore where you'll find many interesting and unusual editions. Art books are a strength.

Fifth Avenue and 57th Street
Although Madison Avenue and SoHo carry the flag for elegant shopping where you can actually buy something, Fifth Avenue south of 59th Street—and its extension on East 57th Street up to Lexington Avenue—is still a hot area for elegant shopping and big names (like Saks and Bergdorf's). Fifth Avenue South, below 23rd Street, is rapidly developing as a more moderate, cool shopping area, competing with SoHo.

For Midtown shopping, take the E/F train to the Fifth Avenue stop and walk south. You'll find some top European Fashion designers, such as **Christian Dior** (712 Fifth Ave., ☎ 212/582-0500), **Chanel** (15 E. 57th St., ☎ 212/355-5050), **Gianni Versace** (647 Fifth Ave. at 54th Street, ☎ 212/317-0224), and **Laura Biagiotti** (4 W. 57th St., ☎ 212/399-2533).

You'll also find some of the top names for accessories and shoes, such as **Ferragamo** (725 Fifth Ave., ☎ 212/759-3822), **Gucci** (685 Fifth Ave. ☎ 212/826-2600), **Hermés** (11 E. 57th St., ☎ 212/751-3181), **Louis Vuitton** (21 E. 57th St., ☎ 212/371-6111), and **Fendi** (720 Fifth Ave., ☎ 212/767-0100).

South Street Seaport and Pier 17
This place is a New York–style mall with all the big favorites, and due to late closing hours (many are open until midnight), you really can shop 'til you drop. The good thing is that there are almost as many (and maybe more) restaurants and bars as there are shops, plus the South Street Seaport Museum and historical ships (see chapter 13) and a branch of the Strand Bookstore (see chapter 14) to give you a nice break or distract the non-shoppers of your party.

Tourist Traps

"Great Sales! Going Out of Business!" The Midtown part of Fifth Avenue in the 30s and 40s is lined with dubious stores announcing their imminent closure. Poor babies, they've been there for years. Although they mainly cater to foreigners, it's a good thing to know that they ARE rip-offs. They mainly sell cheap electronics that you'll be able to find at better prices (and with warranties) at good, reliable stores (see the section "Electronics" later in this chapter).

New York Stories

The recent development of a shopping stretch south of 23rd Street on Sixth Avenue is reviving the very same area where, more than 100 years ago, ladies would come for the latest fashions in New York. The elegant "Ladies' Mile" ran between 14th and 23rd streets and was lined with top elegant stores such as Tiffany and Co. Today's heirs are inhabiting the same beautiful cast-iron buildings and include shops and chains such as **Bed Bath & Beyond** (620 Sixth Ave. at 18th Street, ☎ 212/255-3550), **Old Navy Clothing Company** (610 Sixth Ave. at 18th Street, ☎ 212/645-0663), and **Barnes & Noble Superstore** (675 Sixth Ave. between 21st and 22nd streets, ☎ 212/727-1227), plus some discount stores such as **Filene's Basement** (see the section "Discount Stores" later in this chapter), **T.J. Maxx,** and the **Burlington Coat Factory.**

🌟Kids 8th Street

From Sixth to First avenues, this is a great spot for shoes (particularly if you want a young, hip look), t-shirts, and souvenirs. It also has some good leather shops. Teenagers in particular find this a shopping haven. When you get to the East Side, check out 9th and 7th streets as well, where you'll find some new designers and funky stores; it's the equivalent of off-Broadway for fashion.

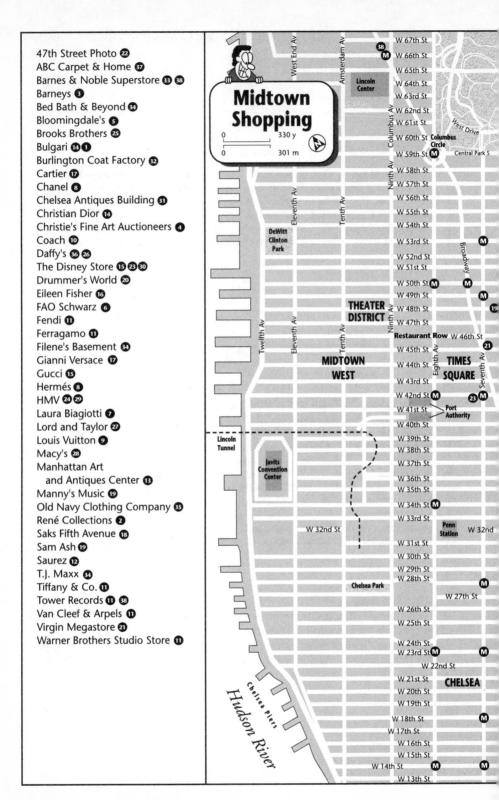

47th Street Photo **22**
ABC Carpet & Home **37**
Barnes & Noble Superstore **33 38**
Barneys **3**
Bed Bath & Beyond **34**
Bloomingdale's **5**
Brooks Brothers **25**
Bulgari **14 1**
Burlington Coat Factory **32**
Cartier **17**
Chanel **8**
Chelsea Antiques Building **31**
Christian Dior **14**
Christie's Fine Art Auctioneers **4**
Coach **10**
Daffy's **36 26**
The Disney Store **15 23 30**
Drummer's World **20**
Eileen Fisher **16**
FAO Schwarz **6**
Fendi **11**
Ferragamo **11**
Filene's Basement **34**
Gianni Versace **17**
Gucci **15**
Hermés **8**
HMV **24 29**
Laura Biagiotti **7**
Lord and Taylor **27**
Louis Vuitton **9**
Macy's **28**
Manhattan Art
  and Antiques Center **13**
Manny's Music **19**
Old Navy Clothing Company **35**
René Collections **2**
Saks Fifth Avenue **18**
Sam Ash **19**
Saurez **12**
T.J. Maxx **34**
Tiffany & Co. **11**
Tower Records **11 38**
Van Cleef & Arpels **11**
Virgin Megastore **21**
Warner Brothers Studio Store **11**

Midtown Shopping

0 — 330 y
0 — 301 m

East Drive

The Pond

Central Park S

Plaza Hotel

Rockefeller Center

Bryant Park

New York Public Library

MIDTOWN EAST

MURRAY HILL

Empire State Bldg.

Madison Square Park

Gramercy Park

FLATIRON DISTRICT

GRAMERCY PARK

Union Square

Grand Central Terminal

Chrysler Building

United Nations

Mitchell Place

Queensboro Bridge

Roosevelt Island Tram

Queens

East River

Queens–Midtown Tunnel

Peter Cooper Village

Stuyvesant Town

From Lower Level

To Upper Level

Tunnel Exit

Tunnel Entrance

E 67th St
E 66th St
E 65th St
E 64th St
E 63rd St
E 62nd St
E 61st St
E 60th St
E 59th St
E 58th St
E 57th St
E 56th St
E 55th St
E 54th St
E 53rd St
E 52nd St
E 51st St
E 50th St
E 49th St
E 48th St
E 47th St
E 46th St
E 45th St
E 44th St
E 43rd St
E 42nd St
E 41st St
E 40th St
E 39th St
E 38th St
E 37th St
E 36th St
E 35th St
E 34th St
E 33rd St
E 32nd St
E 31st St
E 30th St
E 29th St
E 28th St
E 27th St
E 26th St
E 25th St
E 24th St
E 23rd St
E 22nd St
E 21st St
E 20th St
E 19th St
E 18th St
E 17th St
E 16th St
E 15th St
E 14th St
E 13th St

Sixth Av
Fifth Av
Madison Av
Park Av
Depew Pl
Lexington Av
Third Av
Second Av
First Av
FDR Drive
York Av
Sutton Pl
Sutton Pl South
Beekman Place
Vanderbilt Av
Broadway
Park Av. S.
Union Sq W
Union Sq
Union Sq E
Irving Pl
ND Perlman Pl
Asser Levy Pl

Subway stop Ⓜ

215

Where to Find That Thingie You Wanted—Specialty Shopping

Antiques

New York is a great place to buy antiques. The choices go from outrageously expensive, museum-quality pieces to affordable minor items.

An important part of the business happens at the various antique shows (see the list of events in chapter 1) and auction houses, such as **Christie's Fine Art Auctioneers** (502 Park Ave. at 59th Street, ☎ **212/546-1000,** N/R train to the Lexington Avenue stop or 4/5/6 train to the 59th Street stop) and **Sotheby's** (1334 York Ave. at 72nd Street, ☎ **212/606-7000,** buses M30/M31/M72 from the West Side).

A prime area for antiques is East 60th Street between Second and Third avenues, where you'll find about a dozen stores. Other good areas are around Broadway and East 12th Street (some are open to the trade only), and a few on Bleecker Street between Seventh Avenue and Hudson.

Two other prime locations are the **Chelsea Antiques Building** (112 W. 25th St. between Sixth and Seventh avenues, ☎ **212/929-3939,** 1/9 train to the 23rd Street stop) and **Manhattan Art and Antiques Center** (1050 Second Ave. at 56th Street, ☎ **212/355-4400,** N/R train to the Lexington Avenue stop or 4/5/6 train to 59 Street stop).

If you're in town on Sunday, make sure to check out the outdoor flea markets centered around Sixth Avenue and 26th Street. Get there early, though—say, around 8am—or the bargains will walk out before you walk in.

Bookstores

From the days when Whitman and Melville lived here to the Beat Generation and beyond, there's always been a serious literary vibe in New York. Innumerable novelists, poets, and playwrights have called the city home, and most of the country's major publishing houses are based here as well.

For years, that kind of concentration meant that independent bookstores flourished in the city, filling literary niches for a small, discriminating clientele of one kind or another. Unfortunately, skyrocketing rents and the pressure exerted by the major national booksellers have killed a lot of these shops in recent years, leaving the city just that much poorer. Thankfully, though, a number of great shops still survive.

The biggest and most mind-boggling is **The Strand,** located at the corner of Broadway and 12th St. (☎ **212/473-1452**); take the 4/5/6/N/R/L train to the 14 St./Union Square stop and walk south. They stock a self-professed "Eight miles of books" on every subject conceivable, both new and used and mostly discounted. There's also a newer, monstrously huge Strand at 95 Fulton St. (☎ **212/732-6070**), near the South Street Seaport (2/3/4/5 train to Fulton St. stop then walk east).

For mystery fans, **Murder Ink** (2486 Broadway at 91st Street, ☎ **212/ 362-8905;** and 1467 Second Avenue between 76th and 77th streets, ☎ **212/ 517-3222**) is the place to be. They stock mystery titles old and new, and also run a mail-order service for out-of-town clients. Ask to be placed on their mailing list.

Rizzoli is a particularly good choice for art books, and also stocks a full selection of other subjects. Their Midtown branch is located at 31 W. 57th Street between Fifth and Sixth avenues (☎ **212/759-2424**); take the N/R to the 57th Street stop and walk east. Their SoHo store is at 454 West Broadway, just below Houston (☎ **212/674-1616**); take the N/R to the Prince Street stop and walk three blocks west.

For a general selection that's heavy on literature, Midtown's **Coliseum Books** is a good bet. Their two floors stock all the newest and most well-reviewed raves plus many obscure and hard-to-find titles. They're located on the corner of Broadway and 57th Street (☎ **212/757-8381**); take the A/B/C/D/1/9 to 59th Street/Columbus Circle.

If travel is your bag—and it must be, since you're reading this book—check out the **Traveler's Bookstore** in the lobby of 22 W. 52nd St. between Fifth and Sixth Avenues (☎ **212/664-0995**), for travel guides, maps, both old and new books of travel commentary, and various travel knickknacks. Take the B/D/F/Q to Rockefeller Center and walk half a block east.

Lastly, there's the giant. Over the last few years, the **Barnes & Noble** superstores—scattered all over town and each with its own Starbucks Coffee Shop—have become a full-fledged institution. The Lincoln Square location (1960 Broadway at 66th St., right across the triangle from Lincoln Center, take the 1/9 to 66th Street; ☎ **212/595-6859**) and the Astor Place location (just east of Broadway, below 8th Street, take the N/R to 8th St. and walk one block south; ☎ **212/420-1322**) are particularly attractive and close to other sightseeing. There are other branches all over town.

Discount Stores
In these stores you'll be able to find famous labels, big names of fashion, and European designers at discount prices. Most of the stores offer a selection of clothing and accessories for men, women, and children, and some also have a small home section.

Century 21. 22 Cortland St. between Broadway and Church Street (☎ **212/ 227-9092**). 1/9 train to Cortland Street stop or C/E train to World Trade Center stop.

Daffy's. The larger store is at 111 Fifth Ave. at 18th Street (☎ **212/ 529-4477**), 4/5/6/L/N/R train to 14 Street/Union Square stop. Other locations are at 335 Madison Ave. at 44th Street (☎ **212/557-4422**) and 135 E. 57th St. between Park and Lexington avenues (☎ **212/376-4477**).

The Way We Were

If you're interested in seeing how the city looked in years past, there's a great series of **historical photo books** on various periods published by Dover Publications. *New York Then and Now* gives you photos of the city in the late nineteenth and early twentieth centuries, contrasted with the way it looked in the 1970s. (It's interesting to note that some of the places from the 1970s look completely different now. The book could use a new edition, but it's still fascinating.) There's also *New York in the Thirties, New York in the Forties,* and *New York in the Sixties,* as well as *New York's Fabulous Luxury Apartments, Maritime New York, Nineteenth Century New York in Early Photographs,* and many others. All of these books are in the $10–$15 dollar range, and can be found at most major bookstores around town (try Barnes & Noble or Coliseum—see the "Bookstores" section for addresses) or at the Museum of the City of New York's bookshop (see chapter 14).

Filene's Basement. 620 Sixth Ave. at 18th Street (☎ 212/620-3100), F train to 23rd Street stop; and 2222 Broadway at 79th Street (☎ 212/873-8000), 1/9 train to the 79th Street stop.

Electronics

Although hundreds of shops in New York sell electronics, many are real rip-offs (see "Tourist Traps" box earlier in this chapter). The following two shops are the best for quality, reliability, choice, and prices.

J & R. 15 Park Row at City Hall Park (☎ 212/238-9100). 4/5/6 train to Brooklyn Bridge/City Hall stop. There are two stores one after the other, both of them with a great selection and good prices; the first is for computers and electric appliances, and the second for music equipment and CDs, tapes, and LPs. They're open daily and you can order from anywhere in the U.S. at ☎ 800/221-8180.

47th Street Photo. 115 W. 45th St. between Sixth and Seventh avenues (☎ 212/398-1530). 1/2/3/7/9/N/R/S train to 42nd Street/Times Square stop. A great store for anything from a computer to a portable CD player, at terrific prices and with all the warranties. The store ships anywhere in the United States by Federal Express at no extra charge, and you can also order by mail or by telephone from anywhere in the United States at ☎ 800/221-7774. Note that the shop is closed Friday after 2pm and all day Saturday.

Food

New York is where you can find food from all over the world. Following are the two largest gourmet shops.

Balducci's. 424 Sixth Ave. at 10th Street (☎ **212/673-2600**). L/F train to the 14th Street stop. A great place for gourmet food with an Italian flavor.

Zabar's. 2245 Broadway at 80th St. (☎ **212/787-2000**). 1/9 train to the 79th Street stop. A gourmandiser's dream, this is *the* spot for a selection of gourmet foods with a Jewish deli heritage and much more (including caviar), plus a whole floor of cooking utensils and appliances.

Java Shopping

If you're a coffee junkie, you owe it to yourself to visit **Porto Rico Importing Company,** a veritable Shangri La of beans, where you can choose your selection from among dozens of burlap sacks full of coffees from around the world. They're just as well-stocked with teas, but it's the coffee that made this place famous. Among their three locations, the main branch at 201 Bleecker St., between Sixth Avenue and MacDougal Street (☎ 212/477-5421), is the largest and most fun, but you'll get a contact buzz at any of them, just from breathing in the coffee aroma. (Their other two branches are in SoHo at 107 Thompson St. between Prince and Spring, ☎ 212/966-5758; and in the East Village at 40½ St. Marks Place, between First and Second avenues, ☎ 212/533-1982.)

Jewelry

Many of the big names are located near **Tiffany** on Fifth Avenue (see the section "The Big Names" earlier in this chapter for directions). **Cartier** (2 E. 52nd St., ☎ **212/446-3459**) is there, as are **Bulgari** (730 Fifth Ave., ☎ **212/315-9000**) and **Van Cleef & Arpels** (744 Fifth Ave., ☎ **212/644-9500**). **Bulgari** also has a branch on Madison Avenue (783 Madison Ave., ☎ **212/717-2300**).

Otherwise, the prime area for wholesale jewelers is West 47th Street between Fifth and Sixth avenues, which is jam-packed with stores.

CDs and Tapes

There are several huge music stores in New York, but the best are **J & R Music World** (see the section "Electronics" earlier in this chapter), **HMV** (565 Fifth Ave. at 46th Street, ☎ **212/681-6700,** 7 train to Fifth Avenue stop; 2081 Broadway at 72nd Street, ☎ **212/721-5900;** and 57 W. 34th St., right across from Macy's, ☎ **212/629-0900**), **Tower Records** (692 Broadway at 4th St., ☎ **212/505-1500,** 6 train to Astor Place stop; 196 Broadway at 66th Street, ☎ **212/799-2500,** 1/9 train to 66 Street/Lincoln Center stop; and 725 Fifth Ave. at 57th Street, inside the Trump Tower on Fifth Avenue, ☎ **212/838-8110,** N/R train to the Fifth Avenue stop), and the **Virgin Megastore** (1540 Broadway at 46th Street, ☎ **212/921-1020,**

1/2/3/7/9/N/R/S train to 42nd Street/Times Square stop, open daily 9am–1am and until 2am Friday and Saturday).

Musical Instruments

If your idea of a good souvenir is a new Les Paul guitar or Selmer sax, West 48th Street between Sixth and Seventh avenues is the place to go. **Sam Ash** (☎ **212/719-2299**) and **Manny's Music** (☎ **212/819-0576**) are the two biggies on the block, but there are several smaller dealers as well. For drums and percussion instruments from around the world, the best place in town is **Drummer's World,** two blocks down at 151 W. 46th St. (☎ **212/ 840-3057**). It's on the 3rd floor, but there's a sign at street-level.

Chapter 16

Battle Plans for Seeing the Sights— Eight Great Itineraries

In This Chapter

➤ Eight itineraries that will show you New York's hot spots

There are many ways to work the major sights of Manhattan into your visit, ranging from the leisurely to the insane. We suggest avoiding the "Bronx is up and the Battery's down" kind of ricochet tour, zooming from the World Trade Center to Museum Mile, boxing the compass from Times Square to the United Nations. If you only have a couple of days, think about reducing your expectations or taking one of the better guided bus tours. Your feet will thank you.

Each of the itineraries we've prepared is meant to end up around nightfall, leaving you in a place where you can easily hop a subway back to your hotel or to the nightlife of your choice: theater, concert, or club.

For more information on each attraction, please refer to chapters 13 and 14.

Itinerary #1—Central Park & the East Side Museums

After breakfast at your hotel or vicinity, take a stroll through Central Park on your way to the Metropolitan Museum of Art. After your visit, have a slice of pizza at Pintaile's Pizza or lunch in the area, and then walk north to the Guggenheim Museum. Alternatively, walk south along the park to the Whitney Museum and lunch at Sarabeth's Restaurant (within the museum) before visiting the art. Remember that this itinerary is good for any day of the week except Mondays, when the Met is closed.

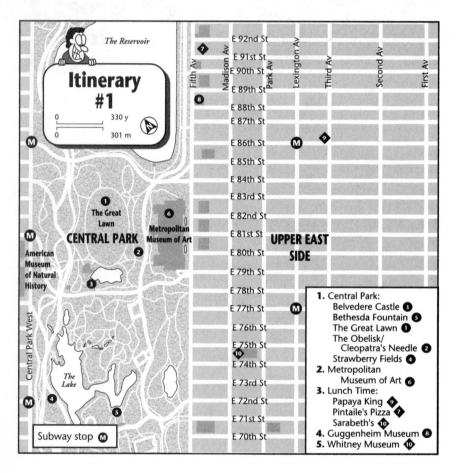

1. **Central Park.** Walk through the park heading toward 84th Street and Fifth Avenue. You can enter the Park at various points along its east, south, or west border (see the Central Park attractions map and chapter 13). According to where you enter, you'll have to allow more or less time for your visit. As a general suggestion, plan to spend up to 1 hour in the Park (one could spend a whole day there), but you can make the stroll much shorter by entering the Park nearer the Met.

2. **Metropolitan Museum of Art.** Plan to arrive at the museum around opening time (9:30am) and remember that the Museum is closed Mondays. Arriving early is a good idea, particularly on weekends, when it gets very crowded (especially at the coat check line in fall and winter). Allow a minimum of 2 hours at the museum. (See chapter 13.)

3. **Lunch Time.** For lunch, have a top-quality pizza at **Pintaile's Pizza,** grab a great hot dog and Papaya juice at **Papaya King** (see chapter 11), or eat at one of the Upper East Side suggested restaurants (see chapters 11 and 12). If you choose step **4b,** have lunch at **Sarabeth's** in the Whitney Museum, a restaurant mostly known for breakfast and brunch but which offers top food at any time (see chapter 11).

4a. **Guggenheim Museum.** If you feel up to it, go in and visit; if you're a little tired, just look at this unique building from the outside and from just within the entrance.

4b. **Whitney Museum.** After the Met (and a quick peek at the Guggenheim if you're a strong and fast walker and don't mind hip-hopping north and then south), go south along the Park to 75th Street, and then head one block east to Madison Avenue and the Whitney Museum (see chapter 14). Allow 1 hour minimum for the visit.

Kids Itinerary #2—The Museums, the Park, & Times Square

Again start at the Metropolitan Museum of Art early in the morning, and then stroll through Central Park. Either proceed southward and have a gourmet lunch at The Boathouse Cafe overlooking the lake, or head west over to the Upper West Side and eat there. After lunch, visit the American Museum of Natural History (alternatively, The Children's Museum or the Cathedral of St. John the Divine). Take the subway or bus to Times Square, eat at one of the restaurants on 46th Street's Restaurant Row, and then see a show in the Theater District if you're still standing. (*Note:* If this itinerary seems sparse, consider that both the Met and the Natural History museum both have millions of objects, so this is a better itinerary for those who want to see them thoroughly than for the "been there, done that" crowd.)

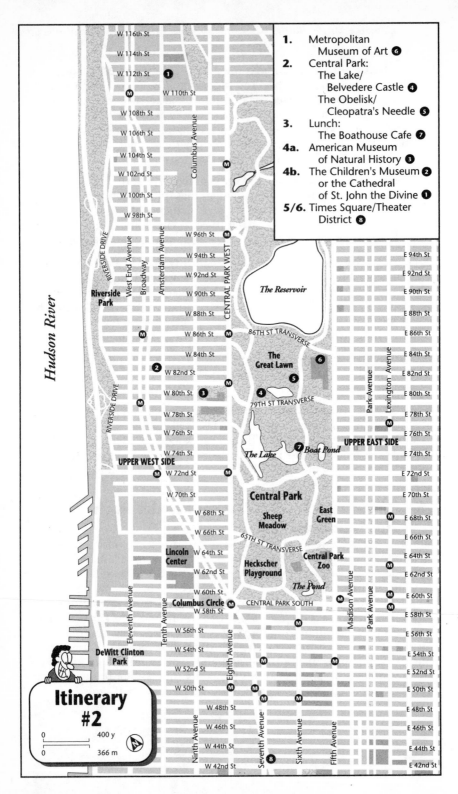

1. Metropolitan
   Museum of Art ⑥
2. Central Park:
   The Lake/
      Belvedere Castle ④
   The Obelisk/
      Cleopatra's Needle ⑤
3. Lunch:
   The Boathouse Cafe ⑦
4a. American Museum
   of Natural History ③
4b. The Children's Museum ②
   or the Cathedral
   of St. John the Divine ①
5/6. Times Square/Theater
   District ⑧

W 116th St
W 114th St
W 112th St ①
W 110th St
W 108th St
W 106th St
W 104th St
W 102nd St
W 100th St
W 98th St
W 96th St
W 94th St
W 92nd St
W 90th St
W 88th St
W 86th St
W 84th St
W 82nd St ②
W 80th St ③
W 78th St
W 76th St
W 74th St
W 72nd St
W 70th St
W 68th St
W 66th St
W 64th St
W 62nd St
W 60th St
W 58th St
W 56th St
W 54th St
W 52nd St
W 50th St
W 48th St
W 46th St
W 44th St
W 42nd St

E 94th St
E 92nd St
E 90th St
E 88th St
E 86th St
E 84th St
E 82nd St
E 80th St
E 78th St
E 76th St
E 74th St
E 72nd St
E 70th St
E 68th St
E 66th St
E 64th St
E 62nd St
E 60th St
E 58th St
E 56th St
E 54th St
E 52nd St
E 50th St
E 48th St
E 46th St
E 44th St
E 42nd St

RIVERSIDE DRIVE
West End Avenue
Broadway
Amsterdam Avenue
Columbus Avenue
CENTRAL PARK WEST
RIVERSIDE DRIVE

Ninth Avenue
Tenth Avenue
Eleventh Avenue
Eighth Avenue
Seventh Avenue
Sixth Avenue
Fifth Avenue
Madison Avenue
Park Avenue
Lexington Avenue

Hudson River

Riverside Park

The Reservoir

86TH ST TRANSVERSE

The Great Lawn ⑥ ⑤ ④

79TH ST TRANSVERSE

The Lake ⑦ *Boat Pond*

UPPER EAST SIDE

UPPER WEST SIDE

Central Park

Sheep Meadow

East Green

65TH ST TRANSVERSE

Lincoln Center

Heckscher Playground

Central Park Zoo

The Pond

Columbus Circle

CENTRAL PARK SOUTH

DeWitt Clinton Park

⑧

Itinerary #2

0   400 y
0   366 m

224

1. **Metropolitan Museum of Art.** As in Itinerary 1, step 2. (Remember that the museum is closed on Mondays.)

2. **Central Park.** Take a leisurely stroll heading southwest, passing by the obelisk and the lake (see chapter 13).

3. **Lunch.** A perfect place to have lunch on this itinerary is the **Boathouse Cafe,** on the lake in Central Park. Alternatively, you can head west and have lunch at one of the many locations in the Upper West Side (see chapters 10 and 11).

4a. **American Museum of Natural History.** Almost directly across the park from the Met and within walking distance from wherever you had lunch, this very interesting museum is great for adults and kids (maybe not toddlers). Plan at least 2 hours for the visit.

4b. **The Children's Museum** or **the Cathedral of St. John the Divine.** If you have toddlers or you're tired of museums, you may choose one of these alternative activities. The Cathedral is a little far north (at 112th Street), but definitely worth visiting (see chapter 13).

5. **Times Square.** After step 4a or 4b, take the subway (1/9 train) or the bus (M10 from the Natural History Museum, M104 from the others) to Times Square. Try to time your arrival to around dusk, when the lights begin to show their effect, and then stay until dark.

6. **Dinner and/or Show.** You are now in a prime spot for a great dinner. Choose between Restaurant Row (see chapter 9) or one of the other great restaurants in the area (see chapters 10 and 11). You're also now in the Theater District, and it could be a perfect opportunity to see a show, either before or after dinner, depending on how tired you are. "But what if we didn't plan ahead?" you ask? Well, you're also just by the TKTS booth, where you can get last-minute tickets (see chapter 18).

Itinerary #3—The Statue of Liberty, South Street, & Chinatown

Start at Battery Park in the morning—the earlier the better. Take the ferry to the Statue of Liberty/Ellis Island. Have a bite at Fraunces Tavern or at South Street Seaport and stop to visit the museum or to shop; then walk across the Brooklyn Bridge. In the summer, catch an evening boat tour of the harbor from the Seaport; otherwise, walk or cab to Chinatown or Little Italy for dinner.

1. **Statue of Liberty/Ellis Island.** Arrive at Battery Park as early as you can (the first ferry leaves at 9:15am), especially in summer when lines may be hours long (see chapter 13). If you decide to visit only the museum on Ellis Island, figure about 2 hours.

2. **South Street Seaport.** Walk from Battery Park to the Seaport area (take Pearl Street all the way to Fulton Street and turn right toward the Seaport). On your way, visit the famous **Fraunces Tavern** (54 Pearl St. at Broad Street, ☎ 212/269-0144); you can stop for a drink or a snack, but we suggest you skip real food, which is mediocre, and instead have lunch at one of the many restaurants around the Seaport. There's also a food court on the third floor of Pier 17, the huge red structure overlooking the water. This is a good opportunity to shop (see chapter 15) and, if you're interested in maritime history, to visit the **South Street Seaport Museum,** with its many vessels.

3a. **Brooklyn Bridge.** Walk west on Fulton to Theater Street, turn right on Theater Street, and walk one block north to Park Row (on the east side of City Hall Park); the pedestrian entrance to the bridge will be on your right (see chapter 13). Walk over the bridge, lingering over the views up and down the East River. Time your walk to be there just before sunset—you'll have one of the most extraordinary views of Manhattan. (By the way, if you plan to shop for electronics or music, this is a good opportunity to stop at **J&R,** located right at the base of the bridge on Park Row—see chapter 15.)

3b. **Evening Cruise.** In the summer, a nice alternative (or an additional activity) is to catch one of the several cruises starting from Downtown Manhattan (see chapter 12)—maybe on a historical sailing ship. Cruising at sunset in the harbor is truly magical.

4. **Dinner.** Take advantage of being Downtown and take a short cab ride to one of the restaurants in **Chinatown** or **Little Italy** (see chapters 9 and 10 to make your choice). In Little Italy you could also just have a drink or dessert at a romantic sidewalk table.

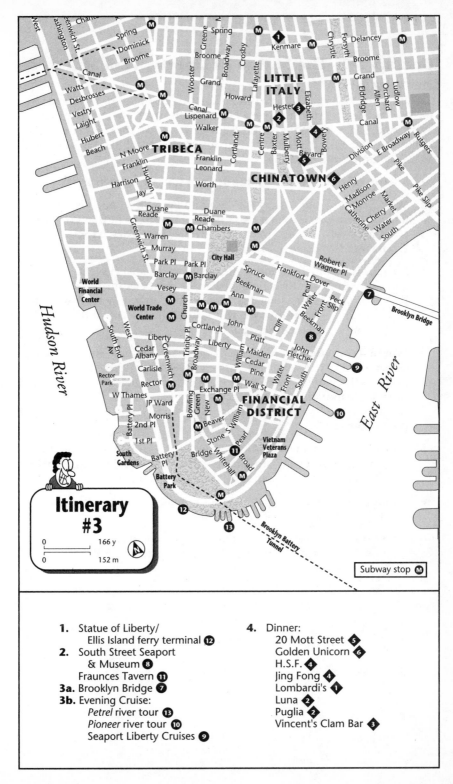

Itinerary #4—The Statue of Liberty, Wall Street, & the Village

As in Itinerary 3, start at Battery Park, taking the first ferry to the Statue of Liberty/Ellis Island. Returning, have lunch around Wall Street, visit Fraunces Tavern, and then walk to the World Trade Center. Take the subway north and stroll up around SoHo. Either stay there for dinner or continue to Greenwich Village for dinner and nightlife.

1. **Statue of Liberty/Ellis Island.** As in Itinerary 3, step 1.

2. **Wall Street.** From Battery Park, walk to Pearl Street and visit the famous **Fraunces Tavern** (see Itinerary 3, step 2). Turn left on Broad Street and walk to Wall Street and visit the **New York Stock Exchange** (see chapter 13) on your left.

3. **Lunch.** Have lunch in one of the places in the area (see chapters 11 and 12) or grab a sandwich, maybe at the most elegant McDonald's you have ever seen (see chapter 13). Alternatively (but only Mon–Fri), proceed directly to **Windows on the World,** on the top of the World Trade Center, for lunch (see chapter 10).

4. **World Trade Center.** Walk west on Wall Street, past Trinity Church and its cemetery (chapter 14), turn right on Trinity Place and continue north to the World Trade Center plaza. You can then go to the top and catch the panoramic views of the city and harbor. Also, just across the street from the World Trade Center is the historical **St. Paul's Chapel** (see chapter 13).

5. **SoHo.** Take the subway (1/9/C/E train) to the Canal Street stop, walk east on Canal Street and stroll up West Broadway and through **SoHo** for art galleries and shopping (see chapters 14 and 16).

6a. **Dinner.** SoHo is also a neat place for a trendy dinner or drink in a street-side cafe (see chapters 10, 11, and 20).

6b. **Greenwich Village.** As an alternative, you could cross Houston Street and continue northwest for dinner and nightlife in the Village (see chapters 10, 11, and 20).

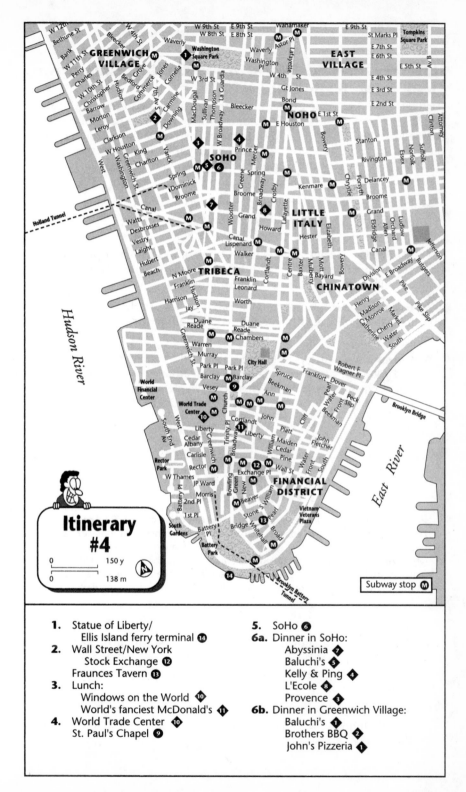

Itinerary #4

0 ——— 150 y
0 ——— 138 m

Subway stop Ⓜ

1. Statue of Liberty/
   Ellis Island ferry terminal ⑭
2. Wall Street/New York
   Stock Exchange ⑫
   Fraunces Tavern ⑬
3. Lunch:
   Windows on the World ⑩
   World's fanciest McDonald's ⑪
4. World Trade Center ⑩
   St. Paul's Chapel ⑨

5. SoHo ⑥
6a. Dinner in SoHo:
   Abyssinia ⑦
   Baluchi's ⑤
   Kelly & Ping ④
   L'Ecole ⑧
   Provence ③
6b. Dinner in Greenwich Village:
   Baluchi's ❶
   Brothers BBQ ❷
   John's Pizzeria ❶

Itinerary #5—The World Trade Center, Chinatown, Little Italy, & the Village

Begin at the World Trade Center in the morning, taking in the view. Walk north, visiting St. Paul's Chapel, passing by City Hall, and then taking a stroll on the Brooklyn Bridge. Stop in Chinatown or in Little Italy for lunch, and then walk up Broadway for shopping. You may then turn west into SoHo or continue north to visit the Guggenheim SoHo. Round out the day in Greenwich Village.

1. **World Trade Center.** Get to the Towers first thing in the morning—a particularly good idea during top tourist months, when lines at the bottom can be quite long—and take in the view.

2. **St. Paul's Chapel.** Walk out of the World Trade Center plaza and cross Church Street to visit Manhattan's oldest church. You see the churchyard first; the entrance is on Broadway.

3. **Brooklyn Bridge.** Head down Park Row toward the bridge. Have a look at **City Hall.** At this point, you're right at the pedestrian entry for the bridge.

4. **Chinatown.** After your bridge walk, head a couple of blocks north and you're in Chinatown. You can stroll around and go for dim sum in one of the great restaurants there (see chapters 9 and 10), or, if that's too far out, walk a little further and eat in **Little Italy.**

New York Stories

If you're walking around Little Italy, stop into the **Marechiaro Tavern** at 176½ Mulberry Street, near the corner of Broome Street. Recognize the place? You probably will if you've seen a lot of Mafia movies (among other things, it was where Al Pacino met Johnny Depp in *Donnie Brasco*). This is a classic Little Italy barroom that looks like it hasn't been redecorated since Roosevelt was in office. During the day it's pretty quiet, but at night it fills up with local regulars.

5. **SoHo.** From Chinatown or Little Italy, walk west to Broadway and turn right (north) to SoHo; you may want to do some shopping here, visit a few art galleries, or visit the **Guggenheim SoHo** at Broadway and Prince Street.

6. **Greenwich Village.** For a perfect end to the day, visit the Village, with its ample choice of restaurants and nightlife (see chapters 10 and 20).

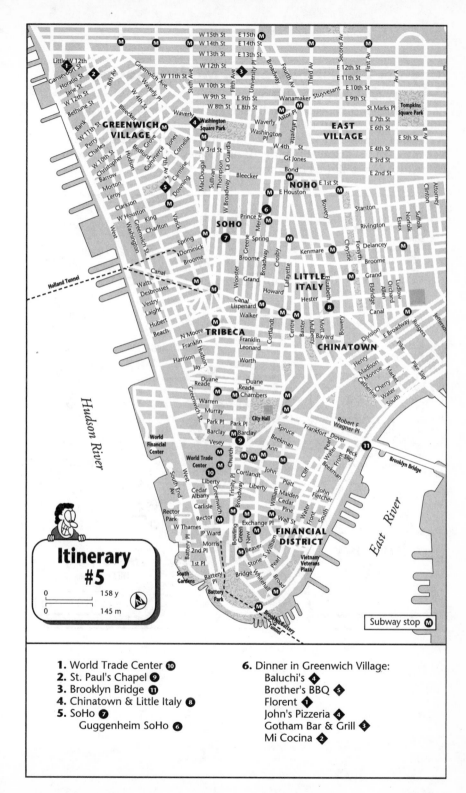

Itinerary #5

0 —————— 158 y
0 —————— 145 m

1. World Trade Center ❿
2. St. Paul's Chapel ❾
3. Brooklyn Bridge ⓫
4. Chinatown & Little Italy ❽
5. SoHo ❼
   Guggenheim SoHo ❻

6. Dinner in Greenwich Village:
   Baluchi's ❹
   Brother's BBQ ❺
   Florent ❶
   John's Pizzeria ❹
   Gotham Bar & Grill ❸
   Mi Cocina ❷

Subway stop Ⓜ

Itinerary #6—Fifth Avenue, MOMA, Rockefeller Center, & Times Square

Start out the morning with a stroll on Fifth Avenue, and then visit the Museum of Modern Art (MOMA). Have lunch and continue south to Rockefeller Center and St. Patrick's Cathedral, and then continue on to the New York Public Library, Bryant Park, and Times Square. See a show in the Theater District, followed by dinner.

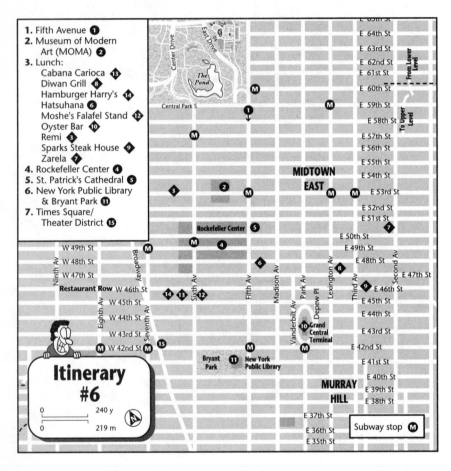

1. Fifth Avenue ❶
2. Museum of Modern Art (MOMA) ❷
3. Lunch:
　Cabana Carioca ❸
　Diwan Grill ❽
　Hamburger Harry's ❹
　Hatsuhana ❻
　Moshe's Falafel Stand ❿
　Oyster Bar ❿
　Remi ❸
　Sparks Steak House ❾
　Zarela ❼
4. Rockefeller Center ❹
5. St. Patrick's Cathedral ❺
6. New York Public Library & Bryant Park ⓫
7. Times Square/ Theater District ⓯

Itinerary #6

0 ——— 240 y
0 ——— 219 m

Subway stop Ⓜ

1. **Fifth Avenue.** From Central Park South and Fifth Avenue, admire the Plaza Hotel, and then stroll downtown, past shops like Bergdorf Goodman, FAO Schwarz, Saks Fifth Avenue, and Tiffany (see chapter 15).

2. **MOMA.** Strolling south on Fifth Avenue, you'll pass half a block from the Museum of Modern Art (on 53rd Street); you may visit it, allowing 1–2 hours, or just do some more shopping at the great Museum Gift Shop.

3. **Lunch.** Stop for lunch at one of the many places in the area (see chapters 10 and 11), before or after steps 4 and 5.

4. **Rockefeller Center.** Stroll around the center and admire the architecture, the shops underground, and (in winter) the skaters on the rink.

5. **St. Patrick's Cathedral.** Located just across the street from Rockefeller Center. It's the one everybody has their cameras trained on.

6. **New York Public Library and Bryant Park.** Continue south on Fifth Avenue to 42nd Street and visit the library. Afterward you may want to stop in the park for a coffee break at one of the restaurants or kiosks, or grab a more substantial snack to fortify yourself until later if you are planning to take in a Broadway show. If it's summer, there may be free entertainment.

7. **Times Square.** Walk west on 42nd Street, arriving at dusk as the lights come up.

8. **Showtime.** A perfect occasion for catching a Broadway show or for simply having dinner in one of the many restaurants of the area (see chapter 10).

Itinerary #7—The Village, the Flatiron District, & the Empire State Building

On a weekend day, start out with brunch in Greenwich Village. Afterward, walk to Washington Square, and then up Fifth Avenue to the Flatiron Building. Take the subway or continue walking to Herald Square/Macy's, and then head east to the Empire State Building. Walk, cab, or take the subway to Gramercy Park, in time for a romantic dinner at one of the area's restaurants. (See chapter 10 for listings.)

1. **Greenwich Village.** This historic neighborhood is particularly delightful on weekend mornings, and it's also a perfect place for breakfast or brunch (see chapter 11). After the meal, stroll in the peaceful streets and walk east to **Washington Square.**

2. **Flatiron Building.** From Washington Square, go straight through the arch and take a very pleasant walk up Fifth Avenue past shops and beautiful buildings to the **Flatiron Building** at the corner of 23rd Street.

3. **Herald Square/Macy's.** If you feel like shopping, this is an opportunity not to miss. Walk up Broadway from the Flatiron Building to 34th Street (or take the N/R subway train from 23rd to 34th) and go for it. If you're hungry, stop for lunch in Koreatown (see chapters 9, 10, and 11).

4. **Empire State Building.** Walk east on 34th Street from Macy's (or north on Fifth Avenue from the Flatiron Building if you decided to skip the shopping) and visit one of the greatest buildings in architectural history.

5. **Gramercy Park.** To end the day on a relaxing and romantic note, take a cab down to Gramercy Park (or walk if your feet still agree). If you wish to take the subway, walk east to Park Avenue and take the 6 train from the 33rd Street stop to the 23rd Street one. Have dinner at one of the area's restaurants (see chapter 10) and take a leisurely after-dinner stroll.

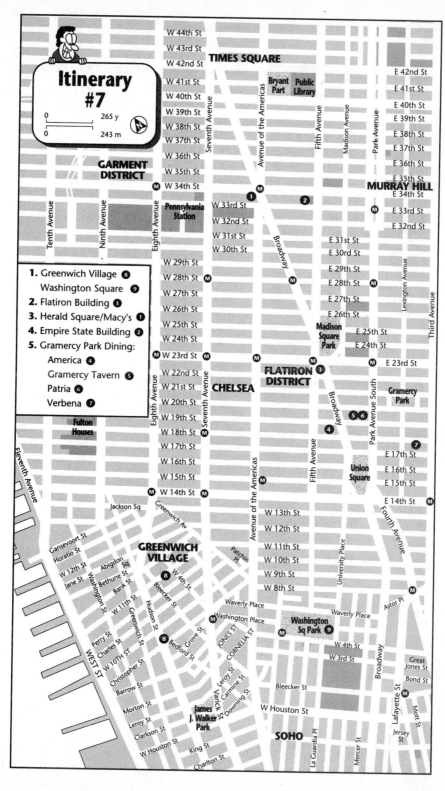

Itinerary #7

0 — 265 y
0 — 243 m

GARMENT DISTRICT

TIMES SQUARE

MURRAY HILL

1. Greenwich Village ⑧
   Washington Square ⑨
2. Flatiron Building ③
3. Herald Square/Macy's ①
4. Empire State Building ②
5. Gramercy Park Dining:
   America ④
   Gramercy Tavern ⑤
   Patria ⑥
   Verbena ⑦

W 44th St
W 43rd St
W 42nd St
W 41st St
W 40th St
W 39th St
W 38th St
W 37th St
W 36th St
W 35th St
W 34th St
W 33rd St
W 32nd St
W 31st St
W 30th St
W 29th St
W 28th St
W 27th St
W 26th St
W 25th St
W 24th St
W 23rd St
W 22nd St
W 21st St
W 20th St
W 19th St
W 18th St
W 17th St
W 16th St
W 15th St
W 14th St
W 13th St
W 12th St
W 11th St
W 10th St
W 9th St
W 8th St

E 42nd St
E 41st St
E 40th St
E 39th St
E 38th St
E 37th St
E 36th St
E 35th St
E 34th St
E 33rd St
E 32nd St
E 31st St
E 30th St
E 29th St
E 28th St
E 27th St
E 26th St
E 25th St
E 24th St
E 23rd St
E 17th St
E 16th St
E 15th St
E 14th St

Bryant Park
Public Library
Pennsylvania Station
Madison Square Park
Gramercy Park
Union Square

Tenth Avenue
Ninth Avenue
Eighth Avenue
Seventh Avenue
Avenue of the Americas
Fifth Avenue
Madison Avenue
Park Avenue
Lexington Avenue
Third Avenue
Broadway
Park Avenue South
Fourth Avenue
University Place

CHELSEA
FLATIRON DISTRICT

Fulton Houses

Eleventh Avenue

Jackson Sq
Greenwich Av

GREENWICH VILLAGE

Gansevoort St
Horatio St
W 12th St
Jane St
Abigdon Sq
Bethune St
Bank St
W 11th St
Perry St
Charles St
W 10TH ST
Christopher St
Barrow St
Morton St
Leroy St
Clarkson St
W Houston St

Washington St
Greenwich St
Hudson St
Bleecker St
W 4th St.

Patchin Pl

Waverly Place
Washington Place
JONES ST
CORNELIA ST
Bedford St
Grove St
Leroy St
Varick St
Carmine St
Downing St

Washington Sq Park ⑨
Waverly Place
Astor Pl

W 4th St
W 3rd St
Bleecker St
W Houston St

James J. Walker Park

King St
Charlton St

SOHO

La Guardia Pl
Mercer St

Broadway
Great Jones St
Bond St
Lafayette St
Mott St
Jersey St

✦Kids✦ Itinerary #8—The U.N., Grand Central, the *Intrepid*, & Times Square

Begin early at the United Nations or coordinate your visit with a lunch at the Delegates Dining Room. Walk to the Chrysler Building and Grand Central Terminal, and then have lunch in the area. After lunch, see the New York Public Library, and then detour up Fifth Avenue to Rockefeller Center, or just continue across 42nd Street by foot or subway to the *Intrepid* Sea-Air-Space Museum or a Circle Line tour. Round out the day with a visit to Times Square, dinner at Restaurant Row, and a Broadway show.

1. **United Nations.** Try to get here relatively early in the morning (the first tour starts at 9:15am) since it gets quite busy at prime tourist times. Plan to spend 1–2 hours visiting the building, grounds, and garden.

2. **Lunch.** If you wish, you can have a luxury buffet lunch at the **Delegates Dining Room** of the United Nations (4th floor, General Assembly building, ☎ 212/963-7625, open Mon–Fri only, reservations mandatory—and dress nicely). Otherwise, have lunch in the area (see chapter 10) or, weather permitting, at **Bryant Park** (behind the New York Public Library).

3. **Chrysler Building.** From the United Nations or from your restaurant—depending on your lunch choices in step 2—walk west on 42nd Street past Third Avenue to get to this architectural jewel.

4. **Grand Central Terminal.** Just half a block west of the Chrysler and another example of a time when people really knew how to build 'em.

5. **New York Public Library and Bryant Park.** Continue on 42nd Street to Fifth Avenue and have lunch here if you so decide, or just visit.

6a. **Rockefeller Center and Fifth Avenue.** Head north on Fifth Avenue to visit the center and do some shopping.

6b. **Intrepid Sea-Air-Space Museum or Cruise around Manhattan.** Alternatively, continue across 42nd Street by foot or bus (M42 stops at every avenue) to Pier 86 for the Museum or Pier 83 for a **Circle Line** tour (3 hours).

7. **Times Square.** Arrive in early evening to see the lights of Times Square, eat at **Restaurant Row**, and take in a Broadway show—or just opt for two out of three if we've worn you out.

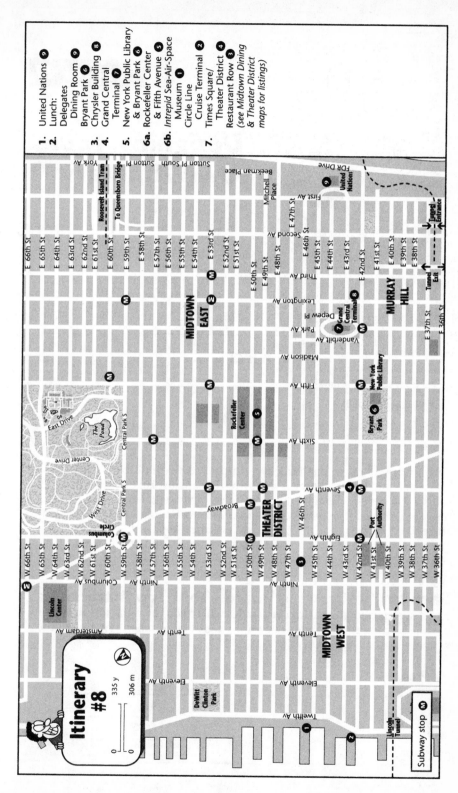

Itinerary #8

335 y
306 m

1. United Nations 9
2. Lunch:
   Delegates
   Dining Room 6
   Bryant Park 6
3. Chrysler Building 8
4. Grand Central
   Terminal 7
5. New York Public Library
   & Bryant Park 6
6a. Rockefeller Center
   & Fifth Avenue 5
6b. Intrepid Sea-Air-Space
   Museum 1
7. Circle Line
   Cruise Terminal 2
   Times Square/
   Theater District 4
   Restaurant Row 3
   (see Midtown Dining
   & Theater District
   maps for listings)

Subway stop Ⓜ

MIDTOWN EAST

MURRAY HILL

THEATER DISTRICT

MIDTOWN WEST

Lincoln Center

Columbus Circle

Central Park

East Drive

The Pond

Center Drive

West Drive

Central Park S

DeWitt Clinton Park

Port Authority

Lincoln Tunnel

United Nations 9

FDR Drive

Tunnel Entrance

Tunnel Exit

Grand Central Terminal 7

Bryant Park 6

New York Public Library

Rockefeller Center 5

Roosevelt Island Tram

To Queensboro Bridge

Mitchell Place

Beekman Place

Sutton Pl South

Sutton Pl

Depew Pl

York Av
First Av
Second Av
Third Av
Lexington Av
Park Av
Vanderbilt Av
Madison Av
Fifth Av
Sixth Av
Seventh Av
Broadway
Eighth Av
Ninth Av
Tenth Av
Eleventh Av
Twelfth Av
Amsterdam Av
Columbus Av

E 66th St
E 65th St
E 64th St
E 63rd St
E 62nd St
E 61st St
E 60th St
E 59th St
E 58th St
E 57th St
E 56th St
E 55th St
E 54th St
E 53rd St
E 52nd St
E 51st St
E 50th St
E 49th St
E 48th St
E 47th St
E 46th St
E 45th St
E 44th St
E 43rd St
E 42nd St
E 41st St
E 40th St
E 39th St
E 38th St
E 37th St
E 36th St

W 66th St
W 65th St
W 64th St
W 63rd St
W 62nd St
W 61st St
W 60th St
W 59th St
W 58th St
W 57th St
W 56th St
W 55th St
W 54th St
W 53rd St
W 52nd St
W 51st St
W 50th St
W 49th St
W 48th St
W 47th St
W 46th St
W 45th St
W 44th St
W 43rd St
W 42nd St
W 41st St
W 40th St
W 39th St
W 38th St
W 37th St
W 36th St

Chapter 17

Designing Your Own Itinerary

In This Chapter

➤ Budgeting your time

➤ Pacing yourself

➤ Tough choices

There comes a time in planning every trip when we sit down and say "I want to see that and that and that..." and realize there just isn't enough time. Of course, you can see more if you organize your days efficiently; disorganized travelers waste a lot of time, show up at the museum on the day it's closed, and end up *waaaaay* out in Queens because they hopped the wrong subway. The worksheets in this chapter are designed to help you decide what to see and to organize yourself so that you can fit it all in.

Back to the Drawing Board—Your Top Attractions

The first step is to go back to chapter 13, where you rated the top attractions from 1–5. Using this list, break down the sights by number: Write in all the #1s, all the #2s, and so on.

#1 Picks

➤ _____

➤ _____

➤ _____

➤ _____

➤ _____
➤ _____
➤ _____
➤ _____
➤ _____
➤ _____

#2 Picks

➤ _____
➤ _____
➤ _____
➤ _____
➤ _____
➤ _____
➤ _____
➤ _____
➤ _____
➤ _____

#3 Picks

➤ _____
➤ _____
➤ _____
➤ _____
➤ _____
➤ _____
➤ _____
➤ _____
➤ _____
➤ _____

#4 Picks

➤ _____
➤ _____

➤ _____

➤ _____

➤ _____

➤ _____

➤ _____

➤ _____

➤ _____

➤ _____

Once you've done this, go back to chapter 14 and pick up the "other fun stuff" that fits your particular interests. Assign these attractions a number, and put them into the preceding lists, too.

You're probably now asking why there are no spaces for the #5s. That's because, if you're a typical visitor, there are so many 1s, 2s, and 3s that you won't need the 5s, and may not even be able to visit the 4s. What if your #1 list above says "Empire State Building, Metropolitan Museum of Art, MOMA, Statue of Liberty, Ellis Island, Circle Line, Central Park"? That would easily fill two days: Day 1 would be your "on the water day," getting up early to see Liberty and Ellis Islands, having lunch, and then doing the 3-hour Circle Line cruise in the afternoon; Day 2 you would start by visiting the Met, and then wander through Central Park and have lunch, see MOMA in the afternoon, and catch the view from the Empire State Building around dusk. You'd still be able to see a show and have a great dinner at night. You'd also be tired.

Budgeting Your Time

An average sight takes two hours to visit. Some (Ellis Island/Statue of Liberty) take more, others (the Chrysler Building, St. Patrick's) take less. Therefore, you can "do" about three or four sights in a day if you're pushing yourself, fewer if you're not.

Add up the number of 1s and 2s in the above list, and then divide by the number of full days in your trip. If the result is a number larger than four, you may have a problem, because you can't see six or eight major sights in a day except superficially. How to get that sights-per-day number down?

➤ Lengthen your visit. This option may or may not be easy for you to do.

➤ Split up. If you are a couple or group, make individual lists as above, and then see if splitting up for a half day or two will provide enough time for everyone to see all his or her favorites.

➤ Axe the 3s. It's our opinion that it's better to see less and see it well than to spend 20 minutes at MOMA, grab a cab to the Cathedral of St. John the Divine, roll down the window for a picture...You get the idea.

240

Am I Staying in the Right Place?

Take your lists of attractions and put them into the following geographical categories:

Uptown

➤ _____

➤ _____

➤ _____

➤ _____

➤ _____

➤ _____

➤ _____

➤ _____

➤ _____

➤ _____

Midtown

➤ _____

➤ _____

➤ _____

➤ _____

➤ _____

➤ _____

➤ _____

➤ _____

➤ _____

➤ _____

Downtown

➤ _____

➤ _____

➤ _____

➤ _____

➤ _____

➤ _____

➤ _____

➤ _____

➤ _____

➤ _____

If your hotel is in the area with the most entries, you're doing well; you'll be able to get to the first item on your daily agenda in a timely manner, even if you aren't up at the crack of dawn. If you can walk to it, so much the better. If, on the other hand, you've reserved at a hotel that's close to very few of the things you want to see, you'll waste a lot of time commuting. Maybe you should change your hotel.

Getting All Your Ducks in a Row

Making your plan concrete may also help make your ideal trip doable. Take a map and mark the locations of all the sights you've listed so far; then mark your hotel. Now try to find clusters of activities that naturally group together. Avoid the Ricochet Rabbit approach to sightseeing (World Trade Center—United Nations—*Intrepid* Museum—Empire State Building). Don't let the city's layout trick you into thinking only vertically, either: You can see the Met in the morning, and then visit Central Park on the way across to the Children's Museum on the Upper West Side.

Time-Savers

Don't forget the season. It's always good in the winter to have a Plan B in case it rains. The weather will also partly determine how much walking you can do (or want to do). At a certain point it will become too cold or raw to ride the ferry or stroll outdoors comfortably. Also take into account what the sun does to your planning: For instance, Times Square's lights are best at night, but night comes down around 5pm in the winter and 9pm in summer.

Fill-Ins

Fill-ins are things you do on the way to someplace else. Shopping is a natural; go back to chapter 15 and pick out the specific stores and neighborhoods you want to spend time in. List them here.

Shopping

➤ _____

➤ _____

➤ _____

➤ _____

➤ _____

➤ _____

➤ _____

➤ _____

➤ _____

➤ _____

Locate these on the map, and figure out what sights they lie in between. Allow different amounts of time depending on whether you're just window shopping or really planning to graze these places. If you intend to buy a suit at Barney's or get all your Christmas shopping done at a major department store, it may become an attraction-length process.

Dining is another fill-in. Leave the question of dinner aside for now. If there are specific places where you want to lunch, locate them on the map in terms of your clusters of sights. If you have no "musts," use the listings in chapters 10 to 11 to pick out some lunchtime options for each of the clusters so you won't go hungry. List the lunch restaurants below:

Lunch

➤ _____

➤ _____

➤ _____

➤ _____

➤ _____

➤ _____

➤ _____

➤ _____

➤ _____

➤ _____

Sketching Out Your Itineraries

Now you're ready to plot some itineraries. At its most basic, an itinerary should be something like this:

Breakfast at [hotel/place/neighborhood]. See [attraction] in the morning. Lunch at [place/neighborhood] or [alternate]. Walk or take the [#] train/bus to [attraction]; visit in the afternoon.

243

Of course, you can fit another attraction into the morning and/or afternoon ("pass through Grand Central and see Chrysler Building on the way to United Nations"), and leave room for shopping ("exit subway at Bloomingdale's, shop like crazy, and then walk to Frick Collection").

Time-Savers

If making itineraries seems like a real drag to you, you can always cannibalize the recommended itineraries in the last chapter. You can mix and match our morning and afternoon activities, or substitute activities from the same neighborhoods and keep the basic structure (put the Museum of the American Indian in place of World Trade Center, for example).

Itinerary #1

➤ _____

➤ _____

➤ _____

➤ _____

➤ _____

Itinerary #2

➤ _____

➤ _____

➤ _____

➤ _____

➤ _____

Itinerary #3

➤ _____

➤ _____

➤ _____

➤ _____

➤ _____

Itinerary #4

➤ _____

➤ _____

➤ _____

➤ _____

➤ _____

Planning Your Nighttime Right

Like Elvis said, "The world is more alive at night—it's like God ain't looking." That's true most everywhere, of course, but it's even more true in New York, and in keeping with that philosophy it might be best to get a little loose in your after-dark itineraries. You could schedule yourself so that when the museum closes at 5pm you come out the door and stand facing that great restaurant you wanted to try, but that would be just a little bit *too* organized —and also exhausting. You'll probably want a little down time between the end of your sightseeing day and the beginning of your evening's activities, so we suggest you head back to your hotel to curl up with a glass of wine and a novel for an hour, or maybe catch a quick snooze to recharge your batteries. This plan also allows you to think about your nightlife plans as a separate mini-itinerary—rather than plan your nightlife by where you end your sight-seeing, you can plan a separate sortie from your hotel and hit the town refreshed, duded up in your evening best (or funkiest), and ready for action.

Spontaneity rules the night, so check out the nightlife recommendations in the following chapters and do what comes naturally—but don't forget to keep track of any dinner reservations or show tickets you've booked in advance. Write them here:

Night #1
➤ _____

➤ _____

Night #2
➤ _____

➤ _____

Night#3
➤ _____

➤ _____

Night#4
➤ _____

➤ _____

For the nights that are blank, you might want to write in tentative options, such as "dinner in [neighborhood]; go to [club/bar/cabaret] afterwards?"

Lastly, keep geography in mind enough so that you don't find yourself finishing up your day at the Brooklyn Bridge only an hour before you have to get to the Theater District. Remember to leave time not only for resting, showering, changing, and dressing, but for that other pleasure of New York: the fortuitous and unexpected things that happen when you finally *slow down.*

Part 6

On the Town—Nightlife & Entertainment

New York at night is like New York during the day—too many things to do to take it all in. There's no other city in the world like it for nightlife; from R&B to S&M, whether your taste runs to bistros or Stroh's, whether you fancy yourself a beatnik or a redneck, there are nighttime activities to suit everyone.

New York's most famous cultural attraction is Broadway. We've already given you some information on reserving tickets for popular shows (see chapter 4), but in the following chapters you'll find more specific information about Broadway and off-Broadway, and how to get tickets at a discount.

Carnegie Hall, Lincoln Center, Radio City, the Village Vanguard, Shakespeare in the Park...the list of cultural institutions and landmarks goes on and on. Entertainment can be found in every corner of the city—some of it expensive, some of it free. Chapters 21 and 22 give you the rundown on a selection of what's out there.

Chapter 18

The Play's the Thing— Theatergoing in NYC

In This Chapter

➤ How to find out what's on

➤ How to get tickets

➤ What to wear

➤ What about dinner?

➤ What if I have kids?

Theater really is THE thing to do in New York. There are 35 theaters on Broadway and more than 300 (300!) off- and off-off-Broadway performance spaces; each year there are more than 600 productions, and in the 1996–97 season, 10.5 million people bought tickets for them—a fact to remember when thinking about and booking your tickets.

Getting Theater Information

If you've been really organized, you've already got a good idea of what's going on in New York from the listings and information you got from the New York Convention and Visitors Bureau (☎ 800/NYC-VISIT or on the Internet at www.nycvisit.com), from reading the New York Times, from checking Web sites, or from using the other information sources we listed in chapters 1 and 4. The New York Times tends to be strong on "high" culture (ballet, opera, and expensively mounted theater), while the Village Voice and New York Press are strong on alternative culture. The listings in New York magazine, The New Yorker, and Time Out are a combination of both. All of these sources also have reviews, of course—though their take on a given production may vary wildly.

Time-Savers

You can get **theater information by phone** by calling **Broadway Line** (☎ **212/563-2929**), **NYC/On Stage** (☎ **800/STAGE-NY**), or the New York Convention and Visitors Bureau (☎ **800/NYC-VISIT**).

Time-Savers

You can get **theater information on-line** at any of these Web sites:

➤ New York Convention and Visitors Bureau   **www.nycvisit.com**

➤ *New York Times*   **www.nytimes.com**

➤ The Paperless Guide to New York City   **www.mediabridge.com**

➤ *Time Out* magazine   **www.timeoutny.com**

➤ *Village Voice*   **www.villagevoice.com**

If you didn't get yourself organized, you can catch up by consulting the same sources listed above and picking up free copies of *New York Press* or *the Village Voice* from their streetcorner boxes; near newsstands; or at book and video stores, laundromats, coffee shops, and the like. *Where in New York* should be available at your hotel.

Buying Your Tickets

The painless way to get tickets is to plan ahead, and then call one of the telephone ticket agencies and buy your seats with a credit card (there will be a small additional charge on top of the seat price):

➤ **Telecharge, ☎ 212/239-6200**

➤ **TicketMaster, ☎ 212/307-4100**

➤ **Tickets and Travel/Tickets Up Front USA, ☎ 800/876-8497** or 317/633-6406

➤ **New York Concierge, ☎ 800/NYS-HOWS** or ☎ 212/239-2591

➤ **Showtix, ☎ 800/677-1164** or ☎ 212/517-4306

(See chapter 4 for addresses and fax numbers.)

If, however, you're winging it, or blew into town on a whim or surprise visit, you still have options. The first is to go to the **TKTS** booth near Times Square (Duffy Square, otherwise known as 47th Street and Broadway), which is run by the Theater Development Fund. TKTS has same-day tickets for Broadway and off-Broadway shows at discount prices (25%–50%). The office is open daily 3pm–8pm, 10am–2pm Wednesday and Saturday (for matinees), and Sunday from 11am–6:30pm. To get to the booth, take any train to Times Square and walk north; look for the low building on an island in the traffic—with a huge line of people in front of it. (TKTS has another location at Two World Trade Center, mezzanine floor. It's open Monday to Friday 11am–5:30pm and Saturday 11am–3:30pm. The lines are smaller here; for matinees, however, you have to buy the tickets a day in advance.)

Another same-day strategy is to call the **box office** of the theater where the show is playing. You can also go there a couple of hours before the performance since the theaters reserve tickets for the press and others, and if they don't show up you can often pick up the seats. In either case, be sure to ask if there are single seats scattered in the house, since breaking up your group will enhance your chances of getting tickets. Also ask whether the ticket you are buying has an obstructed view. Look for theater phone numbers in the advertisements in the *Times* or in one of the information newspapers/magazines listed previously in this chapter.

Getting the Right Seats

As a general rule, try to get seats that face the stage directly—not in the side aisles—either in the orchestra or the first row of each balcony. Avoid the upper balcony levels: The stage looks really tiny from up there, the air is thin, and you have to contend with mountain goats. These strategies should protect you from getting either of the two main types of really bad seats: those with an obstructed view and those too far away to see a thing. The types of seats we've recommended are also the most expensive, but it's better to pay a little more than not enjoy the show.

Dollars & Sense

Don't forget that many theaters set aside special tickets for seniors and full-time students; they generally go on sale the day of the performance.

If those seats are sold out, or if you're after cheap tickets, you can still get good seats. One key is to know if the seats you're getting are cheap because of a special offer, or if they're always cheap because they're bad seats. Ask the clerk if the cheap orchestra seat you're getting happens to be behind a column; he or she should know which seats are good deals. Also, look carefully at the plan of the house, try to figure out what you'll see from the seats you're being offered, and ask about the relative merits of each.

Enter the Ticketmonger

If these options have failed, you may be tempted to go to a **ticket broker** or scalper. Many of them advertise in the newspaper and in the phone book. According to law, they're supposed to charge you only $5 or a 10% commission, whichever is less. Of course, the old saw "rules were made to be broken" is acted out every day in New York, and some brokers really gouge the customer, so beware.

Also check with **your concierge** at the hotel, who may have show tickets to dispose of.

Dollars & Sense

Another cheap way to get a seat is not to have one: **Standing room** is available at some theaters for about $20. If you have good legs (in the structural rather than aesthetic sense), this is a last-ditch way to see a show if you have no other options. Someone may leave at intermission and you can sit down, but don't count on it.

Broadway

Chances are, these big shows will still be playing when you get here (and long after we're all dead, probably): *Cats*, the show David Letterman and most other New Yorkers love to hate; *Phantom of the Opera*, another Andrew Lloyd Webber blockbuster; and *Les Miserables*. Also count on *Rent*, the low-rent musical from off-Broadway that made it Uptown and even won a Tony; *Bring in 'da Noise, Bring in 'da Funk*, another award-winning homegrown musical; and *Ragtime*, based on the E. L. Doctorow novel. Broadway also regularly takes past hits out of the mothballs and serves 'em up; recent successes in this vein have been *A Funny Thing Happened on the Way to the Forum*, *Grease*, *Victor/Victoria*, and *Guys and Dolls*.

Off-Broadway

Because the cost of mounting a Broadway production has become ridiculous, off-Broadway and off-off-Broadway have come into their own as venues, particularly for drama. You'll find the listings for these shows alongside the Broadway shows in the newspapers and magazines. Off-Broadway productions range from the **New York Shakespeare Festival** at the Public

Theater (see the list below for the address) to performance art like the **Blue Man Group** (see chapter 21) and one-man or one-woman shows. Here are some of the main theaters:

➤ **Orpheum Theatre,** Second Avenue at 8th Street (☎ **212/477-2477**)

➤ **New York Theatre Workshop,** 79 E. 4th St. (☎ **212/460-5475**)

➤ **Actors Playhouse,** 100 Seventh Ave. South (☎ **212/463-0060**)

➤ **Mitzi E. Newhouse Theatre,** in Lincoln Center, 150 W. 65th St. (☎ **212/239-6200**)

➤ **Manhattan Theatre Club,** at City Center, 131 W. 55th St. (☎ **212/581-1212**)

➤ **LaMama E.T.C.,** 74A E. 4th St. (☎ **212/475-7710**)

➤ **The Public Theater,** 425 Lafayette St. (☎ **212/260-2400**)

➤ **Duffy Theatre,** 1553 Broadway (☎ **212/695-3401**)

Dressing for the Big Show

Of course, you will want to be beautiful for a special night at the theater, but don't feel obliged to do so if you're not in the mood. The night scene in the Big Apple has become much less formal than in the old days, and in most places men can get away with a jacket and tie and women with any nice outfit. At theaters, though, except for first nights, you don't even need to do that, and you can pretty much just dress as you wish. In the worst case—let's say if you go with your checkered knickers, clown shoes, and a bright pink hat—people might briefly stare at you, but with no hard feelings. Night life in New York is extravagant and you are much more likely to be surprised by other people's outfits than they are to be shocked at yours.

Tourist Traps

Be careful about buying cheap tickets: They might be cheap because from those seats YOU CAN'T SEE ANYTHING. I remember once when my parents were coming to town and I got tickets for a new show in a theater I didn't know. We spent the whole performance folded in two, trying to see the upper part of the stage from underneath the slope of the ceiling. I got a real good view of the actors' shoes, though!

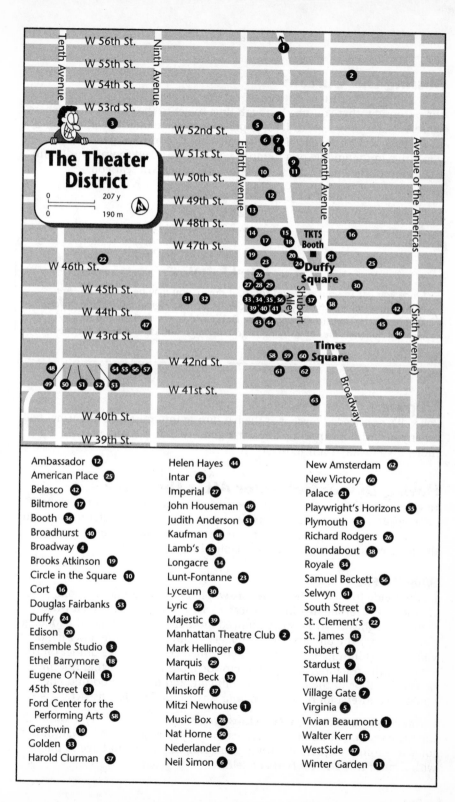

The Theater District

0 — 207 y
0 — 190 m

W 56th St.
W 55th St.
W 54th St.
W 53rd St.
W 52nd St.
W 51st St.
W 50th St.
W 49th St.
W 48th St.
W 47th St.
W 46th St.
W 45th St.
W 44th St.
W 43rd St.
W 42nd St.
W 41st St.
W 40th St.
W 39th St.

Tenth Avenue
Ninth Avenue
Eighth Avenue
Seventh Avenue
Avenue of the Americas (Sixth Avenue)
Broadway
Shubert Alley

TKTS Booth
Duffy Square
Times Square

Ambassador **12**
American Place **25**
Belasco **42**
Biltmore **17**
Booth **36**
Broadhurst **40**
Broadway **4**
Brooks Atkinson **19**
Circle in the Square **10**
Cort **16**
Douglas Fairbanks **53**
Duffy **24**
Edison **20**
Ensemble Studio **3**
Ethel Barrymore **18**
Eugene O'Neill **13**
45th Street **31**
Ford Center for the Performing Arts **58**
Gershwin **10**
Golden **33**
Harold Clurman **57**

Helen Hayes **44**
Intar **54**
Imperial **27**
John Houseman **49**
Judith Anderson **51**
Kaufman **48**
Lamb's **45**
Longacre **14**
Lunt-Fontanne **23**
Lyceum **30**
Lyric **59**
Majestic **39**
Manhattan Theatre Club **2**
Mark Hellinger **8**
Marquis **29**
Martin Beck **32**
Minskoff **37**
Mitzi Newhouse **1**
Music Box **28**
Nat Horne **50**
Nederlander **63**
Neil Simon **6**

New Amsterdam **62**
New Victory **60**
Palace **21**
Playwright's Horizons **55**
Plymouth **35**
Richard Rodgers **26**
Roundabout **38**
Royale **34**
Samuel Beckett **56**
Selwyn **61**
South Street **52**
St. Clement's **22**
St. James **43**
Shubert **41**
Stardust **9**
Town Hall **46**
Village Gate **7**
Virginia **5**
Vivian Beaumont **1**
Walter Kerr **15**
WestSide **47**
Winter Garden **11**

Missing the Curtain

Be aware that the curtain does go up on time in New York, so be there on time. Consider that you need enough time to get to the theater from where you are, claim your seats (if it's a popular show there might be a line), and, in winter, check your coat. If you're really late to a musical performance, and you arrive in the middle of a number, you may be asked to wait until it finishes or until the end of the scene before the usher will seat you.

Extra! Extra!

Once you get to your seat and try to sit down, you may be perplexed. *Are New Yorkers all very thin?* you'll wonder. That's the logical assumption, given the size of the seats in most theaters. Don't add to the lack of comfort by wearing bulky clothes or carrying large handbags, and do use the coat check in winter.

Tipping

Relax, it's not needed (except at the bar during intermission). The usher will usher you without expecting any extra gratuity than a thank you—and a smile, if you really want to overdo it.

Having Dinner Before or After the Show

Having dinner before or after the show mainly depends on your personal preference. If you're not ravenous beforehand, you might prefer to wait and dine in all tranquillity; you might also want to take advantage of a pre-theater special at a restaurant (see chapter 11).

When to Eat

If you decide to dine **before the show,** plan to have dinner by 6pm. Consider that restaurants in the Theater District are likely to be crowded with fellow theater-goers, so you'll need more time to order, get the food, get the check, pay the bill, and, in winter, get your coats. On the other hand, you'll be within walking distance of your theater. If you have dinner on the East Side, the restaurant will be less crowded, but remember that finding a taxi at that time of the night is very difficult, and once you do find one, you'll encounter a lot of traffic on your way to the Theater District.

If you decide to dine **after the show,** you won't have to worry about making the curtain, but do make a reservation or you might have to wait in line for a very long time before getting your meal, or you might have to put up with a bit of ride and eat farther afield.

New York Stories

The Fantasticks, which opened in 1960 and is the longest-running musical in theater history, is still playing at the Sullivan Street Theater in the Village. *The Perfect Murder*, the longest running off-Broadway play still up, is at the Duffy Theater.

Where to Eat

The Theater District offers an ample choice of restaurants for pre- and post-theater dining (see chapters 10, 11, and 12 for a discussion of the area and restaurants listings), and you don't have the hassle of trying to rush from the restaurant to the theater. You can eat early on the East Side, which will be less crowded, and try to sneak across to the West Side in time for your show. If you're eating downtown, better to be on the West Side already; having to fool around getting across, in addition to up, can ruin your schedule.

Wherever you eat, make a reservation. When you arrive at the restaurant, tell the host or your waiter (or both) that you are going to the theater and need to be out by *X* time. What else can we say, except make up your mind fast when you get that menu, and don't order something that takes forever to prepare.

What to Eat

Many restaurants in Midtown—both east and west—offer interesting pre- and post-theater *prix fixe* menus. Be aware, though, that they're of very uneven quality: Some restaurants offer really good meals at advantageous prices, while others offer only a parody of a dinner, in which cases you're much better off choosing from their regular dinner menu (see chapter 11 for the good deals).

We prefer to eat a light meal if it's before the show, so that we don't risk falling asleep during the performance. Also, we can treat ourselves to a luscious dessert later at one of the terrific places on the West Side (see chapter 13). But it's nice to go for a real, leisurely dinner after the show, provided there's time enough to enjoy it.

If you're taking a child along to the theater, of course, you will need to eat something before the show or you may be faced with a child who is cranky, fidgety, or just plain hungry. Which brings us to…

Taking Your Children to the Theater

To get information about shows and performances of special interest to children, check the "For Children" column in the Weekend entertainment section of the Friday *New York Times*. Other sources of information are the children's sections of the other magazines mentioned at the beginning of this chapter and in chapters 1 and 4.

As a rule of thumb, children usually will enjoy some of the longstanding productions that are cute, scary, or goofy, and that will still be there when you come:

➤ *Cats,* at the Winter Garden Theater (Broadway between 50th and 51st streets, ☎ 800/432-7250)

➤ *The Fantasticks,* at the Sullivan Street Theater (181 Sullivan St. between Bleecker and Houston streets, ☎ 212/674-3838)

➤ *The Blue Man Group: Tubes,* at the Astor Place Theater (434 Lafayette St. between East 4th and East 8th streets, ☎ 212/254-4370)

➤ *Beauty and the Beast,* at the Palace Theater (Broadway and 47th Street, ☎ 212/730-8200)

Other all-time children's favorites are seasonal events, such as **Radio City Hall Holiday Shows** (1260 Sixth Ave. at 50th Street, ☎ 212/247-4777), which features a **Christmas Spectacular** from early November to the first week of January, and a **Spring Spectacular** in April; and *The Nutcracker* at the New York State Theater in Lincoln Center (Broadway and 64th Street; ☎ 212/870-5570) during December. *A Christmas Carol* is performed in November and December at the Paramount in Madison Square Garden (Seventh Avenue between 31st and 33rd streets, ☎ 212-465-MSG1). If you plan to be in town at those times, make reservations a few weeks in advance: Tickets are in big demand.

Other theaters with productions for children include the **New Amsterdam Theater,** 214 W. 42nd St. between Seventh and Eighth avenues (☎ 800/432-7250 or 212/282-2900); the **New Victory Theater,** 209 W. 42nd St. between Seventh and Eight avenues (☎ 212/564-4222); and the **New York Children's Theater,** 250 W. 65th St. (☎ 212/877-6115), for weekend shows—magic, puppets, and so on—for ages 3–9, from September–April, at various sites in Manhattan. Call for details.

New York Stories

Broadway is one of the world's longest streets: It originates at the southern end of Manhattan at Bowling Green and ends (under the pseudonym Highway 9) 150 miles away, up in Albany.

Chapter 19

The Performing Arts

In This Chapter

➤ What to see

➤ Where to see it

➤ How to get the tickets

New York offers an almost endless list of concerts, dance, cabaret, and any other possible kind of live performance, in addition to the equally large number of theater shows. It's home to companies of world fame, such as the Metropolitan Opera and the New York Philharmonic, providing an opportunity not to be missed for the passing visitor. Even if you don't shoot for the top, the number of great performances is so large that you'll have lots of choices.

One thing to remember, though: You're competing with millions of others to get the best seats for each performance, so it's important to buy tickets in advance for the popular ones. If you're very keen about one particular performance, you should really try to book it well in advance.

Finding out What's On

Here it's pretty much the same story as for Broadway and off-Broadway (see chapter 18): You'll find information on shows and performances in all of New York's major information papers and Web sites.

Check the **New York Times,** especially the Friday and Sunday issues, and their Web site at **www.nytimes.com**. Get **New York** magazine or the **New Yorker** for nicely organized listings and interesting articles. Consult the list of various information sources in chapters 1 and 4.

Call the New York Convention and Visitors Bureau at ☎ **800/NYC-VISIT** or visit their Web site at **www.nycvisit.com** to receive listings and information over the phone or by mail. Also, call **NYC/On Stage** at ☎ **800/ STAGE-NY** for schedules, descriptions, and directions. (You also have the option to be transferred to one of the telephone services listed below to buy your ticket over the phone.)

The best Web sites to consult to find out what's going on are **The Paperless Guide to New York City** at **www.mediabridge.com**, the site of the magazine *Time Out* at **www.timeoutny.com**, the *Village Voice* site at **www.villagevoice.com**, and **www.newyork.sidewalk.com**.

Once you're in New York, pick up a free copy of *New York Press* or the *Village Voice* from street corner bins; near newsstands; and at book and video stores, laundromats, coffee shops, and the like. You should be able to get *Where in New York* at your hotel. This publication gives listings and reviews, but remember that if you want to see something hot, make those reservations before leaving home.

Getting Your Tickets

When you know what you want to see, call the box office or write to get tickets. You also can buy tickets from **TicketMaster** at ☎ **212/307-4100** for concerts and some performances—including Radio City and the Rockettes—or **Tele-charge** (some concerts), or from agencies such as **Tickets and Travel/Tickets Up Front USA,** (☎ **800/876-8497** or 317/633-6406), **New York Concierge** (☎ **800/NYS-HOWS** or 212/ 239-2591) and **Showtix** (☎ **800/677-1164** or 212/517-4306). See chapter 4 for addresses and fax numbers.

To get last-minute tickets once you're in New York, an organization similar to the TKTS booth for Broadway shows (see chapter 18) is the **Bryant Park Dance and Music Ticket Booth** at 42nd Street and Sixth Avenue, at the corner of Bryant Park (☎ **212/382-2323**). They list whatever they have available and sell it at a discount. Also, always check with the box office for cancellations, particularly at the last moment.

Remember that some discount tickets are for seats with an obstructed view (see "Getting the Right Seat" in chapter 18); this consideration might not be as important for a concert, but it certainly is for the opera or a dance performance.

For Every Thing There Is a Season

The performance season goes on full steam from October to May, when the major performances are scheduled. January and February are usually slow months, when even top shows might not have a full house. During the summer it's far from quiet, though, and that season also has what most New Yorkers absolutely love: free open-air performances.

The Metropolitan Opera and the New York Philharmonic perform in Central Park (usually two performances each; call for schedules); the New York Opera holds a series of performances at the **Summer Stage** (☎ **212/360-2777**), also in Central Park; and all kinds of events take place in the outdoor spaces of Lincoln Center (☎ **212/546-2656** for information on all events, indoors and outdoors), from the **Midsummer Night Swing** in the plaza with live music and dancing to the free concert and dance performances in Damrosch Park on the south side of the Center.

Extra! Extra!

If you're visiting during the summer, you may be able to catch one of the many free or low-cost concerts put on by **Central Park SummerStage.** You might see big-name pop and jazz acts, reggae festivals, poetry readings, or world music acts like the Master Musicians of Jajouka. Concerts are held on the park SummerStage, toward the east side of the park at 72nd Street. Call ☎ **212/ 360-2777** for information.

Other events take place during the summer in other public spaces around the city, such as Bryant Park, the Winter Garden at Battery Park City, and the South Street Seaport. Call the New York City Visitor Bureau for schedules and locations (☎ **800/NYC-VISIT**).

For Every Venue There Is a Subway

Most of the time you'll want to get to performance venues by cab—being nicely dressed and all. But if you happen to enjoy public transportation, here are the directions for the major destinations:

➤ **Lincoln Center,** Broadway and 64th Street: 1/9 train to 66 Street/Lincoln Center stop, or M104 bus (running east/west on 42nd Street, north on Sixth Avenue, and south on Broadway), M5 and M7 (running up Sixth Avenue and Broadway), and M66 (across town running west on 67th Street).

➤ **Carnegie Hall,** 57th Street and Seventh Avenue: N/R train to 57th Street stop or B/D/E to Seventh Avenue stop; M57 bus (cross-town on 57th Street) and M6 and M7 down Seventh Avenue.

➤ **City Center,** 131 W. 55th St. (between Sixth and Seventh avenues): Same as for Carnegie Hall (see above).

➤ **Radio City Music Hall,** Sixth Avenue and 50th Street: B/D/F/Q train to 47–50 streets/Rockefeller Center stop; M5, M6, and M7 up Sixth Avenue and M50 across town (eastbound on 50th Street and westbound on 49th Street).

Where Classical Music Is King

If you like classical music, New York is the place to be. There concerts are
everywhere: concert halls, churches, high school auditoriums, and museums.
You'll be able to find information on these in the sources we mentioned earlier in this chapter. There are, however, some concerts not to miss.

Of course, the **New York Philharmonic** at Avery Fisher Hall in Lincoln
Center (Broadway and 64th Street; ☎ **212/875-5030**) is THE place to go for
wonderful concerts. They also have a summer season in July. Tickets go from
$6–$60.

But then, how not to go to **Carnegie Hall** (57th Street and Seventh Avenue,
☎ **212/247-7800**), probably the most famous performance space in the
world (and one of the greatest acoustically), offering concerts by world-class
visiting orchestras and soloists. The price of the tickets depends on the performance.

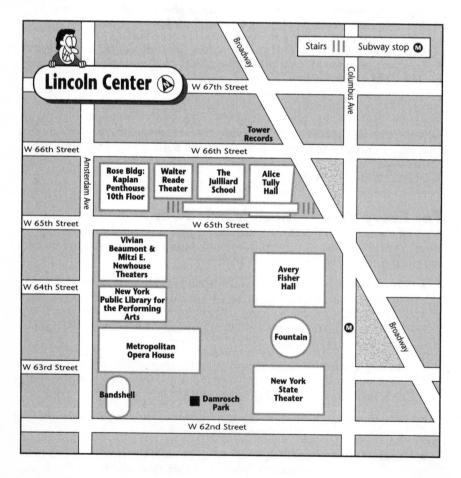

A Night at the Opera

Most capitals in the world have one opera house and are proud of it. Naturally, New York has three. Of these, one is a somewhat more intimate twist on grand opera than you're probably used to.

World-class singers, marvelous sets and costumes, and a wonderful repertoire put the **Metropolitan Opera Company** at the top of world rankings (sorry, La Scala). You'll find them in Lincoln Center at Broadway and 64th Street at the Metropolitan Opera House (☎ **212/362-6000**). Tickets range from $23–$137.

Ranking right below is the **New York City Opera,** a less highbrow company with a wonderful repertoire. They are at Lincoln Center as well, at the New York State Theater (☎ **212/870-5570**). The price range for seats is $20–$85.

The third one, the **Amato Opera Company** (319 Bowery at 2nd Street, ☎ **212/228-8200**) is a smaller opera house that has been in existence since 1948 and is firmly anchored in classic Italian opera—Rossini, Verdi, Puccini, and so on—with some limited exceptions. It has only 100 seats (which sell for about $20) and they get booked fast. If you're interested, make your reservations at least 2–3 weeks ahead.

New York Stories

"Come vanno le vostre lezioni di italiano?" Even if that went over your head, you'll still be able to enjoy the opera and actually understand what the fat guy on the left is murmuring in the ears of the lady, and why her husband stabs him to death. The Metropolitan Opera has equipped the back of each seat with a **subtitle screen** that displays English translations as the opera plays out.

Music That Defies the Melting Pot

New York is home to every ethnic group in the world, from well-established immigrant communities like the Irish, Jewish, Italians, and Chinese to up-and-coming groups like the Koreans, Arabs, Bukharans, and Indians, all of whom bring their distinct artistic heritage to the urban mix. The **World Music Institute** presents the music of these cultures at various concert venues throughout the city, and whether your interest is West African griot songs, Portuguese fado, Persian classical music, or Pakistani qawali, there's a good chance they're presenting it during the year, and an even better chance that they've got recordings of it available at their offices (49 W. 27th St., suite 930). Concerts of one kind or another are held almost every week of the year—often several in any given week. For a schedule of events, call ☎ **212/545-7536**.

Dance (and We Don't Mean the Funky Chicken)

Among all the performing arts, it's in dance that New York offers the most compared to any other city in the world. Some of the major companies and schools that have brought new developments to the history of dance are based here, and the variety of the performances offered is enormous.

For ballet lovers, the **New York City Ballet** performs at the New York State Theater, sharing this space with the **New York City Opera** (see previously). They have a great repertoire to which they regularly add new performances (using both classical and modern music), and all their work is beautifully staged.

Their neighbors, the **American Ballet Theater,** perform at the Metropolitan Opera House and share their space with the **Metropolitan Opera** (see previously). Their repertoire also includes some modern works and they regularly host world-famous guest companies and dancers.

City Center, 131 W. 55th St. between Sixth and Seventh avenues (☎ 212/581-7907), regularly hosts performances by major companies, such as Alvin Ailey American Dance Theater and Martha Graham company, while the **Joyce Theater,** 175 Eighth Ave. at 19th Street (☎ 212/242-0800), has rapidly grown during the past years to become an important venue for a large and diverse series of dance events, including big names such as the Erick Hawkins Dance Company and Meredith Monk.

From Blue Men to Can-Can—All Those Other Performing Arts

Besides the major established arts, New York is the scene of a number of very interesting events that fail (marvelously) to fall into strict categories.

One long-standing production that escapes clear-cut definition but continues to attract people of all ages is the off-off-Broadway show **Blue Man Group: Tubes,** at Astor Place Theater (434 Lafayette St. between East 4th and East 8th streets, ☎ 212/254-4370). The mix of music, percussion, mime, and other stage effects has brought this trio of blue men success, and it is likely to continue. We've yet to meet someone who didn't like their show (and kids love it, too).

Another longstanding tradition in New York that needs no introduction is the **Rockettes,** who perform at Radio City Music Hall (1260 Sixth Ave. at 50th Street, ☎ 212/247-4777).

If you want to go for something really out of the ordinary, there's **Tony 'n' Tony's Wedding,** a funny "production" that features a tacky, wacky wedding and its guests (you), at St. John's Church at 81 Christopher St. in the Village. (Tickets are available through **Telecharge**—see previously.)

Finally, don't forget that New York is home to many TV shows as well, and that you can attend some of the tapings for free. So if you want to see Sally Jessy Raphael (☎ 212/582-1722), Geraldo (☎ 212/265-8520), David

Letterman (☎ **212/975-5853**), or *Live with Regis and Kathy Lee* (**212/ 456-3054**), call them up—but remember to do it in advance if you're really keen on a specific show. And of course, as anyone who's up early knows, the *Today Show* broadcasts from a glass-walled studio in Rockefeller Center (corner of 49th Street and Rockefeller Plaza) from 7–9am. That could be *you* in the crowd of shivering tourists Katie Couric talks to.

Wait a Minute—What About Movies?

If you're a movie lover, there are films playing in New York that will never make it to the town where you live. All the big Hollywood stuff is here as well, of course, but why bother? You can use the **MoviePhone** (☎ **212/ 777-FILM**) to get movie listings for the whole city and to reserve tickets (for a $1 charge). Or you can call directly the houses that show foreign/ alternative/independent/revival/scandalous/provocative films that don't circulate widely in the rest of the country. In addition to the **New York Film Festival,** conducted by Lincoln Center in the early fall (call ☎ **212/ 875-5050** for information), give a call to these houses: **Film Forum** (209 W. Houston St., off Sixth Avenue, ☎ **212/727-8110**), which is often running a revival festival in one room and independent or obscure films in the others; **Anthology Film Archives** (32 Second Ave. at 2nd Street, ☎ **212/ 505-5181**), which is currently the best place in town for foreign films; **Angelica Film Center** (West Houston at Mercer Street, ☎ **212/505-5181**), which is strong on foreign films and "indies" and has several (small) screens; the **Walter Reade Theater** (at Lincoln Center, ☎ **212/875-5600**), which always has some interesting series and vintage films showing; and the theater at **MOMA** (11 W. 53rd Street, between Fifth and Sixth avenues, ☎ **212/ 708-9480**), which also always has something good playing. This list only scratches the surface; check the newspapers and magazines for further choices.

Chapter 20

Hitting the Clubs & Bars

In This Chapter

➤ Where to hear your kind of music live

➤ Where to dance to your kind of music

➤ Where to have a drink in your kind of place

➤ Where to have some fun

➤ Where to wait for dawn

Whether you want to spend the evening dancing, chatting over drinks at a bar or lounge, or checking out the music scene, New York has the venue for you. Following is a list, by category, of some of the spots you might hit if you have a particular interest beyond the big four discussed in the last two chapters (theater, classical music, opera, and dance). We'll start with music, which you can find in New York in any form you can imagine, from straight pop, smokin' jazz, gutbucket blues, and smooth ballads to microtonal accordion music and Tuvan throat singing. As for watering holes, New York might not rival Dublin, where you can walk from one end of the city to the other and pass a bar in every block, but that's only because we're way bigger and more spread out—you won't want for a whistle-wetting spot while you're in town, believe us.

Hey, Hepcats—Where to Go for Jazz

The good news is that many of the old clubs are still there, and some new ones have also come along. In the Village, you have **Blue Note,** at 131 W. 3rd (☎ **212/475-8592**), which consistently books the biggest names in the business—but may hit you with a whopping cover charge almost as high as a Broadway show, and a drink minimum to boot. (The elbow room is ample, too—if you're a rhesus monkey.) **The Village Vanguard** (178 Seventh Ave. S. at 11th Street; ☎ 212/255-4037) is justly famous for greats like John Coltrane and Miles Davis who have played and recorded there. Just down the street at 88 Seventh Avenue South is **Sweet Basil** (☎ 212/242-1785), which may also draw some big names but is generally more low-key; it also has a jazz brunch.

Another Greenwich Village institution, the **Village Gate,** died a few years ago and has been reborn in Midtown (240 W. 52nd St. between Broadway and Eighth Avenue, ☎ 212/307-5252), and is quite a bit cheaper than the sometimes tourist-clogged icons of the Village. Also moved to Midtown is **Birdland** (315 W. 44th St. between Eighth and Ninth avenues, ☎ 212/581-3080). Speaking of Bird, also look for the reopening of Minton's Playhouse in Harlem (scheduled for 1998), at 118th Street and Adam Clayton Powell Boulevard, a landmark of the bebop era. Lastly, right across from Lincoln Center in the basement of the Merlot restaurant you'll find **Iridium** (48 W. 63rd., ☎ 212/956-4676 or 212/582-2121 for reservations), which looks like something out of *Alice in Wonderland* but presents some good sounds.

Shake Your Booty—Where to Go to Dance

If you're into ballroom dance, you may be able to get to **Roseland** (239 W. 52nd St., ☎ 212/247-0200) before it succumbs to some developer's next nightmare for New York. This venerable, cavernous, and somewhat tattered old place has been hanging on by its fingernails for years; dancing on Thursdays and Saturdays from 2:30–11pm, with an $11 cover. If you visit in July, you can dance for free at **Midsummer Night's Swing** right in front of Lincoln Center (Broadway and 64th Street), and even get in on the free lesson. Different dances and styles are featured on different nights of the week. Check the paper, or call **Lincoln Center** (☎ 212/546-2656). At the opposite end of the spectrum, **Rainbow & Stars,** on the 65th Floor of Rockefeller Plaza (49th Street, ☎ 212/632-5000), with its elegant art deco interior, revolving dance floor, and top entertainment, is like something from a 1930s musical. Jacket and tie required. The cost is $40, plus a lot more if you have dinner (see the Rainbow Room listing in chapter 10).

For Latin dancing, the **Copacabana** (617 W. 57th St. between Eleventh and Twelfth avenues, ☎ 212/582-2672) is a more established locale; for something younger, check out **S.O.B's** (see the section "The World Music Scene" later in this chapter).

Getting the Blues

Chicago B.L.U.E.S. (73 Eighth Ave., just south of 14th Street, ☎ 212/924-9755) offers the real thing: big names like Pinetop Perkins as well as hosts of others. At the opposite end of town is the other blues stronghold, **Manny's Car Wash** (1558 Third Ave. between 87th and 88th streets,

☎ 212/369-BLUES), which gets similar acts. Here is as good a place as any to mention: **The Bottom Line** (15 W. 4th St., at Mercer, ☎ 212/228-7880), whose stage has seen everything from the Ramones to Sonny Rollins. Check the paper or call to find out what blues/rock/jazz/folk acts are playing. The **Mercury Lounge** (see the section "Lawdy Miss Claudy—The Rock and Roll Scene" later in this chapter) also has blues acts sometimes.

Life Is a Cabaret—and So Are These Places

If you're into the cabaret scene, then you already know that Bobby Short plays at the **Cafe Carlyle** in the Carlyle Hotel (781 Madison Ave. at 76th Street, ☎ 212/744-1600). Admission is $50, and if you add drinks (there's no minimum) and dinner, better bring your plastic. Also playing at the Cafe Carlyle now is Woody Allen, whose regular gig used to be at Michael's Pub on Monday nights. The night is the same, only the place has changed (you'd better reserve in advance). Another hotel, the Algonquin (59 W. 44th St. between Fifth and Sixth avenues, ☎ 212/840-6800) has a classy but less hyped cabaret, the **Oak Room,** which also gets some fine performers. In the Village, you have **Eighty Eights** (228 W. 10th St. between Bleeker and Hudson streets, ☎ 212/924-0088), which has both a piano bar and a cabaret, as well as the larger and glitzier **Duplex Cabaret** (61 Christopher St., ☎ 212/255-5438), right in the middle of Sheridan Square.

Country, Folk, & Bluegrass in New York? You Bet

The Bitter End (147 Bleecker St., between La Guardia Place and Thompson Street, ☎ 212/673-7030) has been around forever, and was part of the folk boom of the early 1960s. Now it has blues and other acts. **The Bottom Line** (see the preceding section, "Getting the Blues") has country and folk acts, too. For real heel-stomping country music, **Denim and Diamonds** (511 Lexington Ave. between 47th and 48th streets, ☎ 212/371-1600) is the place. Come before 8pm and get a free two-step lesson. The **Rodeo Bar** (375 Third Ave. at 27th Street, ☎ 212/683-6500), with appropriate 'aw shucks decor, has live music every night, including some pretty big names in country.

Where to Go if You Could Use a Laugh

Caroline's (1626 Broadway between 49th and 50th streets, ☎ 212/956-0101) has moved Uptown from its original Downtown location and is the reigning champ of the comedy scene, drawing the big comedians. Cover charges vary depending on how big that name is—ask when you reserve. **The Comic Strip** (1568 Second Ave. between 81st and 82nd streets, ☎ 212/861-9386) has produced its share of stars, including Jerry Seinfeld. The **Comedy Cellar** (117 MacDougal St. between Bleecker and West 3rd treets, ☎ 212/254-3480) has earned a place at the top of the list because of its high-quality and high-profile acts.

The World Music Scene

From Tito Puente to Ismael Lo, **S.O.B.'s** (204 Varick St. at West Houston Street, ☎ 212/243-4940) has seen every kind of music from every corner of the globe, though South American music is the hub of the wheel; the name stands for Sounds of Brazil. The food is overpriced for what it is, but you don't have to eat—or drink for that matter. You can gyrate on the dance floor or lean against a post in the tropically decorated interior. Lots of other venues have world music from time to time, but not as a regular thing; check the newspaper and check the schedule of the **World Music Institute** (☎ 212/545-7536), which programs concerts on most weekends at various venues throughout the city.

Lawdy Miss Claudy—The Rock & Roll Scene

Now that Sonic Youth has played Lincoln Center, you can hear rock just about anywhere, and you don't have to hang around in places where your feet stick to the floor. The **Bottom Line** (see the earlier section "Getting the Blues") is one concert-like, rather than club-like, venue. The **Mercury Lounge** (217 E. Houston St., at Essex Street, ☎ 212/260-4700) is more upscale and attracts a lot of acts who have already made it—and it's not restricted to rock, either. Another favorite of New Yorkers is **Tramps** (51 W.21st St. between Fifth and Sixth avenues, ☎ 212/727-7788), which has a variety of music.

Where the Avant Garde Is Probably Old Hat

For the musically adventurous, **The Knitting Factory** (74 Leonard St., four blocks below Canal, between Broadway and Church streets, ☎ 212/219-3055, Web site www.knittingfactory.com) is a must. On any given night you might hear cutting-edge rock 'n' roll, seriously far-out jazz, minimalist legends like LaMonte Young or Philip Glass, or someone creating sound collages using turntables and kitchen chairs.

Where Have All the Pubs Gone?

Looking for an old-fashioned New York saloon with a long, polished wood bar, tin ceiling, and no ferns? The **Old Town Bar** (45 E. 18th St., between Broadway and Park Avenue, ☎ 212/529-6732) is a nice place to soak up the historical flavor as well as a pint. Not far away is **Pete's Tavern** (129 E. 18th St. at Irving Place, ☎ 212/473-7676), opened during the Civil War and where O. Henry supposedly sat and wrote. **McSorley's Old Ale House** (15 E. 7th St. between Second and Third avenues, ☎ 212/473-9148) claims to be 10 years older than Pete's and thereby the oldest tavern in town. It serves great ales in a boggy atmosphere; beware of the hordes (and lines) of fresh-faced NYU'ers on weekends.

Martinis & Manhattan

If you're looking for someplace classy to have a highball—maybe even with the city spread out below your feet—the obvious choice is **The Rainbow Promenade** (30 Rockefeller Plaza between 49th and 50th streets, ☎ 212/632-5100) at Rockefeller Center. Hotel bars (the good ones, anyway) have that clubby/comfy/pricey/paneled feeling; try the **King Cole Room** at the St. Regis (2 E. 55th St. at Fifth Avenue, ☎ **212/339-6721**) and the **Oak Bar** at the Plaza (768 Fifth Ave. at 59th Street, ☎ **212/546-5320**).

Other Watering Holes

Merchant's New York (112 Seventh Ave. at 17th St., ☎ **212/366-7267**) has a young, mixed crowd that reflects the surrounding neighborhood. Sophisticated without being pretentious, it also has a roaring fireplace you can stare into. Another interesting room is **Fez** (380 Lafayette St. at Great Jones Street, ☎ **212/533-3000**), in the back of the Time Cafe. With Moroccan decor and overstuffed vintage couches (not Jennifer Convertibles), it's a great place for a late afternoon drink (after that it gets crowded). For something a little odder, try **Siberia** (251 W. 50th St. at Broadway, ☎ **212/333-4141**), which is underground in the entrance to the 50th Street 1/9 subway station, and has a warm atmosphere despite Cold War decor. **Elaine's** (1703 Second Ave. between 88th and 89th streets, ☎ **212/534-8103**) is one of the few places to have a drink (skip the chow) where you might see a celebrity and where they'd let you in, too.

Gay Clubs & Bars

Gay nightspots are concentrated in but not restricted to the Village and Chelsea.

For Men: Stonewall (114 Christopher St. just East of Seventh Avenue South, ☎ **212/463-0950**) is a new place on the famous old site. **Ty's** (114 Christopher St. at Bedford Street, ☎ **212/741-9641**) is a few blocks down the road and has been there for ages. There a lot of other places in between. In Chelsea, try **g.** (223 W. 19th St. between Seventh and Eighth avenues, ☎ **212/929-1085**) or **Splash** (50 W. 17th St. at Sixth Avenue, ☎ **212/691-0073**).

For Women: in the Village, **Henrietta Hudson** (438 Hudson St. at Morton Street, ☎ **212/243-9079**) has a small dance floor and a good jukebox, while **Crazy Nanny's** (21 Seventh Ave. S. at Leroy Street, ☎ **212/366-6312**), only a few blocks away, is more footloose and very diverse.

Time-Savers

You won't be able to find the hottest "clubs" like the lesbian **W.O.W. Bar** on a map because they're traveling parties that alight in various spots depending on the day. For example, W.O.W. is a Friday-night party, and you have to call ☎ **212/631-0588** to learn the location. Gay publications (listed in chapter 1) are your best bet—other than word of mouth—for up-to-the-minute club information.

Staying out Late—The Velvet-Rope Scene

The most "in" clubs and bars are always the ones where the average Joe will be left pining away on the wrong side of the velvet ropes. Hence, our friend who actually built the beautiful interior of **Pravda** (281 Lafayette, between Prince and Houston streets, ☎ **212/226-4696**) might get turned away. But you never know; if you're really into seeing famous jet-setters, it might be worth the humiliation you'll be subjected to.

Here are a few places where you'll most probably get in: **Decade** (1117 First Avenue at 61st Street, ☎ **212/835-5979**), an all-night dance and supper club for old people (over 30); **Nell's** (246 W. 14th St. between Seventh and Eighth avenues, ☎ **212/675-1567**), a venerable, comfortable place that attracts all kinds; and **Roxy** (515 W. 18th St. at Tenth Avenue, ☎ **212/645-5156**), a wild and diverse scene, but with such "normal" touches as martini and cigar bars.

New York A to Z— Facts at Your Fingertips

AAA: General, ☎ **212/757-2000;** emergency road service, **800/222-4357.**

Ambulance: Call **911.**

American Express: Several locations, including Macy's, in Herald Square (Sixth Avenue at 34th Street, ☎ **212/695-8075**); for others, call ☎ **800/ AXP-TRIP.**

Baby sitters: Baby sitting is discussed in chapter 1. Baby Sitters Guild (☎ **212/682-0227**); the Frances Stewart Agency (☎ **212/439-9222**).

Camera Repair: Berry Camera Repair (139 Fourth Ave. between 13th and 14th streets, ☎ **212/677-8407**); Citi-Photo (636 Lexington Ave. at 54th Street, ☎ **212/980-5878**); Professional Camera Repair Service, Inc. (37 W. 47th St. between Fifth and Sixth avenues, ☎ **212/382-0550**); Westside Camera Inc. (2400 Broadway at 88th Street, ☎ **212/877-8760**).

Doctors: With the way health care is now, you'd better know how much red tape your HMO or provider wraps you in when you leave home. (We know someone who needed an emergency gall bladder operation and the folks back home didn't want to authorize it.) For an emergency, go to an emergency room at a hospital (see below). Walk-in clinics can handle minor ailments. One example is **New York Healthcare Immediate Care** (55 E. 34th St., between Park and Madison, ☎ **212/252-6001**), which is open Mon–Fri 8am–7pm, Sat–Sun 9am–2pm, and charges $100 for a visit. **Doctors on Call** connects you with doctors who make house calls (☎ **212/ 737-2333**) and is available 24 hours per day.

Emergencies: For police, fire, and ambulance, call **911.** For the **Poison Control Center,** call ☎ **212/764-7667** or 212/340-4494.

Hospitals: From the Battery up, here are the numbers of specific hospitals: New York Downtown Hospital (170 William St. at Beeckman Street, ☎ **212/ 312-5000**); St. Vincent's Hospital (Seventh Avenue at 11th Street, ☎ **212/ 604-7000**); Beth Israel Medical Center (First Avenue at 16th Street, ☎ **212/ 420-2000**); Bellevue Hospital Center (First Avenue at 27th Street, ☎ **212/ 562-4141**); New York University Medical Center (First Avenue at 33rd Street,

☎ **212/263-7300**); Roosevelt Hospital Center (10th Avenue at 58th Street, ☎ **212/523-4000**); St. Luke's Hospital Center (Amsterdam Avenue at 113th Street, ☎ **212/523-4000**); New York Hospital Emergency Pavilion (York Avenue at 70th Street, ☎ **212/746-5050**); Lenox Hill Hospital (77th Street between Park and Lexington avenues, ☎ **212/434-2000**).

Hotlines: 24-hour Crime Victim Hotline is ☎ **212/577-7777;** Sex Crime Report Line ☎ **212/267-7273;** for local police precinct numbers, call ☎ **212/374-5000;** Department of Consumer Affairs ☎ **212/487-4444.**

Information: For tourist information, call the New York Convention and Visitors Bureau at ☎ **800/NYC-VISIT** or see chapter 1; for telephone directory information dial **411** or the area code plus **555-1212.** These calls are free from Bell Atlantic public pay phones.

Liquor Laws: The minimum legal age to buy and consume alcoholic beverages in New York is 21. Liquor and wine are sold only in licensed stores, which are closed on Sundays, holidays, and election days while the polls are open. Beer can be purchased in grocery stores, delis, and supermarkets 24 hours, except Sundays before noon.

Maps: Transit maps for both subway and buses are available free at token booths inside subway stations; bus maps are also available on the buses. To buy all kinds of maps, go to **Hagstrom Map and Travel Center,** 57 West 43rd St. between Fifth and Sixth avenues (☎ **212/398-1222**); open Mon–Fri 9am–5:30pm). For simple New York City maps, go to any of the many bookstores in town.

Newspapers/Magazines: The three major daily newspapers are the *New York Times,* the *Daily News,* and the *New York Post.* Two weekly newspapers distributed free in the city are *New York Press* and the *Village Voice* (Wednesdays). Two useful magazines are *The New Yorker* and *New York.*

Pharmacies: There are two 24-hour pharmacies in the city, and they're both **Duane Reades:** Broadway and 57th Street (☎ **212/541-9708**) and Third Avenue and 74th Street (☎ **212/744-2668**). Kaufman's (Lexington Avenue and 50th Street, ☎ **212/755-2668**) is open until midnight.

Police: Dial **911** for emergencies and ☎ **212/374-5000** for the number of the nearest precinct.

Restrooms: There are public facilities in all transportation terminals, Grand Central Terminal, Penn Station, and the Port Authority Bus Terminal; in Central Park and Bryant Park; and in the New York Public Library and other branch libraries—but be careful about hygiene. Department stores, museums, and large hotels have wonderful restrooms (we love those in Saks Fifth Avenue and the Plaza), as does Trump Tower at 56th Street and Fifth Avenue. Some large coffee shops such as Dean & Deluca and Au Bon Pain, and some chains such as McDonald's and Houlihans, also have nice restrooms. Otherwise it's a bit of a problem, and you have to rely on your imagination—it's so much of a problem that someone even published a little book on the subject, called *Where to Go in New York.*

Safety: See the section on **Safety** in chapter 1.

Taxes: The tax on food and other goods is 8.25%. Hotel taxes are 13.25% plus a room charge of $2 per night.

Taxis: Taxis will cost you $2.00 just for stepping in the door, plus 30¢ per ⅕ mi. or 20¢/min. stuck in traffic. (The average fare in Manhattan is $5.25.)

Time Zone: New York is in the Eastern Standard Time zone.

Transit Info: For transportation to and from airports call Air-Ride (☎ 800/ 247-7433); for mass-transit call New York City Transit Travel Information Center (☎ 718/330-1234 6am–9pm). For other numbers, see chapter 1.

Toll–Free Numbers & Web Sites for Airlines & Hotels

Airlines

Air Canada
☎ 800/776-3000
www.aircanada.ca

Alaska Airlines
☎ 800/426-0333
www.alaskaair.com

America West Airlines
☎ 800/235-9292
www.americawest.com

American Airlines
☎ 800/433-7300
www.americanair.com

British Airways
☎ 800/247-9297
☎ 0345/222-111 in Britain
www.british-airways.com

Canadian Airlines International
☎ 800/426-7000
www.cdair.ca

Carnival Airlines
☎ 800/824-7386
www.carnivalair.com

Continental Airlines
☎ 800/525-0280
www.flycontinental.com

Delta Air Lines
☎ 800/221-1212
www.delta-air.com

Hawaiian Airlines
☎ 800/367-5320
www.hawaiianair.com

Kiwi International Airlines
☎ 800/538-5494
www.jetkiwi.com

Midway Airlines
☎ 800/446-4392

Northwest Airlines
☎ 800/225-2525
www.nwa.com

Southwest Airlines
☎ 800/435-9792
iflyswa.com

Tower Air
☎ 800/34-TOWER (800/348-6937) outside New York;
(☎ 718/553-8500 in New York)
www.towerair.com

Trans World Airlines (TWA)
☎ 800/221-2000
www2.twa.com

United Airlines
☎ 800/241-6522
www.ual.com

USAirways
☎ 800/428-4322
www.usair.com

Virgin Atlantic Airways
☎ 800/862-8621 in Continental
U.S.
☎ 0293/747-747 in Britain
www.fly.virgin.com

Major Hotel &
Motel Chains

Best Western International
☎ 800/528-1234
www.bestwestern.com

Clarion Hotels
☎ 800/CLARION
www.hotelchoice.com/cgi-bin/
res/webres?clarion.html

Comfort Inns
☎ 800/228-5150
www.hotelchoice.com/cgi-bin/
res/webres?comfort.html

Crowne Plaza Hotels
☎ 800/227-6963
www.crowneplaza.com

Days Inn
☎ 800/325-2525
www.daysinn.com

Doubletree Hotels
☎ 800/222-TREE
www.doubletreehotels.com

Econo Lodges
☎ 800/55-ECONO
www.hotelchoice.com/cgi-bin
res/webres?econo.html

Fairfield Inn by Marriott
☎ 800/228-2800
www.fairfieldinn.com

Hampton Inn
☎ 800/HAMPTON
www.hampton-inn.com

Hilton Hotels
☎ 800/HILTONS
www.hilton.com

Holiday Inn
☎ 800/HOLIDAY
www.holiday-inn.com

Howard Johnson
☎ 800/654-2000
www.hojo.com/hojo.html

Hyatt Hotels & Resorts
☎ 800/228-9000
www.hyatt.com

ITT Sheraton
☎ 800/325-3535
www.sheraton.com

Marriott Hotels
☎ 800/228-9290
www.marriott.com

Quality Inns
☎ 800/228-5151
www.hotelchoice.com/cgi-bin/
res/webres?quality.html

Radisson Hotels International
☎ 800/333-3333
www.radisson.com

Ramada Inns
☎ 800/2-RAMADA
www.ramada.com

Residence Inn by Marriott
☎ 800/331-3131
www.residenceinn.com

Travelodge
☎ 800/255-3050

Index

A

ABC Carpet & Home,
146, 206
Abigail Adams Museum,
203
Abyssinia, 124
Accommodations,
45–81
with the best service,
76
budgeting, 17
for business travelers,
71
with children, 55, 66
choosing, 53–54
with data access, 52
free Continental
breakfast, 54
getting best room,
54–55
for health and fitness,
78
intimate and quiet, 74
with a kitchenette, 21,
55
location and,
46–50
location index, 58, 62
minibars and, 51
money-saving tips, 21,
50–51
price index, 62
pricing of, 50
reservation services,
55–56
room service and, 53
smoking and, 55
taxes, 20, 51
telephones and, 51
travelers with disabili-
ties, 55, 77
Web sites and toll-free
numbers, 274
worksheet, 80–81

Aerial Tramway,
Roosevelt Island, 183
Afternoon tea, 145
Airports, 30, 84
traveling to/from, 30,
86–89
Air-Ride, 84, 272
Air travel
airfares, 20, 28–29
airlines, 29–30, 32,
273–74
carry-on luggage,
42–43
money-saving tips, 20
package tours, 27–28
telephone numbers,
useful, 273–74
tips on, 30–31
Web sites, 29–30,
273–74
worksheets, 33–36
Algonquin, The, 266
Allen, Woody, 266
Alphabet City, 104
Amato Opera Company,
261
America, 125
American Ballet Theater,
262
American Express, 15–16,
270
American Indian,
National Museum of
the, 202
American Museum of
Natural History, 40, 92,
170, 223, 225
Ameritania, The, 64
Amtrak, 32
Angelica Kitchen, 125
Anglers and Writers,
145–46
Anthology Film Archives,
263

Antiques, 5, 216
Architecture, books
about, 157
Arizona 206, 125
Arizona Cafe, 126
Artepasta, 106
Art galleries, 40, 105,
210, 228
Gallery Guide, 40
International Fine Arts
Fair, 6
Art museums, 164,
196–97
the Cloisters, 99,
196–97
Frick Collection, 197
Guggenheim
Museum, 180, 223,
230
International Center
of Photography, 202
Metropolitan Museum
of Art, 181–82, 223,
225
Museum of Modern
Art (MOMA), 182,
233, 263
Whitney Museum,
197, 223
Astor Place, 204
Astor Place Theater, 262
ATM machines, 14–17
Attractions, 163–89,
196–204. See also
Itineraries
admission prices, 18
budgeting for, 18
for children, 171,
203–04
free museum nights,
18, 22
location index, 164
by type, 164, 170
worksheet, 190–95

Auctions, 216
Auto Show, Greater New York International, 5

B

Babysitters, 9, 270
Bagels, 108, 110, 147
Bakeries, 152–53
Balducci's, 219
Ballet, 256, 262
Baluchi's, 106, 126–27
Barbizon, The, 64
Barnes & Noble, 146, 217
Barneys, 207
Bars, 267–68
Baseball, 201
Basketball, 201
Battery Park City, 99, 171
Beacon, Hotel, 68
Beard, James, House, 104
Beauty and the Beast (theater), 256
Bed Bath & Beyond, 213
Bed & breakfasts, 54
Beer, 153. *See also* Bars, Microbreweries, 153
Belgian fry places, 150–51
Belvedere Fountain (Central Park), 174
Bergdorf Goodman, 207
Big Apple Circus, 7
Big Apple Greeters, 3, 162
"Big Apple," use of term, 11
Big Onion Walking Tours, 160–61
Bleecker Street, 104, 152–53
Bloomingdale's, 146, 207
Bluegrass music, 266
Blue Man Group, 252, 256, 262
Blues music, 265–66
Boat cruises, 158–60. *See also* Staten Island Ferry
Boathouse Cafe (Central Park), 106, 127, 225
Boating, 174

Boat Show, New York National, 5
Bombay Dining, 127
Bookstores, 199, 216–18
Bowling, 199
Bridge, Brooklyn, 171, 226, 230
Broadway, 83
about, 256
theater, 4, 18, 248–49, 251
Bronx Zoo/Wildlife Conservation Park, 197
Brooklyn Academy of Music, 7
Brooklyn Bridge, 171, 226, 230
Brooklyn Heights, 171–72
Brooklyn Heights Promenade, 99, 172
Brooks Brothers, 207
Brothers BBQ, 128
Bryant Park, 182, 233, 236
Budgeting, 17–19
worksheet, 23
your time, 240
Buses, 97–98
to/from airports, 30, 87–88
to New York City, 32
subway transfers from, 95
tours, 26–27, 157–58
Web site, 97
Business hours, 206

C

Cabana Carioca, 128
Cabaret, 266
Cabs. *See* Taxis
Cafe Carlyle, 266
Café des Artistes, 106
Calendar of events, 4–7
Camera repair, 270
Canal Street, 174
Carey Transportation, 87–88

Carlyle Hotel, 65, 266
Carmine's, 128–29
Carnegie Delicatessen and Restaurant, 129
Carnegie Hall, 259–60
Caroline's, 266
Car rentals, 17, 37
Car services, 88–89
Car travel to New York City, 31–32
Casablanca Hotel, 65
Cathedral of St. John the Divine, 173, 225, 240
Cats (theater), 251, 256
Central Park, 92, 99, 174, 223
restaurants, 127, 141
Strawberry Fields, 173
SummerStage, 174, 259
walking tour, 222–23, 225
Zoo/Wildlife Conservation Center, 197–98
Central Park South, 47
Central Park West, 173
Century 21, 217
Channel Gardens, 184
Chanterelle, 105
Chelsea, 90
accommodations, 62, 65–66, 69
Chelsea Antiques Building, 216
Chelsea Brewing Company, 153, 200
Chelsea Piers Sports and Entertainment Complex, 199–200
Chelsea Pines Inn, 65–66
Children, 8–9
accommodations, 55, 66
air travel with, 31
attractions, 9, 171, 203–04
restaurants, 124
theater, 256
Children's Museum of Manhattan, 204, 225

Chinatown, 5, 89–90,
174, 226, 230
restaurants, 108–09,
113, 121, 130, 226
Chinatown Ice Cream
Factory, 151
Chinese New Year, 5
Christie's Fine Art
Auctioneers, 216
Chrysler Building, 176,
236
Churches index, 170
Cinema. *See* Movies
Circle Line Sightseeing
Cruise, 158–59
Circuses, 5, 7
City Center, 259, 262
City Hall, 200, 230
Classical music, 260
Climate, 3–4
Cloisters, the, 99, 196–97
Clothing. *See also*
Department stores
designer, 208, 210,
212
discount stores,
217–18
packing tips, 41–43
Coffee beans, 146–47,
219
Coffeehouses, 146–47,
152
Columbus Circle,
47, 97
Comedy Cellar, 266
Comedy clubs, 266
Comedy Nation, 133
Comic Strip, 266
Concerts, 260. *See also*
Music
Convenience costs,
21–22
Cost of everyday items,
19
Country music, 266
Credit cards, 16
Crime, 13
Crowne Plaza
Manhattan, 66
Cruises, 158–60. *See also*
Staten Island Ferry

Current events, 39–40,
93, 248–49, 257–58
Customs House, U.S.,
201
Cybercafes, 52

D

Daffy's, 217
Dakota Apartments, 173
Danal, 145–46
Dance troupes, 256, 262
Dancing, 265, 269
Midsummer Night
Swing, 259, 265
Dean & Delucca, 146,
149
Delis, 148–49
De Niro, Robert, 105, 142
Department stores, 146,
206–07, 213
Designer clothing, 208,
210, 212
Diamond district, 219
Dining. *See* Restaurants
Dinner cruises, 160
Dinosaurs, 170
Disabled travelers, 10–12
accommodations, 55,
77
public transportation,
98
Discos, 265, 269
Discount stores, 217–18
Disney Store, 207
Diwan Grill, 129
Doctors, 38–39, 270
Dog Show, Westminster
Kennel Club, 5
Doubletree Guest Suites,
66–67
Doughnuts, 147
Downtown, 49–50,
89–90. *See also*
Chinatown; Greenwich
Village; Little Italy;
SoHo; TriBeCa; Wall
Street
accommodations,
49–50, 62, 70–72
attractions, 164

restaurants, 113, 143
walking tours,
226–28, 230
guided, 160–61
self-guided, 198
Drake Swissôtel, 67
Drugstores, 271

E

Easter Parade, 5
East Village, 90
restaurants, 104, 113,
125, 127, 132, 134,
136, 140, 142
8th Street, shopping, 213
EJ's Luncheonette, 107
Electronics, 213, 218
Ellis Island, 176, 226
El Museo del Barrio,
202
Elysee, Hotel, 68
Emergencies, 270
Empire State Building,
47, 176–77, 234
Entertainment, 247–69.
See also Bars; Movies;
Music; Performing arts;
Theater
budgeting, 18
current events, 39–40,
93, 248–49, 257–58
tickets, 39, 41, 249–51

F

Fake watches, 210
Falafel, 106, 150, 152
Families. *See* Children
Fantasticks, The (theater),
256
FAO Schwarz, 207
Farmer's market, 199
Fashion designers, 208,
210, 212
Fast food chains,
149–50
Federal Hall National
Memorial, 198
Ferry, Staten Island,
185–86

Festivals, 4–7
Fifth Avenue, 233, 236
  shopping, 212–13,
    219
57th Street
  shopping, 212
  theme restaurants,
    133
Filene's Basement, 218
Financial District, 89. *See
  also* Wall Street
Flatiron Building,
  177–78, 234
Flatiron District, 177–78,
  234
  restaurants, 105
Flea markets, 216
Fleet Week, 6
Florent, 129–30
Flower Show, New York,
  5
Folk music, 152, 266
Food, 148–49, 218–19
  Wild Food Tours, 161
Fort Tryon Park, 99,
  196
48th Street West, 220
42nd Street, guided walk-
  ing tour, 162
47th Street West, 219
46th Street West
  (Restaurant Row), 48,
  105, 223, 236
Fourth of July, 6
Fraunces Tavern, 198,
  226, 228
French fries, Belgian-
  style, 150–51
Frick Collection, 197
Frozen yogurt, 151
Fulton Fish Market, 185

G

Gay men and lesbians,
  12–13
  accommodations,
    65–66, 69
  Lesbian and Gay Pride
    Week and March, 6
  nightlife, 268–69
  sailing tea dance, 160
  Wigstock, 7
Geraldo, 262
Gold, Joyce, 161
Golden Unicorn, 130
Golf, 199
Gotham Bar & Grill, 130
Gourmet food, 148–49,
  218–19
Grace Church, 184, 201
Gracie Mansion, 200
Gramercy Park, 90, 178,
  234
  restaurants, 105, 116,
    125, 131, 142
Gramercy Tavern (Tavern
  Room), 105, 131
Grand Central
  Partnership, 93, 162
Grand Central Terminal,
  178, 236
  restaurants, 137
Grand Hyatt New York,
  67
Grant's (Ulysses S.)
  Tomb, 198
Gray Line Air Shuttle,
  87–88
Gray Line New York
  Tours, 157–58
Greenmarket, Union
  Square, 199
Greenwich Village, 49,
  90, 178–79, 228, 230
  accommodations, 62
  attractions, 164
  coffeehouses,
    146–47
  nightclubs, 264–67
  pizza, 148–49
  restaurants, 103–04
  shopping, 8th Street,
    213
  walking tour,
    233–34
Greenwich Village
  Halloween Parade, 7
Guggenheim Museum,
  180, 223
Guggenheim SoHo, 230
Guided tours. *See* Tours

H

Hamburger Harry's, 107
Hard Rock Cafe, 133
Harlem
  guided walking tours,
    161
  restaurants, 113, 141
Harlem Spirituals, 161
Harley-Davidson Cafe,
  133
Hatsuhana, 131
Hayden Planetarium, 170
Health concerns, 38–39
Hell's Kitchen, 92
Herald Square, 47, 207,
  234
  accommodations, 47,
    67–68
  restaurants, 143
Herald Square Hotel,
  67–68
Heritage Trails, 198
Historic buildings, 170
Hospitals, 270–71
Hot dogs, 150
Hotels. *See*
  Accommodations
Hot lines, 271
Houston Street, 180
Hudson Canyon, 158
Hudson River, cruises,
  159–60
Hudson River Park, 171
Hudson Street, 104

I

Ice cream, 151
Ice skating, 174, 183, 200
Il Cortile, 131–32
IMAX theater, 170
Incentra Village House,
  69
Indian, National
  Museum of the
  American, 202
Indochine, 132
Information sources, 2–3,
  92–93, 271. *See also*
  Web sites

Insurance, 38
International Center of
  Photography, 202
Intrepid Sea-Air-Space
  Museum, 6, 180, 236
Irving, Washington, 159
Iso, 132
Itineraries
  designing your own,
    238–46
  suggested, 221–36

J

James Beard House, 104
Javits Convention
  Center, 5
Jazz music, 264–65
Jefferson Market
  Courthouse, 179
Jekyll & Hyde Club, 133
Jewelry stores, 219
Jewish Museum, 202
Joe Allen, 105
John's Pizzeria, 106, 133
Jolly Madison Towers
  Hotel, 69
Joyce Theater, 262
Jules, 134

K

Kelley and Ping, 134
Kennedy Airport, 30, 86
Kimberly, The, 69–70
Knicks, 201
Knitting Factory, 267
Koreatown, 109, 143
Krispy Kreme doughnuts,
  147

L

Ladies' Mile (Sixth
  Avenue), 213
La Guardia Airport, 30,
  86, 89
*Late Show with David
  Letterman,* 262–63
Layout of New York,
  89–92

L'Ecole, 134–35
LemonGrass Grill, 107
Lennon, John, 173
Letterman, David,
  262–63
Libraries, 182, 199, 233
Limousines, 88–89
Lincoln Center, 259, 263
  Festival, 6
  Midsummer Night
    Swing, 259, 265
  restaurants near, 106,
    113, 133, 137, 140
Liquor laws, 271
Little India (6th Street
  East), 104, 108, 127
Little Italy, 90, 180, 230
  restaurants, 109, 113,
    131–32, 135, 143,
    226
*Live with Regis and Kathy
  Lee,* 263
Lodgings. See
  Accommodations
Loeb Boathouse (Central
  Park), 174
Lombardi's, 135
Lord and Taylor, 207
Lotfi's, 105
Lowell, The, 70
Lower East Side, 90
Lower East Side
  Tenement Museum,
  203

M

MacDougal Street, 152
Macy's, 207, 234
  Thanksgiving Day
    Parade, 7
Madison Avenue, shop-
  ping, 208, 210
Madison Square Garden,
  5, 201, 256
Mafia movies, 230
Magazines, 39–40, 271.
  *See also specific maga-
  zines*
Manhattan Mall, 93
Maps, 271

Marathon, New York
  City, 7
Marechiaro Tavern, 230
Mark, The, 70
Markets. *See* Farmer's
  market; Flea markets
Mark's, 135
Marriott World Trade
  Center, 70–71
Mary Ann's, 107
Mass transit. *See*
  Transportation
Mayflower Hotel on the
  Park, 71
Mayor's residence, 200
Medical concerns,
  38–39
Membership discounts,
  21
Metro, Hotel, 68–69
MetroCard, 21–22, 96,
  98
Metropolitan Museum of
  Art, 181–82, 223, 225
  the Cloisters,
    196–97
Metropolitan Opera, 259,
  261–62
Mets, 201
Michelangelo, The,
  71–72
Mi Cocina, 136
Microbreweries, 153
Midsummer Night's
  Swing, 259, 265
Midtown, 46–47, 90
  accommodations,
    46–47
  restaurants, 105, 255
  walking in, 99
  walking tour, 232–33,
    236–37
Midtown East, 47
  accommodations,
    47, 58, 67–68,
    69–70, 72–73, 75,
    78–79
  attractions, 164
  restaurants, 113, 129,
    131, 137, 139, 141,
    144

Midtown West, 47–48, 90, 92. *See also* Times Square
  accommodations, 58, 64–69, 71–77
  attractions, 164
  restaurants, 113, 116, 124, 128–29, 133, 138–39
  walking tour, 223–25
Millenium Hilton, 72
Modern Art, Museum of (MOMA), 182, 233, 263
Money matters, 14–23
Money-saving tips, 20–22
Montague Street (Brooklyn), 172
Montrachet, 105
Morgans, 72
Moshe's Falafel, 106, 150
Movies, 263
  MoviePhone, 263
  New York Film Festival, 7, 263
Mulberry Street, 109, 180, 230
Murray Hill, 47
  accommodations, 47
Museo del Barrio, 202
Museum of Modern Art (MOMA), 182, 233, 263
Museum of Television and Radio, 202–03
Museum of the City of New York, 161, 198
Museums
  free nights, 18, 22
  index, 164
Music
  avant garde, 267
  bluegrass, 266
  blues, 265–66
  Central Park Summer-Stage, 174, 259
  classical, 259–60
  country, 266
  festivals, 6
  folk, 152, 266
  jazz, 264–65
  nighttime cruises, 159
  opera, 259, 261
  rock & roll, 267
  shopping for, 219–20
  world music, 267
  World Music Institute, 261, 267
Musical instruments, 220

N

National Museum of the American Indian, George Gustav Heye Center, 202
Natural History, American Museum of, 40, 92, 170, 223, 225
NBC Studios, 183
Neighborhoods, 84, 89–92, 170. *See also specific neighborhoods*
  guided walking tours, 160–62
Newark International Airport, 30, 86
Newspapers, 39–40, 271. *See also specific newspapers*
New Year's Eve, 7
New York, Museum of the City of, 161, 198
New York Apple Tours, 157
New York City Ballet, 262
New York City Opera, 261–62
New York City Transit Museum, 161
New York Convention and Visitors Bureau, 2–3, 248, 258, 271
New York Film Festival, 7, 263
New York Knicks, 201
New York Marriott Marquis, 73
New York Mets, 201
New York Philharmonic, 259–60
New York Press, 249, 258, 271
New York Public Library, 182, 233, 236
New York Shakespeare Festival, 251–52
New York Sports Club, 200
New York Stock Exchange, 183, 228
New York Then and Now, 218
New York Times, 39, 248, 256–57, 271
  Web site, 3, 40, 249
New York Waterways, 159–60
New York Yankees, 201
Next Wave Festival, 7
Nightclubs, 264–67, 269
Nightlife. *See* Bars; Dancing; Entertainment; Music; Nightclubs; Theater
Nobu, 105
NoHo, 90
  restaurants, 104, 113, 132, 136
NoHo Star, 136
Novotel New York, 73

O

Odeon, The, 136
Old Navy Clothing Company, 146, 213
Olympia Trails, 88
Opera, 259, 261
Organized tours. *See* Tours
Orso, 105
Oyster Bar, 137

P

Package tours, 20, 27–28, 39
Packing, 41–43
  checklist, 43
  tips on, 20
Pamir, 106

Parks, 164, 170, 182, 233, 236. *See also* Central Park
Gramercy Park, 90, 178, 234
Washington Square Park, 178, 187–89, 234
Park Slope Brewing Company, 153
Pastries, 152–53
Patria, 105
Pearl River Chinese Department Store, 174
Penn Station, 32, 93, 147
Performance venues, 259, 262
Performing arts, 257–63. *See also* Dance; Music; Theater
current events, 39–40, 93, 257–58
seasons for, 258–59
tickets, 39, 41, 258
Persepolis, 106
Petrel, 160
Phantom of the Opera (theater), 251
Pharmacies, 271
Photography, International Center of, 202
Picholine, 137
Pickwick Arms Hotel, 73
Pier 16, 159
Pier 17, 185, 212
Pier 40, 160
Pier 83, 159
Pierpont Morgan Library, 199
Pierre, The, 74
Pioneer, 160, 185
Pizza, 108, 148–49
Planetarium, Hayden, 170
Planet Hollywood, 133
Plaza Hotel, 74, 145, 268
Police, 271
Port Authority Bus Terminal, 32
Portland Square Hotel, 74–75

Promenade at Rockefeller Center, 184
Provence, 138
Public Theater, 251–52
Pubs, 267

Q

Quality Hotel and Suites Rockefeller Center, 75
Quality Hotel Fifth Avenue, 75

R

Radio, Museum of Television and, 202–03
Radio City Music Hall, 183, 259, 262
special shows, 256
Radisson Empire Hotel, 75–76
Rainbow Promenade, 268
Rainbow Room, 138–39
Rainbow & Stars, 265
Rainfall, average monthly, 4
Ramble, The (Central Park), 174
Ray's Pizza, 149
Remi, 139
Rent (theater), 251
Reservations, 39, 41
accommodations, 55–56
restaurants, 41, 111, 255
Restaurant Row (46th Street West), 48, 105, 223, 236
Restaurants, 101–52
brunch, 103, 146
budgeting, 17–18
for businesspeople, 131
with children, 124
by cuisine, 117, 120–21
in department stores, 146
dinner cruises, 160
dress code, 111

ethnic neighbor-hoods, 108–09
for exotic dining experiences, 135
gourmet, 138
for the homesick, 134
hygienic conditions, 148
location and, 103–06
location index, 113, 116
money-saving tips, 21–22
with multiple locations, 107
price index, 116–17
prices and, 109–10
prix fixe menus, 255
reservations, 41, 111, 255
for a romantic interlude, 126
smoking, 111
taxes, 111
for theater, before or after, 254–55
theme, 133
tipping, 111
trends in, 102–03
24 hours, 129
Restaurant Week, 6
Restrooms, 271
Riverside Park, 99
Rock climbing, 199–200
Rockefeller Center, 183–84, 200, 233, 236
accommodations, 75
Christmas Tree Lighting, 7
Flower and Garden Show, 6
restaurants, 138–39
Rockettes, 183, 256, 262
Rock & roll, 267
Roosevelt Island Aerial Tramway, 183
Royalton, The, 76

S

Safety tips, 13
Sailing ships, 160

St. John the Divine,
Cathedral of, 173, 225,
240
St. Mark's Place, 204
St. Patrick's Cathedral,
184, 233
St. Patrick's Day Parade,
5
St. Paul's Chapel, 184,
228, 230
St. Regis, 268
Saks Fifth Avenue, 146,
207
Salad bars, 148–49
Sales tax, 206
Salisbury Hotel, 76
Sally Jessy Raphael, 262
Saloon, The, 106, 140
Sea-Air-Space Museum,
Intrepid, 6, 180, 236
Seaport Liberty Cruises,
159
Seasons, 3–4
traveling in off, 4, 20,
51
Second Avenue Deli,
140
Seinfeld, 151
Senior citizen travelers,
9–10, 50, 159, 250
Seventh Regiment
Armory, 5–6
Shabu Tatsu, 140
Shakespeare Festival,
New York, 251–52
Shea Stadium, 201
Sheep Meadow (Central
Park), 174
Sheraton New York Hotel
and Towers, 77
Shopping, 205–20
budgeting for, 18
Showtix, 41, 250
Sidewalk.com, 3, 40
Sightseeing. *See*
Attractions
6th Street East (Little
India), 104, 108, 127
Skateboarding, 204
Skating, ice, 174, 183,
200

Smith, Abigail Adams,
Museum, 203
SoHo, 49, 90, 185, 228,
230
accommodations, 62,
77
art galleries, 228
attractions, 164
restaurants, 104–05,
113, 124, 126–27,
134–35, 138
shopping, 210, 212
SoHo Grand Hotel, 77
Solomon R. Guggenheim
Museum, 180, 223
Sony Wonder
Technology Lab, 203
Sotheby's, 216
Soup, 151
Soup Kitchen
International, 151
South Street Seaport,
159, 185, 226
shopping, 212
South Street Seaport
Museum, 185, 226
Souvenirs, 21
Sparks Steak House, 141
Special events, 4–7
Sports complex, 199–200
Starbucks, 146
Staten Island Ferry,
185–86
Statue of Liberty, 186,
226
Stock Exchange, New
York, 183, 228
Strand Bookstore, 199,
216
Strawberry Fields, 173
Street vendors, 150, 210
Student travelers, 250
Subway, 94–97
bus transfers from, 95
safety tips, 13
tips for, 96–97
Web site, 95
SummerStage, 174, 259
Surrey Hotel, 77–78
Sylvia's, 141
Symphonies, 259–60

T

Tavern on the Green,
106, 141
Taxes, 206, 272
Taxis, 8, 13, 272
to/from airports, 30,
86–87
tips for, 87
Tea, afternoon, 145
Telecharge, 41
Telephone numbers, use-
ful, 40–42, 93, 271
Television and Radio,
Museum of, 202–03
Television tapings,
262–63
Temperatures, average
monthly, 4
Tenement Museum,
Lower East Side, 203
Tennis Championships,
U.S. Open, 6
Theater, 248
Broadway, 4, 248–49,
251
budgeting, 18
for children, 256
current events, 39–40,
93, 248–49
curtain time, 254
dinner before or after
the show, 254–55
dressing for, 252
information sources,
248–49
Off-Broadway, 251–52
performance art, 262
seat sizes, 254
standing room, 251
telephone numbers,
useful, 40, 93, 249
tickets, 39, 41, 249–51
Web sites, 249
Theater District, 90, 92,
225, 254–55
accommodations, 64,
71, 73–74, 76
restaurants, 105, 116,
128–29, 139
Theme restaurants, 133

34th Street Partnership, 93, 162

32nd Street West (Koreatown), 109, 143

TicketMaster, 41, 249, 258

Tickets, 39, 41, 249–51, 258
  brokers and concierges, 251
  getting right seats, 250–51
  money-saving tips, 250
  tips on, 250–52

Tiffany & Co., 207, 219

Time Out, 40, 248–49, 258

Times Square, 47–48, 186–87, 225, 233, 236
  accommodations, 47–48
  guided walking tour, 162
  New Year's Eve, 7
  walking tour, 223–25

Times Square Visitor & Transit Information Center, 92

Tipping, 19, 111, 254

TKTS booth, 225, 250

Today Show, 263

Toilets, 271

Tony 'n' Tony's Wedding, 262

Tourist information, 2–3, 92–93, 271. *See also* Web sites

Tours, 157–62. *See also* Walking tours
  by boat, 158–60
  by bus, 157–58
  escorted, 26–27
  escorted versus on own, 25–27
  package, 27–28, 39

Tower Building, 177

Tower Records, 219

Train travel to New York City, 32

Transit Information Center, 94, 272

Transit Museum, New York City, 161

Transportation, 21, 94–98
  to/from airports, 30, 84, 86–89
  budgeting, 17
  with children, 8
  maps, 271
  MetroCard, 21–22, 96, 98
  money-saving tips, 21, 95, 98
  transit information, 94, 272
  travelers with disabilities, 98
  Web sites, 95, 97

Travel agents, 24–25

Traveler's checks, 14, 15

Traveling to New York City, 28–32

Travel insurance, 38

TriBeCa (Tribeca), 89
  restaurants, 105, 116, 136, 142

TriBeCa Grill, 105, 142

Trinity Church, 201

Trump International Hotel and Tower, 78

TV tapings, 262–63

20 Mott Street, 121

"21" Club, 124

U

Union Square, 105
  restaurants, 105, 116, 125, 130–31, 142

Union Square Greenmarket, 199

United Nations, 187, 236

Upper East Side, 49, 92
  accommodations, 49, 58, 64–65, 70, 74, 77–78
  attractions, 164
  restaurants, 106, 116, 125–26, 133, 135, 140

shopping, Madison Avenue, 208, 210
  walking tour, 222–23

Upper West Side, 48, 92
  accommodations, 48, 58, 68, 71, 75–76, 78
  attractions, 164
  restaurants, 106, 116, 126—29, 133, 137, 140–41

U.S. Open Tennis Championships, 6

V

Verbena, 142

Veselka, 142

Village, The. *See* Greenwich Village; West Village

Village Voice, 40, 248, 258, 271
  Web site, 249, 258

Vincent's Clam Bar, 143

Virgin Megastore, 219–20

Visitor information, 2–3, 92–93, 271. *See also* Web sites

W

Waldorf-Astoria and Waldorf Towers, 78–79

Walking, 99

Walking tours
  organized, 160–62
  free, 161–62
  self-guided, 198

Wall Street, 49, 89, 183, 187–88, 228

Warner Bros. Studio Store, 207

Washington, George, 184, 198, 200

Washington Arch, 189

Washington Square Hotel, 79

Washington Square Park, 178, 187–89, 234

Watches, fake, 210

Water, bottled, 22
Water Shuttle, 89
Weather, 3–4
    forecasts, 42
Web sites, 3
    airlines, 30, 273–74
    air travel, 29–30
    for children, 8
    New York City Beer
    Guide, 153
    publications, 40
    subway, 95
    tickets and reserva-
    tions, 41
Westminster Kennel Club
Dog Show, 5
West Village, 90. *See also*
Greenwich Village
    accommodations,
    65–66, 69, 79
    ATM machines, 16
    restaurants, 103–04,
    113, 126–30, 133,
    136
Whitney Museum, 197,
223

Wigstock, 7
Windows on the World,
    143
Winter Garden, 171
Wollman Rink (Central
    Park), 174, 200
Won Jo, 143
Woolworth Building, 201
World Music Institute,
    261, 267
World Trade Center, 189,
    228, 230
    accommodations,
    70–72
    restaurants, 143
Wright, Frank Lloyd, 180

X-Y-Z

Yankees, 201
Yankee Stadium, 201

Zabar's, 219
Zarela, 144
Zen Palate, 107
Zoos, 197–98